KT-146-652

Makers of Contemporary Islam

WITHDRAWN FROM
THE LIBRARY

UNIVERSITY OF
WINCHESTER

KA 0271942 8

MAKERS OF CONTEMPORARY ISLAM

John L. Esposito
John O. Voll

OXFORD
UNIVERSITY PRESS
2001

OXFORD

UNIVERSITY PRESS

Oxford   New York
Athens   Auckland   Bangkok   Bogotá   Buenos Aires   Calcutta   Cape Town
Chennai   Dar es Salaam   Delhi   Florence   Hong Kong   Istanbul   Karachi
Kuala Lumpur   Madrid   Melbourne   Mexico City   Mumbai   Nairobi   Paris
São Paulo   Shanghai   Singapore   Taipei   Tokyo   Toronto   Warsaw

and associated companies in
Berlin   Ibadan

Copyright © 2001 by John L. Esposito and John O. Voll

Published by Oxford University Press, Inc.,
198 Madison Avenue, New York, New York 10016

Oxford is a registered trademark of Oxford University Press.

All rights reserved. No part of this publication may be reproduced,
stored in a retrieval system, or transmitted, in any form or by any means,
electronic, mechanical, photocopying, recording, or otherwise,
without the prior permission of Oxford University Press.

Library of Congress Cataloging-in-Publication Data
Esposito, John L.
Makers of contemporary Islam / John L. Esposito and John O. Voll.
    p.   cm.
Includes bibliographical references and index.
ISBN 0-19-514127-x; 0-19-514128-8 (pbk)
1. Scholars, Muslim—Islamic countries—Biography.   2. Intellectuals—Islamic
countries—Biography.   3. Islam and secularism—Islamic countries.
4. Islam—20th century. I. Voll, John Obert, 1936–   II. Title.
BP70 .E86   2001
297.2′092′2—dc21   00-056674
[B]

KING ALFRED'S COLLEGE
WINCHESTER

297.2
/ESP   KA·2719428

9 8 7 6 5 4 3 2

Printed in the United States of America
on acid-free paper

*For Jeanette P. Esposito
and Sarah P. Voll*

ACKNOWLEDGMENTS

The research support for this study came from a generous grant from the National Endowment for the Humanities. We are grateful to the endowment, which is, of course, not responsible for any of the views expressed in this work. The result of our travels, interviews, and research was both *Islam and Democracy* and *Makers of Contemporary Islam*. We are indebted to all those connected with the project who were generous with their time and candid in their responses. In addition, we are grateful to the Council on Foreign Affairs in New York for permission to publish an earlier and now expanded version of Valla Vakili's chapter Abdolkarim Soroush and Critical Discourse in Contemporary Iran, whose original title was "Debating Religion and Politics in Iran: The Political Thought of Abdolkarim Soroush" and to *The Muslim World* for permission to publish a revised version of our "Khurshid Ahmad: Muslim Activist-Economist." Natana De-Long-Bas, research assistant for parts of this project, did an excellent job. Cynthia A. Read, our editor at Oxford and her colleagues have been especially helpful in expediting publication. Finally, a special thank you to Jeanette P. Esposito and Sarah P. Voll.

John L. Esposito
John O. Voll
Washington, D.C.

CONTENTS

Makers of Contemporary Islam

INTRODUCTION

*Muslim Activist Intellectuals
and Their Place in History*

Socrates challenged the thinking of Athenians in the classical age and Confucius attempted to bring a new vision of society to the "Warring States" of China. Luther's concepts and visions altered Western Christendom, and Lenin's combination of intellectualism and activism transformed world history in the twentieth century. Throughout history, people of ideas who have become involved in the civic and political affairs of their day, as activist intellectuals, have attempted to play roles in the transformation of their societies. In the late twentieth century, a number of intellectuals in Muslim societies have played similar roles. They criticize existing institutions and mentalities and work to provide some alternative.

From the United States to North Africa, the Middle East, and Southeast Asia, these Muslim activist intellectuals serve in important ways as the makers of contemporary Islam. Their ideas provide the foundations for many of the programs of Islamic movements throughout the world. Even for those who disagree with them and dispute their claims, these activist thinkers have shaped the conceptual world and set the terms of most debates in the Muslim world. These people, their organizations, and their modes of thinking have been part of the heart of what has come to be called the Islamic resurgence of the end of the twentieth century.

Intellectuals play crucial roles in the contemporary Islamic resurgence. They are both its primary formulators and its most articulate opponents. This situation reflects the complexity of the impact of intellectuals in Muslim societies in the modern world. The actions and influence of Muslim intellectuals in the modern era are similar to the experiences of intellectuals throughout the world. At the same time, they represent a distinctive example of how intellectuals work within the context of their broader cultural heritages to respond to the challenges of the modern world experience.

Although many people have noted the activities of intellectuals throughout history, remarkably little has been written about the role of intellectuals, as intellectuals, in the movements of Islamic resurgence in the final decades of the twentieth century. Intellectuals committed to the cause of active renewal and reform in contemporary Muslim societies represent an interesting combination of the older role of the religious scholar in Muslim societies and the role of "intellectual" as understood in more secular, modern societies, a work that is not simply an eclectic bringing-together of a number of different activities. This synthesis is characteristic of a type of intellectual that is different from the other types of intellectuals active within Muslim societies. It may also provide an important example of the activist, politically involved intellectual who may be seen in many different societies in the contemporary world.

Intellectuals have been described and analyzed in many different and often contradictory ways. There is, despite this diversity, some vague sense of agreement on the important elements that define intellectuals and their roles in societies. Two important aspects of this broader understanding are a sense that "intellectuals" are somehow a distinctive grouping of people within a society, set apart from the majority, while at the same time they are a crucial element *in society*, defining and articulating the communal agreements that provide a sense of legitimacy and basic principles for societal operation and survival. These two dimensions' separation and involvement have been both complementary and contradictory as intellectuals have interacted with their societies throughout history.

Intellectuals as Separate

What is an "intellectual"? Most discussions of intellectuals at least start with an emphasis on their separation from most of society. Intellectuals are the people who are specialists in ideas, images, and symbols. The often-cited definition by Edward Shils provides a careful statement of this:

> Intellectuals are the aggregate of persons in any society who employ in their communication and expression, with relatively higher frequency than most other members of their society, symbols of general scope and abstract reference, concerning man, society, nature, and the cosmos. The high frequency of their use of such symbols may be a function of their own subjective propensity or of the obligations of an occupational role.[1]

The result of this is that intellectuals are viewed as "persons possessing knowledge, or in a narrower sense those whose judgment, based on reflection and knowledge, derives less directly and exclusively from sensory perception than in the case of non-intellectuals."[2] In the writings of pioneering social scientists like Max Weber, intellectuals "are understood as politically disinterested, socially unattached individuals who, in their subjective intentions, pursue knowledge for its own sake."[3]

This image of separateness was perhaps most fully portrayed by Julien Benda in the 1920s in a book that continues to have great influence. Benda argued that, side by side with the general masses of people, there was a class of people

> whose activity essentially is *not* the pursuit of practical aims . . . who seek their joy in the practice of an art or a science or metaphysical speculation, in short in the possession of non-material advantages, and hence in a certain manner say: "My kingdom is not of this world." Indeed, throughout history, for more than two thousand years until modern times, I see an uninterrupted series of philosophers, men of religion, men of literature, artists, men of learning (one might say almost all during this period), whose influence, whose life, were in direct opposition to the realism of the multitudes.[4]

These were the intellectuals or, in Benda's terms, "the clerks."

The primary responsibility and role of intellectuals in this perspective is to provide a constant critique of the activities of the majority and the institutions of society. In this perspective, such a critique is essential. Benda argued that "civilization" is "possible only if humanity consents to a division of functions, if side by side with those who carry out the lay passions and extol the virtues servicable to them, there exists a class of men who depreciate these passions and glorify the advantages which are beyond the material."[5] Dissent is at the heart of the definition of an intellectual, and qualitative dissent, the presentation of new ideas and perspectives or the fundamental rearrangement of old ones, is the "*raison d'etre* of intellectuals."[6] Edward Said, himself a prominent public intellectual, notes that the "intellectual is an individual endowed with the faculty for representing, embodying, articulating a message. . . . And this role has an edge to it, and cannot be played without a sense of being someone whose place it is publicly to raise embarrassing questions, to confront orthodoxy and dogma."[7]

This dissent of the intellectuals is not simply a negative opposition to existing conditions: "intellectuals as dissenters are not always trying to change a status quo (though more often they are) but may also be defending it by arguing for a different arrangement of components."[8] The intellectuals' critiques and interests arise not from more specific, material issues but "from the need to perceive, experience, and express . . . a general significance in particular, concrete events"[9] and are made "on the basis of universal principles."[10]

These activities—the creation of ideas and concepts that can provide broad principles for criticizing existing conditions and institutions and also provide the general foundations for the transformation of society—are of extreme importance for the development and survival of societies. Benda, for example, points to Socrates, Jesus, and Thomas Aquinas, among many others,[11] as illustrating the crucial significance of the intellectual's role.

Although people of ideas have been important throughout history, the use of a single term, "intellectuals," for this grouping is relatively recent.[12] It is, in fact, often identified with a particular type, the "secular intellectual." The rise of the secular intellectual is a new phenomenon and an important part of the development of modern society. "It is true that in their earlier incarnations as priests, scribes and soothsayers, intellectuals have laid claim to guide society from the very beginning. But as guardians of hieratic cultures . . . their moral and ideological innovations were limited by the canons of external authority and by the inheritance of tradition."[13] However, the development of modern society resulted in a decline in the influence of the older style of intellectuals and the emergence of the secular intellectual.

> For the first time in human history, and with growing confidence and audacity, men arose to assert that they could diagnose the ills of society and cure them with their own unaided intellects: more, that they could devise formulae whereby not merely the structure of society but the fundamental habits of human beings could be transformed for the better. Unlike their sacerdotal predecessors, they were not servants and interpreters of the gods but substitutes.[14]

Modern secular intellectuals have themselves been criticized for allowing their ideas and broader interpretive principles to become dogmatic ideologies or "secular religions."[15] However, for most people, in modern society, "the true intellectual is a secular being. However much intellectuals pretend that their representations are of higher things or ultimate values, morality begins with their activity in this secular world of ours."[16] In this perspective, many people feel that "religious" thinkers and leaders are not "true intellectuals."

The first element of understanding the nature and role of the modern "Muslim activist intellectual" is recognition of the tradition of the intellectual as a special and distinct type of person within Muslim society. Intellectuals provide important critiques of the mental and societal orders in any society as a part of their function. While it is possible to identify such people in most societies throughout history, this role has taken a distinctive form in modern societies, especially as they have developed in Western Europe and North America in the past two centuries. The "modern" intellectual is usually a social radical (of either the Left or the Right) and in some significant way is identified as "secular" rather than "religious."

On the face of it, if "intellectual" is defined solely in terms of this "modern-secular" interpretation, then "Muslim activist intellectual" is an internally contradictory concept. Instead of simply rejecting the term on this basis, it is important to see the "modern-secular" intellectual as part of a broader historical pattern that provides an important aspect of the leadership of the Islamic resurgence in the final decades of the twentieth century. However, from "a societal or a social-theory point of view the meaningfulness of intellectuals can be gauged only in their social setting," and explanations must involve analysis of "the three-cornered relationship between certain types of ideas, their articulators, and the social structure of their environment."[17] It also is important, in other words, to define the traditional structures and styles of intellectual activities in Muslim societies, which have provided the social setting for the "Muslim activist intellectuals."

People of Knowledge in Premodern Muslim Societies

Intellectuals are intimately involved in the fundamental structures of power and authority in their societies and do not live in total isolation. Intellectuals are those people in a society who define, develop, and express the broader principles on which the basic institutions are based. In the influential analysis of Max Weber, they are those people "who by virtue of their peculiarity have special access to certain achievements considered to be 'cultural values,'" and, as a result, represent "the leadership of a 'culture community.'"[18]

Intellectuals in this way have a dual role. On the one hand, the "capacity for criticism, for rejection of the status quo is not simply a matter of preference by some critical intellectuals" but is "built into the very nature of the occupational roles."[19] On the other hand, "most intellectuals involved in such roles are also engaged in activities that involve reaffirming and transmitting aspects of existing culture."[20] Intellectuals have both innovative and integrative roles, which are complementary, since while they seek to engage in creative and innovative activity, they "seek their final fulfillment in integrating these into the wider domain of the society."[21] Confucius was not alone in hoping to persuade the rulers of his day to adopt his ideas and visions.

The integrative activities of intellectuals and the way they express broad principles show that throughout history there is a profound connection between religion and the intellectuals. Indeed, Shils argues that

> [i]ntellectual work arose from religious preoccupations. In the early history of the human race, it tended, in its concern with the ultimate or at least with what lies beyond the immediate concrete experience, to think with religious symbols. . . . [T]he tradition of awesome respect and of serious striving for contact with the sacred, is perhaps the first, the most comprehensive and the most important of all the traditions of the intellectuals.[22]

Weber, in his analyses of the sociology of religion spoke of "the fact of fundamental importance that all the great religious doctrines of Asia are creations of intellectuals."[23]

As the institutions of the Muslim community of believers developed in the early centuries of the Islamic era, the people of knowledge, or *ulama*,[24] emerged as a major grouping within Muslim societies. General and theoretical discussions of intellectuals recognize this important role. Shils, for example, observes: "In the great religious cultures of Islam, Buddhism, Taoism, and Hinduism, prior to the emergence of a differentiated modern intellectual class, the care of the sacred through the mastery, interpretation, and exposition of sacred writings, and the cultivation of the appropriate mental states or qualities were the first interests of the intellectuals."[25]

The ulama were not an ordained priesthood, and their organizations and associations were not "churches." The key element that identified them was the fact that they were "people of knowledge." In the early Islamic community, following the death of the Prophet Muhammad in 632 c.e., the most visible institution was the caliphate, which was the structure of political authority and coordination. However, much of the tone and intellectual content of cultural life was set by the "piety-minded representatives of the Islamic hope for a godly personal and social order."[26] Those pious people, among all groups within the Islamic Community, came to be identified as the ulama and "worked out what we may call the Shari'ah-minded programme for private and public living centered on the Shari'ah law." Although some areas were not exclusively ulama-defined, their work "gave a certain dignity to the whole social edifice. As a whole, that edifice reflected the aspirations of the 'ulama', and the intellectual and social patterns that followed therefrom, more than it reflected any other set of ideals."[27]

The importance of the ulama within Islamic society is reflected in an often-quoted Tradition of the Prophet Muhammad, who is reported to have said, "The scholars are the heirs of the prophets." The famous fourteenth-century Muslim scholar Ibn Khaldoun, explained that this meant that the

> early Muslim scholars represented the religious law in all its aspects, and were identified with all of it and were known to have a thorough practical knowledge of its ways. . . . People who combine the theoretical and practical knowledge of the law are religious scholars, the real heirs, such as the jurists among the people of the second generation, the ancient Muslims, the four founders of the schools of law, as well as those who took them as models."[28]

The ulama were not, as ulama, officially part of the political structure of the caliphate. They acted as critical intellectuals, often providing powerful critiques of existing conditions. "The ulema regarded themselves as the collective voice of the conscience of society."[29] When some Abbasid caliphs in the ninth century attempted to establish the role of the caliph as the final authority in determining the correctness of theological positions, it was the ulama who provided the main opposition. The heroic prototype of this nonmilitary opposition to state interference in matters of Islamic interpretation was Ahmad Ibn Hanbal, who was later viewed as the founder of one of the four great schools of law in Sunni Islam.[30]

It was often argued that direct participation in the government would somehow taint the piety of the scholar. In a well-known Tradition, the Prophet Muhammad says, "The nearer a man is to government, the further he is from God."[31] Islamic law developed as a discipline and a system of sociomoral legitimacy outside of the state structures. The political-military controllers of the state came to be viewed as legitimate to the extent that they supported and protected the Shariah (Islamic law), but they had no role in defining the content or the interpretation of that law. This was true both of the early imperial leaders who held the title of caliph, or *khalifah* ("successor"), of the Messenger of God and of the later politico-military "authorities," or *sultans*. It was the ulama who emerged as the controllers, interpreters, and articulators of Islamic law and the definition of the Islamic community.

Through the first millennium and more of the history of the Islamic community,

> we cannot but be struck with the remarkable consistency and tenacity with which the Muslim thinkers had pursued their main objective. The historic caliphate had lost its power and perished, military conquerors had imposed their rule over every Muslim people, a rigid class structure had replaced the fluid social order of the early days, but through all vicissitudes the principles of Muslim government remained unchanged.[32]

Within this historical framework, the ulama emerged as part of the established structure of authority in Muslim societies. This means that the "ulama establishment" developed as something different from simply being the people of knowledge, acting as "intellectuals," in Muslim societies. By the era of the peak of power of the Ottoman Empire in the sixteenth century, the "official" ulama were a significant part of the state structure and the institutions of the status quo.

Within the ulama, as a result of the evolution of Muslim societies, there developed a variety of different modes of operation. Already by the thirteenth and fourteenth centuries, the lines were relatively clearly drawn between what might be thought of as the ulama bureaucrats and the ulama intellectuals. For some, the conviction developed that it was better to accept the decisions of earlier thinkers rather than engage in independent informed interpretation, while others saw such independent analysis as the continuing responsibility of appropriately learned scholars. This was the conflict over *taqlid* ("imitation") versus *ijtihad* ("independent judgment"). While some argued that the "Gate of Ijtihad" had been closed, others maintained that properly informed intellectuals could, and should, continue to engage in ijtihad.

On the issue of submission to political authority, a similar difference developed. In the political and military instability of the thirteenth and fourteenth centuries, many ulama adopted positions of political "realism" like that of Badr al-Din Ibn Jama'a (1241–1333), "who declared military power pure and simple as constituting the essence of rulership."[33] He argued that "Self-investure by armed force is lawful, and obedience is due to such a ruler."[34] In this perspective, "authority is preferable to anarchy. The old-established principle that the caliph can be deposed if he acts contrary to the *Shari'a*, or that if he issues regulations contrary to it he must be disobeyed, has been quietly abandoned in favour of obedience to any lawfully constituted authority."[35]

A contemporary of Ibn Jama'a, Taqi al-Din Ahmad Ibn Taymiyya (1263–1328), represents a different perspective, which maintained the role of the intellectual as critic. While Ibn Taymiyya also accepted the need to avoid anarchy and obey those in power,[36] he stressed the need for all Muslims, both rulers and ruled, to follow the obligations of their faith. No one was to be free from the obligation to encourage virtue and condemn vice. Early in his career as a scholar in the Mamluk domains of Syria and Egypt, he refused to accept important posts, probably in order "to remain free to criticize practices he deemed not in keeping with the tenets of Islam."[37] Throughout his life he was "a forceful advocate of a reform of the administration in the spirit of the ideal *Shari'a*. This brought him into conflict with the authorities and frequently into prison."[38]

Ibn Taymiyya claimed the right of ijtihad and used his independent judgment in rearticulating the general principles provided by the Quran and the Sunnah (the Traditions of the Prophet and the general path of the early Community). In his strong criticism of both the political and communal life of his time, and in the way he articulated that critique, he helped to define the intellectuals' alternative to the stable ulama establishment that was emerging by the thirteenth century.

Ibn Taymiyya is a classic representative of a distinctive style of the Islamic intellectual critic. In Muslim societies, the most visible and historically significant form of the intellectual tradition of critical separation from existing conditions involved a call for the renewal of the community by a return to, or strict application of, the Quran and Sunnah. This process of renewal, or *tajdid*, is a longstanding and important tradition within Islamic history.[39] Reformers for centuries have identified themselves with this tradition of tajdid, with scholars and historians developing lists of the great renewers (*mujaddids*) of Islamic history.[40]

The history of intellectuals in Muslim societies provides an important foundation for activist reforming intellectuals in the twentieth century.

The roots of the tradition lie in the emergence of the people of knowledge, the ulama, as a significant force within the Islamic community. The ulama as a whole represent in important ways the activities of intellectuals in Muslim societies, and the full complexities of the many different roles of intellectuals can be seen in the many different ways that ulama gradually responded to changing conditions over the centuries. Shils, who has defined "traditions of intellectuals" largely as they developed in Western European societies, defines the context of these scientist, romanticist, populist, apocalyptic, and anti-intellectual traditions in a way that also applies to Muslim intellectuals:

> The tension between the intellectuals and the powers—their urge to submit to authority as the bearer of the highest good—whether it be order or progress or some other value—and to resist or condemn authority as a betrayer of the highest values—comes ultimately from the constitutive orientation of the intellectuals towards the sacred. Practically all the more concrete traditions in the light and shadows of which intellectuals have lived express this tension.[41]

In this tension, the contrasts between the traditions represented by Ibn Jama'a and Ibn Taymiyya can be clearly seen. Within Islamic traditions, the critical Muslim intellectual tradition takes a "tajdid/ renewalist" rather than a "romantic" or "scientistic" mode.

In the "paradigm" for understanding roles of intellectuals suggested by Lipset and Basu, the tajdid tradition tends to be a "moralist" one in which "the intellectual is both the examiner and the evaluator . . . the conscience of society. . . . The moralists hold up the society to scorn for failing to fulfill basic agreed upon values. They challenge those running the society with the crime of heresy."[42] In contrast, the more establishment or bureaucratic ulama operate more in the style of intellectuals as "preservers" and "caretakers."[43]

The structures and contexts of Muslim societies have important resources for the intellectuals of the modern era. The general evolution of the roles of ulama in the Islamic world and the specific development of the tajdid tradition as a style of intellectual activity provide an important foundation for the emergence of the Muslim activist intellectuals of the late twentieth century.

Intellectuals in the Modern Muslim World

During the past two centuries, Muslim societies, like all other societies around the globe, have experienced significant transformations. The lives and roles of intellectuals in every society have been radically changed as a part of these transformations. In the Muslim world, three developments have been of special importance in the emergence of the Muslim activist intellectuals during the final decades of the twentieth century. As a part of the interaction with the West and the consequent Westernization and modernization of significant sectors in Muslim societies, a grouping (or "class") of "secular intellectuals" emerged. These people were similar to, and possibly both inspired and created by, their counterparts in the evolving modern societies of western Europe and North America. Second, there was a significant decline in the importance of the classically defined ulama among the intellectuals in Muslim societies. Third, by the end of the nineteenth century, a new type of Muslim intellectual began to develop in which many of the characteristics of both the modern secular intellectual and the tradition ulama were visible, at first, often, in uncomfortable compromise and then in increasingly effective synthesis.

Emergence of Secular Intellectuals

At the beginning of the nineteenth century in many parts of the Muslim world, people began conscious efforts to reshape and reform their societies. There was a growing sense of inadequacy and weakness in the face of the expanding European imperial and industrial powers. These reforms involved not only changing structures of government but also increasingly important efforts to provide the information and knowledge necessary for such modernizing (at first almost exclusively "Westernizing") efforts. Schools of a new type were established, and by the final decades of the nineteenth century the result was the development of "a new educated class looking at itself and the world with eyes sharpened by western teachers, and communicating what it saw in new ways."[44]

This "new class" was different from the ulama in training, institutional loyalties, and visions of the world and represented the emergence of a new type of intellectual in Muslim societies. The experience in the Arab world had many special characteristics, but in its general trends it was representative of the broader Muslim world's experiences.

> Not since the high Middle Ages had an educated elite arisen in the Arab world that was distinctly separate from the closed religious stratum of the *ulema*, who for generations had monopolized learning and intellectual activity. The impact of education and of the new ideas slowly but inexorably broke this monopoly; by the end of the nineteenth century a new intelligentsia had emerged.[45]

The development of this new intellectual class was a relatively long process, but it emerged as a grouping of "secular intellectuals" similar to what had emerged in Western Europe. This secular character was a fundamental part of this "New Class" as it developed earlier in Western Europe.

An "episode decisive in the formation of the New Class" was "a process of secularization in which most intelligentsia are no longer trained by, living within, and subject to close supervision by churchly organization. . . . Secularization is important because it de-sacralizes authority-claims and facilitates challenges to definitions of social reality made by traditional authorities."[46]

There were many different approaches among the intellectuals in the Muslim world of the late nineteenth century, with some making significant efforts to maintain a clear identification with older formal articulations of the Islamic tradition. However, these more Islamically oriented intellectuals were pushed to the periphery, and following World War I, the "intellectual and social orientation shifted toward an irreversible westernizing and secularist direction. . . . Islam, among the educated strata, was absorbed into secular ideology," and in the interwar period the group that "gained undisputed political ascendancy in both Egypt and the Fertile Crescent was the Muslim secularists."[47]

The domination of a secularist orientation for elite intellectuals in Muslim societies increased during the middle of the twentieth century. In what many observers saw as the Muslim country that was the most successful in its modernizing transformation, Turkey, the political system was officially secular, and most of the intellectual and political elites in the Muslim world accepted and supported that perspective. One popularizing tract on "muslim heroes of the twentieth century" written by a Sri Lankan Muslim included Mustafa Kemal Ataturk, the Turkish reformer who created the secular republic.[48] Similarly, Anwar al-Sadat, who in the 1970s proclaimed himself to be the "believing president" of Egypt, spoke of his love and admiration for Ataturk.[49] Elsewhere secularism was less explicit and official, but it was the dominant tone. A well-informed analysis of Middle Eastern politics noted, in the early 1970s, that in "every Middle Eastern country, political and social change must accomodate itself to the *lingering religious consciousness* of its inhabitants" but affirmed that the dominant tone and path was set by the fact that the "twentieth century is a secular age."[50] A later edition of this book said that by "the 1960s Arab nationalism appeared to have triumphed . . . [although] [s]ecular Arab nationalism had never been firmly established as the undisputed state-ideas of countries such as Egypt, Iraq, and Syria."[51] By 1990, it was clear that the secular intellectuals and the political elite of which they were a part had been unable to transform their secularist and semisecular ideologies into mass movements or to reconstruct the worldviews of the majorities in their societies in a more fully secularist way. However, the modernizing and westernizing secular intellectuals succeeded in providing the worldviews and visions for the political elite that has been created by the transformations of the past two centuries. Most states in the contemporary Muslim world are based on ideological foundations provided by the secular intellectuals in Muslim societies.

The secular intellectuals were products of new modes of education and the transformations resulting from the dynamics of Westernization and modernization and were a separate "new class." They emerged as the dominant intellectual grouping in the first half of the twentieth century, reaching possibly a peak of influence and power in the days of the worldwide emergence of various forms of "radical socialism" during the 1960s. However, their generic political secularism did not become the hegemonic worldview in societies in the Muslim world (or elsewhere), and by the 1990s, the older style of a relatively "pure" secularism was being challenged significantly, even in some of its most solid bastions like Turkey.

The "secular intellectual" remains an important factor in the Muslim world. The contemporary role of the secular intellectuals is almost "classic" in these societies as a separated, sometimes alienated, grouping. They are most visible as active critics of authorities and policies in the emerging postsecularist world. The "new class" of secular intellectuals first developed as a small minority within the strata of intellectuals in modern Muslim societies. In that context, the major alternative to them was the traditional "religious intellectual" grouping among the ulama. The success of the secular intellectuals in the twentieth century is related both to the needs of modernizing societies and also to the weaknesses of the ulama in the modern era.

Decline of the Ulama

As the ulama developed as a special grouping within Muslim society, they became identified with established institutions and were more preservers and caretakers than moral critics. Already by the fourteenth century, the ulama as a class were coming under criticism. Ibn Khaldoun argued that the scholars of his own time could not be thought of as "the heirs of the prophets." The standing of the scholars simply "reflects an affectation of respect for their position in the royal councils, where it is desired to make a show of reverence for the religious ranks. . . . The jurist who is not pious . . . has not inherited anything. He merely makes rulings for us as to how to act. This applies to the majority of contemporary jurists."[52]

In some major areas, like the Ottoman Empire, the ulama had become an institutionalized part of the ruling system. This gave real power to the scholars but opened the way for the organizations of scholars to become closely tied to political institutions that were subject to decline. In Ottoman domains, there was a long-term decline of the prestige and effectiveness of the bureaucratic, preserving ulama through intellectual rigidity tied to a standardized official educational system, corruption in the operation of offices, and the emergence of a wealthy and hereditary Ottoman "Molla aristocracy."[53] Although it is clear that the modernizing transformations of the nineteenth century had a major negative impact on the role of the ulama, the roots of the decline are deeper. By the eighteenth century, it

> is difficult to avoid the impression that in reality the position of the
> *Ulema* was gravely undermined. Though they still preserved the ap-
> pearance of power, it was beginning to wear thin. . . . The pitiable
> spectacle which the *Seyhs* [teachers] were to present during the
> nineteenth century was not solely the result of the rapid overthrow
> of the old social order. It was the sudden culmination of a long
> process that had gradually sapped their moral position.[54]

Some of the most important criticism of and opposition to the ulama establishments throughout the Muslim world came from ulama in the tajdid tradition. At the beginning of the nineteenth century in West Africa, the great jihad led by Uthman dan Fodio involved a "constant attack" on "the evil scholars" (*ulama al-su*) who had compromised in practice with local non-Islamic traditions.[55] In the same era, one of the leading intel- lectuals in Yemen whose works were widely known, Muhammad al- Shawkani (d. 1834), argued that the rigid adherence of ulama to the texts of their law schools (taqlid) was a form of idolatry, which made those ulama unbelievers.[56]

During the nineteenth century, the most active ulama were those within the tajdid tradition of Muslim intellectuals. While they clashed with the emerging secular intellectual, they had, in the long run, little direct im- pact on the direction in which their societies were moving. They did have a very important indirect effect by keeping alive authentically indigenous traditions of critical intellectual life that could provide inspiration for the later Muslim activist intellectuals.

The majority of the ulama in most Muslim societies emerged in the nineteenth and twentieth century as a declining conservative force. The educational institutions under their control lost resources, students, and influence and in many places were simply taken over by the states, which were increasingly dominated by secularist modernizers. Perhaps the major symbolic culmination of this trend was the nationalization in 1961 of the great historic Islamic university of al-Azhar in Cairo. The justification was the need to "train a new generation committed to and capable of con- tributing to modernization and development. As a result, the university lost much of its independence both academically and politically."[57]

The basic fact about the role of the "traditional" ulama in the modern world is "that the *'ulama* as a group lost their position as an uncontested intellectual elite in the Arab world,"[58] and this is true elsewhere as well. Except "for a few bold spirits . . . the *'ulama'* responded to the challenge of modernity by withdrawing into a defensive conservatism"[59] at the same time that the modernizing secular intellectuals were emerging as a major force. The old-style ulama proved to be unable to provide inspiration or help for the emerging modern-educated Muslims in the context of the rising influence of secularism.

The experience of Hasan al-Banna as recounted in his autobiography illustrates this weakness well. In the 1920s, al-Banna was a modern-educated Egyptian who was training to be a schoolteacher. He was concerned by what he saw as the increasing moral corruption of his society caused by Western intellectual and political domination. Al-Banna went to leading ulama in hopes of finding ways of resisting this growing corruption and instead was advised to retreat quietly into his own personal world of religious thought.[60] It was only after this disillusionment with the leading ulama that al-Banna began to organize his own activist (and non-ulama) association dedicated to strengthening Islamic faith and practice.

The failure of the old-style ulama to provide any real alternative to the secular intellectuals in the nineteenth and early twentieth century may be the single most important aspect of the rise of the contemporary Muslim activist intellectual. The conservative ulama have not had much success in maintaining their influence either in the days of imperial rule or under the conditions of political independence.

> The colonial and postcolonial moment in the Arab world has led to a noticeable erosion in the religious and social position of the "*ulama*" as the traditonal intelligentsia class in the world of Islam. The function of the traditional '*alim* is to preserve and transmit religious knowledge. A new type of Muslim intellectual (the Islamist) is being born—one who is critical of the "*ulama*," yet who, nevertheless, shares nearly the same world-view of Islam. The new Muslim intellectual takes a more activist role, and is forced, therefore, to interpret the contents of Islam in a new way.[61]

In the final decades of the twentieth century, it was the challenge from the new Muslim intellectuals rather than from the Westernizing secular intellectuals that was transforming the role of the old-style ulama most dramatically. The secular intellectuals were unable to create effective ties with the masses or with the new, increasingly large, educated classes in Muslim societies. Secularist nationalism and radicalism also were unable to coopt the old-style ulama and transform them. Even though the states could secure their grudging cooperation in issuing appropriately nationalist or socialist rulings, few of the old ulama establishment ever were convincingly converted to radical socialism or secularist nationalism.

The ineffectiveness of the traditional ulama meant that the way was open for the emergence of a new style of Muslim intellectual who would work to create a modern but not secularist alternative to both the conservative ulama and the secular intellectuals. To a remarkable degree, the new intellectual perspectives peripheralized the old secular intellectuals and converted the traditional ulama into more activist Islamic advocates and reformers.

Modern Muslim Activist Intellectuals

Many modern-educated Muslims were and are dissatisfied with the alternatives represented by both the new secular intellectuals and the traditional ulama. The secularist Westernizing vision did not provide a satisfactory tie to the cultural foundations of the Muslim intellectual's identity. In addition, by the late nineteenth century, the West meant not just modern ways of doing things but also imperial domination and control of Muslim societies, so the intellectual who was "too secular" in a Westernizing sense might be seen as an agent of imperialism. However, many in the ruling elites and virtually all of the new educated class recognized the absolute necessity of reform and modernization. As a result, the static conservatism of most of the old-style ulama was seen as dangerous, and the tajdid tradition was still represented, in much of the nineteenth century, by ulama who maintained a nonmodern vision of the world.

Between these two alternatives, there were people who worked to create a Muslim approach to modernity that could be both authentically Islamic and effectively modern. In the early part of the nineteenth century, it seemed that such a synthesis might be possible without too much difficulty. This possibility is shown by the experience of Rifa'a al-Tahtawi (1801–1873), an Egyptian scholar with the traditional training for ulama, who spent five years (1826–1831) in Paris as the imam of an educational mission sent by the Egyptian reforming leader, Muhammad Ali. Tahtawi believed that the ulama "are not simply guardians of a fixed and established tradition. . . . He believed that it was necessary to adapt the *Shari'a* to new circumstances and that it was legitimate to do so. . . . If the *'ulama'* are to interpret the *Shari'a* in the light of modern needs, they must understand what the modern world is."[62] In his efforts, which included translations and writing a variety of studies, Tahtawi

> did not devote much time to reconciling what he advocated with the Qur'an. Tahtawi was fortunate enough to write at a time when Western imperialism was not yet making serious incursions into his native Egypt. He did not face the dilemma that wracked so many later Muslim intellectuals—how to advocate modernization without encouraging servility to the West and discouraging confidence in one's own cultural resources.[63]

By the final decades of the nineteenth century, the dilemmas created by European imperial expansion and the recognized need for modernization made a "middle position" much more difficult. The alternatives were, in general terms, to accept the sheer power of European imperialism and try to articulate a "modern Islam" or to organize militant opposition to European expansion with a minimum of Westernization. Efforts to accomplish the former came to be called Islamic modernism, while the latter was the most visible activity of the people engaged in nonmodern tajdid as they confronted European imperialism. In either case, the situation was dominated by the fact of the overwhelming might of the Western powers.

During the nineteenth century the older dynamics of the history of the tajdid tradition produced a number of movements and groups that had little relationship to the efforts to bring together Western and Islamic elements. However, once established, these movements at times became important in providing the basis for resistance to Western imperial expansion. An important example is the development of Sufi brotherhoods in the tradition of Ahmad ibn Idris (1750?–1837), a North African scholar who taught in Mecca for a long time and whose students organized a remarkable number of important Islamic movements during the nineteenth century.[64] One of his students, Muhammad bibn Ali al-Sanusi, established the Sanusiyyah brotherhood, which played an important role in resistance first to French imperial expansion in Africa and then to the Italian conquest of Libya in the twentieth century and whose head finally became the first king of independent Libya in 1952.

Many other teachers who combined being scholars with being leaders of effective brotherhood organizations were important in resisting European expansion. It was the Amir Abd al-Qadir, a Qadiriyyah shaykh, who led Muslim resistance to the French conquest of Algeria in the 1830s and 1840s and Amir Shamil (1796–1871) of the Naqshbandiyyah who led the fighting against the Russian conquest of the Caucasus. The Mahdi in the Sudan was a quiet scholar in the tajdid tradition who led a movement in the 1880s that established an "Islamic state" after driving Egyptian and British forces out of the country. All of these movements represented a resistance to European expansion that was firmly within the tajdid tradition but gave virtually no recognition to the need to "rethink" basic ideological positions. Unaware of the "need to modernize," such movements ultimately were defeated. They provided inspiration but no intellectual content for later nationalists. They did, however, keep alive the indigenous tradition of tajdid that could become a resource for later Muslim activists.

The most influential, in modern terms, of the efforts to create a middle position between the secular intellectuals and the old-style ulama were those that created what has come to be called Islamic modernism. While this involved some resistance to European imperialism, it was primarily an effort to create a synthesis of modern Western and Islamic intellectual traditions. The most prominent of these new Islamic modernist intellectuals is Jamal al-Din al-Afghani (1838–1897), who traveled throughout the Muslim world calling for the creation of Pan-Islamic unity in opposition to the

West and a modern-style rationalist interpretation of the Islamic tradition. "His legacy of reinterpretation of Islam in a modernist, pragmatic, anti-imperialist direction and his political activism have been of great importance to the modern Muslim world."[65]

Al-Afghani was more politically oriented than most of the Islamic modernists of the end of the nineteenth century. The major expressions of this modernist position were presented by intellectuals who accepted the fact of foreign (non-Muslim) rule in their society and worked to create an effectively modern interpretation of Islam. The leading figures in this were Muhammad Abduh in Egypt, Sir Sayyid Ahmad Khan in India, and Ismail Gasprinskii in the Russian Empire. Each of these men accepted rule by non-Muslims and worked to develop programs of modern and authentically Islamic education and interpretation. Both secular intellectuals, who adopted a more nationalist tone, and the conservative ulama, who opposed the modernist rationalism, rejected the Islamic modernists and their efforts.

For a brief period of time in the early twentieth century, the Islamic modernists looked like they might play a major role in the development of Muslim societies. The journal of the modernists in Egypt, *al-Manar*, was read throughout the Muslim world and inspired many imitators, from magazines in the islands of southeast Asia to discussion groups in North Africa. The Islamic modernist mode had some appeal but strong opposition. The modernist ulama "found themselves opposed not only to the reactionary traditionalists 'who resisted all change,' but to the young 'renegades' who wanted 'to westernize Islam . . . to make Muslims forget their history and abandon their heritage.'"[66] In this context, following the deaths of the major figures of the late nineteenth century, there was a tendency for Islamic modernism to develop in two different and contradictory directions. Some, like Rashid Rida, the editor of *al-Manar*, tended to emphasize the need to defend a more traditionally articulated Islam and moved modernism in a more traditionalist direction. Others, like Qasim Amin, stressed the modern elements of this tradition and essentially became secular intellectuals and participated in their triumph in the interwar era.

The secular intellectuals did not fully desert the task of presenting Islam, but they presented a romanticized version that would fit comfortably into a secularist worldview. The affirmation of a nonsecularist version of Islam became the task of a new kind of intellectual who could be seen as an heir to al-Afghani and Abduh but was quite different from them. Egypt, as is common, provides the prototype of this person and movement in Hasan al-Banna and the Muslim Brotherhood.

In the interwar era, a new type of Muslim intellectual began to emerge. This person was heir to the modernist efforts of al-Afghani and Abduh (and Ahmad Khan and others) but was different in terms of the evaluation of the West. While Abduh emphasized the importance of a rational articulation of Islam and accepted the validity of Western rationalist thought, as well as accepting the fact of British rule in Egypt, al-Banna was actively anti-imperialist and saw much of the Western intellectual heritage as encouraging unbelief and undermining Islam. Similarly, in South Asia, Abu al-Ala al-Mawdudi began to present a position that was in contrast not only to the West-accepting rationalism of Ahmad Khan but also the more mystical philosophical positions of the twentieth-century Indian Islamic modernist Muhammad Iqbal. Mawdudi's work eventually resulted in the creation of the Jama'at i-Islami as a parallel to the Muslim Brotherhood in Egypt.

The people who joined the Muslim Brotherhood and the Jama'at were modern-educated Muslims who were unable to believe the traditional ulama but were unwilling to accept the secularist positions of the Westernizers. Al-Banna and Mawdudi were not content simply to provide intellectual formulations for people to read; they established organizations that people could join. These leaders represented a new kind of Islamic intellectual, committed to and relatively knowledgable in Islam but not traditional ulama. They were, instead, modern-educated and able to speak to the growing proportion of Muslim societies who were also modern-educated but not willing to become secularists.

In the era of anti-imperialist nationalism, the secularist intellectuals spoke for nationalist aspirations. They provided the intellectual foundations both for the liberal nationalisms that achieved independence and the radical nationalism that succeeded them in countries like Egypt. In this context, al-Banna, Mawdudi, and others like them were on the fringes of power and public visibility. However, at the end of the 1960s, there was a profound discouragement with the lack of achievements by the radical secularist elites. The secular intellectuals were unable to produce a new version of secular modernity that could cope with this crisis.

By the 1970s, virtually all Muslims were directly involved in the increasingly global, modern world. The "modern-educated" classes in Muslim societies were a growing proportion of Muslim societies, and these societies were rapidly urbanizing. The old elitist visions of the secularists, which had few roots in the Islamic traditions and which were important to the newly educated and urban masses, and the social and political institutions that had been created by Western-style modernizers had proven to be woefully inadequate. Among the modern educated classes, a new style of Muslim intellectual emerged, who was committed to effective transformation of society but within the framework of ideologies and programs that could be identified as authentically Islamic. In spirit, these new Muslim intellectuals were a continuation of the radical tajdid tradition in Islam. In practice, they built on the accomplishments of the early Islamic modernists and the new-style Muslim associations created by Mawdudi and al-Banna. They created activist programs of reform and social transformation that could be clearly identified as Islamic but, at the same time, went far beyond the traditionalism of the remaining conservative ulama establishment.

This new alternative attracted people from both the old secular intellectual establishment and the more traditional ulama organizations. Mustafa Mahmoud, a former Marxist, could become a prominent figure in Islamic revivalist life in Cairo and could speak of "my trip from doubt to faith."[67] Khalid Muhammad Khalid, the Egyptian intellectual who caused a major debate in the 1940s with a book calling for the separation of religion and politics, joined those calling for an Islamic state in the 1980s. The key to this new development was the emergence of the Muslim activist intellectuals and the perspectives that they articulated.

These Islamically oriented activist intellectuals are the subject of this book. They are people whose lives are in many ways very different; however, at the core, they share a number of important characteristics. While they are all well informed in Islamic traditional studies, they are not traditional ulama. Although they are real intellectuals in their general interest and work in defining and expressing concepts and symbols, they are activists in that they are directly involved in political and social affairs rather than standing aloof as intellectual critics. There are many individuals throughout the Muslim world who are among this emerging group, and only a few could be discussed in a single volume, so the coverage obviously is not comprehensive. The individuals included in this book illustrate important dimensions of the role of the activist intellectuals in shaping contemporary Islamic life and can be divided into three groups: the early activists after the middle of the century who articulated important foundations for the Islamic resurgence; the "second generation" who became an important part of the resurgence in the 1970s and 1980s; and a third group, whose work in the 1990s represents a further development of intellectual and political involvement in the context of the Islamic resurgence as part of the established mainstream.

Three individuals reflect the early articulation of the activist intellectuals' contributions at the beginning of the era of the Islamic resurgence, creating new modes of organizing Islamic thought. Ismail al-Faruqi became a prominent scholar in Western universities and traveled widely in the Muslim world. He was an important figure in the development of the Islamization-of-knowledge project, which provides a significant intellectual foundation for much of the late-twentieth-century Islamic resurgence. Khurshid Ahmad is part of the Jamaat-I Islami tradition in South Asia and was both an activist and a prominent intellectual in the definition of a new disciplinary vision of Islamic economics. Maryam Jameelah is an American convert to Islam who became, by the early 1960s, a highly visible articulator of a postapologetic Islamic discourse. The "second generation" became important as the Islamic resurgence became a major factor in Muslim world developments. Hasan Hanafi, an Egyptian philosopher, extended the efforts of redefining intellectual methods and, in the global context of the 1960s and 1960s, worked to define an Islamic liberation theology. Rashid Ghannoushi and Hasan Turabi became leaders of Islamist movements in Tunisia and Sudan, with Ghannoushi ending up in exile as the leader of a major opposition movement and Turabi coming to power as the leading idealogue for an Islamically oriented military regime.

In the 1990s, Islamic intellectuals emerged in new relationships to political power. The Islamic Republic had been in existence for more than a decade in Iran, and Abdolkarim Soroush provides an example of a rethinking of the Islamic revolutionary tradition. In Malaysia, the former leader of an activist Islamic student organization, Anwar Ibrahim, became deputy prime minister and then, following arrest and a political trial, the leading symbol of opposition. In Indonesia, Abdurrahman Wahid, a leader of one of the largest Islamic organizations in the world and a prominent intellectual, became president of the country following the downfall of the long-standing regime of Suharto. These people represent important trends in Islamic intellectual life, reflecting the continuing globalization of Islamic life and the articulation of activist perspectives regarding diversity and the changing nature of modern and postmodern society.

These nine individuals through their activist lives and intellectual contributions represent highly significant forces within the contemporary Muslim world. In many ways, they can be viewed as makers of contemporary Islam.

I
ISMAIL RAGI AL-FARUQI
Pioneer in Muslim-Christian Relations

Ismail Ragi al-Faruqi's untimely death (murdered with his wife, Lois Lamya al-Faruqi, a scholar of Islamic art, on May 24, 1986) cut short the life of a creative mind, productive scholar, and provocative colleague. He was a pioneer in the development of Islamic studies in America and in interreligious dialogue internationally and an activist who sought to transform the Islamic community at home and abroad.

Faruqi's Palestinian roots, Arab heritage, and Islamic faith made the man and informed his life and work as a scholar. Issues of identity, authenticity, acculturation, and Western political and cultural imperialism, so common in recent years, were continuous themes in his writing, though he addressed them differently at different stages in his life. His early emphasis on Arabism as the vehicle of Islam was tempered by a later centrality accorded to Islam and Muslim identity. He would draw on these sources intellectually, religiously, and aesthetically throughout the rest of his life.

Early Life and Education

After an early traditional Islamic education at the mosque school, al-Faruqi attended a French Catholic school, College des Freres (St. Joseph) in Palestine. This was followed by five years at the American University of Beirut, where he earned his bachelor's degree in 1941. He entered government service and in 1945, at twenty-four, became governor of Galilee; the future direction of his life seemed set. All came to an abrupt end with the creation of the state of Israel in 1948, and Faruqi became one of thousands of Palestinian refugees, emigrating with his family to Lebanon. His life and career as an administrator in Palestine now tragically ended, he, like many other Palestinians, turned to academia to rebuild his life and career. America became the training ground where he prepared himself by earning master's degrees at Indiana and Harvard and in 1952 a doctorate in philosophy from the University of Indiana. These were difficult years; added to the trauma of exile from his homeland was the struggle to survive and support himself in his studies.

Although Faruqi successfully completed a doctoral degree in Western philosophy, both a scarcity of jobs and an inner drive brought him back to his Islamic intellectual heritage and roots. He left America for Cairo, where for four years, from 1954 to 1958, he immersed himself in the study of Islam at Cairo's famed al-Azhar University. Returning to North America, he became a visiting professor of Islamic Studies at the Institute of Islamic Studies and a fellow of the Faculty of Divinity at McGill University from 1959 to 1961, where he studied Christianity and Judaism. He then began his professional career as professor of Islamic studies at the Central Institute of Islamic Research in Karachi from 1961 to 1963. During the following year he returned to America as a visiting professor of the history of religions at the University of Chicago. In 1964, he obtained his first full time permanent position as associate professor in the Department of Religion at Syracuse University. He finally moved to Temple University in 1968 to become professor of Islamic studies and history of religions, a post he retained until his death in 1986. During an extremely active and productive professional life that spanned almost thirty years, he authored, edited, or translated twenty-five books, published more than one hundred articles, was a visiting professor at more than twenty-three universities in Africa, Europe, the Middle East, and South and Southeast Asia, and served on the editorial boards of seven major journals.

Arabism and Islam

Ismail al-Al-Faruqi's Arab/Palestinian Muslim identity was at the center of the man and the scholar. For him, Arabism and Islam were intertwined; yet it is possible to identify two phases or stages in his life and thought. In the first, Arabism was the dominant theme of his discourse. In the second, Islam occupied center stage as he assumed the role more and more of an Islamic activist intellectual, functioning both as an academic and a Muslim leader nationally and internationally. The first phase of his thought is epitomized in his book *On Arabism: Urubah and Religion.*

Here, Arabism is the central reality of Islamic history, faith, and culture. It is "as old as the Arab stream of being itself since it is the spirit which animates the stream and gives the momentum."[1] Indeed, it is the soul of the Arab stream of being, molded by the consciousness that God is and that he is one.

The borders of Arabism, for Faruqi, were indeed far-flung and inclusive, embracing the entire Islamic community (*ummah*) and non-Muslim Arabs alike. For Faruqi, Arabism was not simply an idea but a reality, an identity, and a set of values, integral to and inseparable from the identity of all Muslims and all non-Muslim Arabs. It was the very spirit of the ummah. Arabism incorporated not only the Arabic-speaking members of the Arab world but also the entire world community of Muslims, since Arab language, consciousness, and values are at the core of their common Islamic faith.

Faruqi read the Quran through Arab eyes. As Arabic is the language of the Quran, so the content of revelation is regarded as a message to the Arabs. Thus, he believed, Arabs are the referent for the Quranic declaration: "Ye are the best people brought forth unto mankind." Regarding this reading as a judgment of faith, he could formulate the following syllogism based on the Quranic mandate to enjoin good and prohibit evil: "To enjoin good, forbid evil and believe in God is to be ethically the best; The Arabs enjoin the good, forbid evil and believe in God; therefore, the Arabs are ethically the best."[2] The Arabs are an elite who ought to be expected to do better than those who are non-Arabic-speaking.

The centrality of Arabism (*urubah*) to Islamic history and civilization in Faruqi's thought can be seen in the titles that he selected for the four projected volumes of his series on Arabism: *Urubah and Religion*, *Urubah and Art*, *Urubah and Society*, and *Urubah and Man*. He regarded Arabness or Arab consciousness as the vehicle for the divine message and its immanence in faith, society, and culture. In this sense, Arabness was central to the history of religion or, more specifically, to the three prophetic faiths. Faruqi could declare that Arabism was cointensive with the values of Islam as well as with the meaning of the Hebrew prophets and Jesus.[3]

Al-Faruqi also maintained that Arabism is the heart of non-Muslim Arab identity, though it is often not recognized as such because of the influence of European colonialism: "[non-Muslim Arabs have] lived every value that Arabism recognized, including the Quranic values, but have regrettably maintained a pseudo-consciousness of a separate identity, under the indoctrination, encouragement and political instigation of foreigners in pursuit of imperialistic aims."[4] Faruqi's position here was rooted in his distinction between Arab Christians and Western Christians. The former have preserved the faith, original Christianity, in its pristine Semitic purity from what he regarded as the accretions and distortions of Jesus' message by the Pauline West. For this, he maintained, they were regarded as heretics and schismatics, persecuted by their coreligionists. Driven from their lands, Arab Christians, he declared, were often more at home and able to function under the aegis of Islam.

Whether in his Arabist or his later Islamic activist period, Ismail Faruqi was a person who believed in and therefore sought to interpret reality as an integrated, interrelated whole. Its foundation and center is belief in God; Islam provides the fullest expression of God's will for humankind and the value system to be followed. If Arabism is the spirit and best expression of Islamic values in a human community, then the pieces that do not seem to fit, such as non-Arab Muslims and non-Muslim Arabs, are to be understood as unconscious or uncultivated expressions of Arabism.[5]

While few questioned Arab influence on non-Arab Muslim faith and culture or Arab Muslim influence on non-Muslim Arabs, the implication that they both find their ultimate expression and fulfillment in Faruqi's interpretation of Arabism was regarded by many others as an attempt to establish the hegemony of Arab Islam or, more precisely, Arab Muslim culture. This attitude is reflected in Faruqi's observation that "[t]his difference between a Muslim and a Christian Arab does not constitute a difference in culture or religion or ethics, but in personality".[6]

As we will show, Faruqi's later work and writing focused on a comprehensive vision of Islam and its relationship to all aspects of life and culture. However, he also continued in later life to maintain the special place of Arabism in Islam based on the integral relationship of Arabic to both the form and content of the Quran: "the Quran is inseparable from its Arabic form, and hence . . . Islam is *ipso facto* inseparable from *urubah*."[7]

Faruqi was quick to distinguish urubah from any form of Arab nationalism or ethnocentrism. He regarded any emphasis on nationality or ethnicity as a modern phenomenon. Thus, Arab nationalism of any kind was to be rejected as a western import introduced by Arab Christians such as Constantin Zurayk and Michel Aflaq under the influence of modern European notions of nationalism. Such narrow ethnocentric nationalisms sharply contrast with Faruqi's understanding of an Arabism rooted in the universal revelation of the Quran, and therefore the common legacy to all Muslims. He believed that these Western-inspired nationalisms constitute a new tribalism *(shuubiyyah)* aimed at undermining the unity and universal brotherhood of the ummah.[8]

During the period just prior to and after the writing of *On Arabism*, Faruqi was often described as a Muslim modernist. His approach in teaching and interpretation bore this out. His course on modern Islam focused on the work and writings of Jamal al-Din al-Afghani, Muhammad Abduh, Sayyid Ahmad Khan, and Muhammad Iqbal, rather than, for example, Hasan al-Banna, Sayyid Qutb, or Mawlana Mawdudi. Living and working in the West, Faruqi tended to present Islam in Western categories to engage his audience as well as make Islam more comprehensible and respected. In explaining Islam through his writing and lectures to an often ignorant, ill-informed, or hostile western audience, Faruqi emphasized the place of the ideal (the principles, beliefs, and values of Islam) over the realities of contemporary Muslim life. In particular, he emphasized reason, science, progress, the work ethic, and private property. Like the fathers of Islamic modernism, he often presented Islam as the religion par excellence of reason, science, and progress. Ironically, though he decried Western cultural penetration and influence, both his choice of categories and his criteria in explaining and defending Islam were Western. Indeed, some have argued that he presented Islam within the worldview of the Enlightenment and the Protestant work ethic.

From Arab Nationalist to Islamic Scholar-Activist

During the 1950s and 1960s, Ismail Faruqi sounded like an Arab heir to Islamic modernism and Western empiricism with his emphasis on Islam as the religion of reason par excellence. In the late 1960s and early 1970s, he progressively resolved this struggle with his identity, assuming the role of an Islamic scholar-activist. Reflecting on this transitional period, he reminisced: "There was a time in my life . . . when all I cared about was proving to myself that I could win my physical and intellectual existence from the West. But, when I won it, it became meaningless. I asked myself: Who am I? A Palestinian, a philosopher, a liberal humanist? My answer was: I am a Muslim!"[9]

This shift in orientation was evident in the recasting of his intellectual framework as well as his activism. Islam replaced Arabism as the primary focus and reference point. The projected series of books on Arabism was replaced by books and articles on Islam. Instead of Arabism and the culture or Arabism and society, it was now Islam and culture, Islam and society, Islam and art, Islamization of knowledge. Islam had always had an important place in Faruqi's writing, but it now became its center and organizing principle. Islam was presented as an all-encompassing ideology, the primary identity and source of unity of an otherwise diverse worldwide community of believers and the guiding principle for society and culture. This approach, this wholistic Islamic worldview, was embodied in a new phase in his life and career as he continued to write extensively, to lecture and consult with Islamic movements and national governments, and to organize Muslims in America. Intellectually, it was epitomized in such works as *Tawhid: Its Implications for Thought and Life* and in his last publication, *The Cultural Atlas of Islam*, which he coauthored with his wife, Lois Lamya al-Faruqi .

Islam: An Ideological Worldview

Faruqi saw the world through the prism of his Islamic faith and commitment, focused on issues of identity, history, belief, culture, social mores, international relations. Whatever the national and cultural differences across the Muslim world, for Ismail al-Al-Faruqi analysis of the strengths and weaknesses (past, present, and future) of Muslim societies began with Islam—its presence in society and its necessary role in development. As we view his writings and activities during the 1970s and 1980s, we see old themes and new concerns, all brought together now under the umbrella of Islam. His analysis of the plight of Muslim societies, its causes and cure, are cast in an Islamic mold. Spiritual malaise, the Westernization of society, education, poverty, economic dependence, political fragmentation, military impotence, the liberation of Jerusalem—all were addressed from within an Islamic context. It was Islam, rather than Arabism or Palestinianism, that was now to be the starting point and primary frame of reference.

Islam and the West

Ismail Al-Faruqi laid the failures of Muslim societies at the doorstep of the West and the Muslim community alike. He believed that the Crusades, European colonialism, Zionism, and superpower (U.S.-Soviet) neocolonialism were the formative influences in the West's attitude and policies and enduring political and cultural realities in the contemporary Muslim world. The Westernization of Muslim societies begun during the colonial era afflicted modern Muslim states and societies. Nationalist governments spread this "despicable Western virus," a variation of the old disease of tribalism (shuubiyyah), which divided and weakened the ummah. Westernization, informed by secularism and based on the principles and values of a spiritually bankrupt West, focused on material progress, neglecting the integral place of the spiritual.[10]

Religion, Faruqi maintained, was marginalized by nationalist governments and modern elites. Modernization programs were uncritically adopted and transplanted from the West, alienating Muslims from their past and making them a caricature of Westerners. A debilitated community was further weakened by its political, economic, military, and cultural dependence on the West. But what of those Muslims and movements that have undertaken Islamic responses to revitalize the ummah? While al-Faruqi was a great admirer of eighteenth- and nineteenth-century revivalist movements, he believed that they were ill prepared to face the challenges from the West. They enjoyed only limited success. Similarly, modern associations like Hasan al-Banna's Muslim Brotherhood in Egypt failed to delineate in sufficient detail their Islamic blueprint for society. Whatever its accomplishments and gains, Faruqi found the condition of the Islamic community in a generally sorry state: divided and dependent, an easy prey to its internal and external enemies. He believed that revival (tajdid) and reform (islah), an Islamic reformation, were the order of the day.

Islamic Reform

An old Christian acquaintance of al-Faruqi once commented that al-Faruqi believed that Islam was in need of a reformation and, he believed, al-Faruqi aspired to be its Luther. In all probability, al-Faruqi would have preferred the term mujahid, a true struggler for Islam, or, more simply, being known as a *muslim*, one whose submission is a lifelong struggle to re-alize or actualize God's will in personal life and in society. The writing and activities of the last decade of his life reveal a man driven by his desire and commitment to reform or change the present and future condition of Mus-lims. Equipped with his knowledge of Islam and Western thought, he never ceased his struggle to provide the "ideational depth" and processes he thought were needed for the inculturation and implementation of Islam in Muslim societies. At the same time, he continued his efforts to present his vision of Islam to the West, convinced that the Children of Abraham (Jews, Christians, and Muslims) had to reach an accommodation on religious as well as political and cultural grounds.

Al-Faruqi combined the spirit of the Islamic modernists such as Egypt's Muhammad Abduh and Pakistan's Muhammad Iqbal with the revivalist outlook of earlier leaders such as Saudi Arabia's Muhammad ibn Abd al-Wahhab. Like ibn Abd al-Wahhab, he was bitterly critical of the corrosive effects of Sufism and outside cultural influences on Islam and convinced of the need to see all of Muslim life as rooted in the doctrine of *tawhid*, God's unity or oneness.[11]

Islam was to be the primary referent in all aspects of life. At the same time, Faruqi was an heir to the Islamic modernist legacy with its emphasis on Islam as the religion of reason. Reason and revelation were means to knowledge of the divine will: "knowledge of the divine will is possible by rea-son, certain by revelation."[12] We can see in Faruqi's writings the twofold in-fluence of Muhammad ibn Abd al-Wahhab and Muhammad Abduh, both of whose works included a study of tawhid. This is particularly evident in Faruqi's *Tawhid: Its Implications for Thought and Life*. Like Abduh and ibn Abdul Wahhab, he grounded his interpretation of Islam in the doctrine of tawhid, combining the classical affirmation of the centrality of God's one-ness with a modernist interpretation (ijtihad) and application of Islam to modern life. Tawhid is presented as the essence of religious experience, the quintessence of Islam, the principle of history, of knowledge, of ethics, of aesthetics, of the ummah, of the family, of the political, social, economic, and world orders. Tawhid is the basis and heart of Islam's comprehensive worldview: "All the diversity, wealth and history, culture and learning, wis-dom and civilization of Islam is compressed in this shortest of sentences—La ilaha illa Allah [There is no God but God]."[13]

The extent to which Faruqi was the product of and bridged two worlds is demonstrated by the ideas and language he employed in his writing and talks for both non-Muslim, Western audiences and his brothers and sisters in Islam. It is particularly striking in *Tawhid*, which was written as a "Mus-lim Training Manual." Here, despite his audience, his presentation of Islam combines Islamic belief and values with Western philosophical/religious issues and language. Some might attribute this simply to the influence of his Western education and his living in the West, but it would probably be more correct to credit it to his desire to present Islam as the only viable response to modern issues that, in his estimation, Western culture has failed to adequately address. This approach met a twofold need. It offered a modern interpretation of Islam and took into account the Western cultural tradition that had increasingly penetrated the education and lives of Muslims. Thus, for example, Islam is presented as the religion of nature, true humanism, ethics, and society. Tawhid provides a unity to nature, personhood, and truth that subordinates them to God and, in turn, resolves any concern about a conflict between religion and science, affirms the ethical dimenson of Islam, and legitimates the need to rediscover the Islamic dimension of all knowledge through a process of Islamization. Al-Faruqi clearly affirmed the integral or essential relationship of Islam to all of reality: "The Islamic mind knows no pair of contraries such as "religious-secular," "sacred-profane," "church-state," and in Arabic, the religious language of Islam, has no words for them in its vocabulary."[14]

His penchant for Western philosophical language can be seen in such statements as: "Hedonism, eudaemonism and all other theories which find moral value in the very process of natural life are [the Muslim's] *bete noire*."[15] It is even more pronounced in his observation that "He [the Muslim] is therefore an axiologist in his religious disciplines of exegesis, but only to the end of reaching a sound deontology, as a jurist."[16] The use of Western categories and language did not betray an uncritical acceptance of and assimilation to Western culture. Indeed, it was to counter such dangers to Islam that Faruqi in his later years in particular focused on what he termed the Islamization of knowledge.

Training a New Generation

A major focus of al-Faruqi's work was the education of a new generation of Muslims, schooled in modern methods but Islamically oriented. Believing that many of the problems of the Muslim world are due to its elites and the bifurcation of education in Muslim societies, he addressed this problem in a variety of ways. Typically, he combined thought with action, ideology with its institutionalization and implementation. He traveled extensively and regularly throughout the Muslim world, lecturing at universities and to Muslim youth groups and carefully recruiting students for his program at Temple University in Philadelphia. Their presence at Temple enhanced the learning experience of non-Muslim students, but, more important, provided an opportunity for Muslims to obtain modern university education combining the study of Islam, the history of religions, and other religious traditions. He and his wife, Lois Lamya Faruqi, enjoyed a transnational extended family. They often looked after the material needs as well as educational requirements of their students, providing for many a home (family) away from home.

Organizationally, al-Faruqi was a leader in the Muslim Student Association, a founder and president of associations of Muslim professionals such as the Association of Muslim Social Scientists, and chairman of the board of trustees of the North American Islamic Trust. Throughout his scholarly life, he combined his commitment to Islam and Islamic studies with his role as an historian of religion and an ecumenist. At the same time that he worked so feverishly to establish Islamic studies programs, recruit and train Muslim students, and organize Muslim professionals, he also established and chaired the Islamic Studies Steering Committee of the American Academy of Religion (AAR; 1976–1982), the largest professional association of professors of religion. For the first time, Islamic studies enjoyed a strong presence in the AAR through a series of panels convened every year at the annual meeting and the publications that resulted from the procedings.[17]

By the late 1970s, Faruqi had become restless and frustrated with his situation at Temple University. Budget cuts, departmental politics, and conflicting priorities kept him from building the kind of program in Islamic studies that had first attracted him to Temple. His own work was moving him more and more in the direction of what may be described as strategic planning for and implementation of Islamic reform. As we have shown, he had increasingly devoted the bulk of his energies to sketching out his interpretation of the meaning of Islam and its implications for Muslim society and to organizing and educating Muslims. He realized that implementing new, non-Western models for the development of Muslim societies and communities, abroad and at home, required the training of new generations of Muslims and the organized efforts of those experts who were available.

In his last years, several projects in particular typified his "mission," consuming the major portion of his time and energies. He established the American Islamic College in Chicago and served as its first president. For more than a decade he had talked about creating a major Islamic university in the United States where Islamic studies and training could be done as he had envisioned them. His plans were grand, and on a number of occasions they seemed close to realization. However, he had to settle for a more modest beginning with a small college in Chicago. At the same time, he realized a long-held dream when, in 1981, he created the International Institute for Islamic Thought in Virginia. He realized that while one might object to the uncritical adoption of Western models of political, economic, social, and educational development, they are the established, entrenched models. Appeals and demands for more Islamically oriented states and societies had to move beyond criticism of the status quo and ideological rhetoric regarding Islamic alternatives. Islamic activism had to be prepared to move beyond opposition to implementation. It no longer was enough to decry what one was against and to proclaim what one was for; it was imperative to possess specific, concrete plans for the new Islamic order.

The growth of Islamic movements and of government appeals to Islam underscored, Faruqi believed, the pressing need for think tanks of experts prepared to bridge the bifurcated world of modern secular elites and more traditional religious leaders. Such organizations could provide the studies and plans needed to address the question of what modern Islamic political, economic, social, and legal systems should look like. At the heart of his vision was the Islamization of knowledge. He regarded the political, economic, and religiocultural malaise of the Islamic community as primarily due to the bifurcated state of education in the Muslim world with a resultant lack of vision. He believed that the cure was twofold: the compulsory study of Islamic civilization and the Islamization of modern knowledge. Here we find his familiar themes, a combination of the influences of the Islamic modernist and revivalist traditions. These include the belief that the weakness and failures of Muslims were the result of the abandonment of ijtihad (interpretation), which is the source of creativity in Islam; the tendency to oppose revelation (*wahy*) to reason (*aql*); the separation of thought from action; and cultural and religious dualism. In typical fashion, Faruqi combined thought and action. He published several pieces, including *Islamization of Knowledge* and "Islamizing the Social Sciences";[18] organized and participated in international conferences on the Islamization of knowledge in such countries as Malaysia and Pakistan; and served as an advisor to both Muslim governments and Islamic organizations and as a consultant to universities from Africa to Southeast Asia.

Faruqi's desire to develop, institutionalize, and implement the Islamization of knowledge was realized in 1981 when he and like-minded colleagues such as Abdul Hamid Abu Sulayman, Taha Jabir Alalwani, and Jamal Barzinji established the International Institute of Islamic Thought (IIIT) in Herndon, Virginia.[19] Believing that Muslim intellectuals and the Muslim community had uncritically followed Western social sciences, rooted in a Western ideological vision and set of values, IIIT sought to provide an Islamic vision that would Islamize knowledge by Islamizing contemporary academic disciplines. In this way, Muslim societies and communities could modernize without becoming Westernized. They could borrow and benefit from the best of science and technology while basing their development on Islamic principles and values. The Institute has throughout the years of its existence promoted its vision and agenda through publications, seminars, and conferences and the creation of a network of offices in Europe, the Middle East, and Asia.

Muslim–Christian Relations

Interreligious Dialogue

As Faruqi traveled around the world in his capacity as an Islamic scholar-activist, so too he was an active participant, a modern Muslim pioneer, in international ecumenical meetings. From the early publication of his *Christian Ethics* in 1967 to *Trialogue of the Abrahamic Faiths*, he demonstrated his enduring interest and commitment to interfaith dialogue. He was a major force in Islam's dialogue with other world religions. During the 1970s he established himself as a leading Muslim spokesperson for Islam, one of a handful of senior Muslim scholars (including Fazlur Rahman and Seyyed Hossein Nasr) known and respected in both Western academic and ecumenical circles. His writings, speeches, and participation and leadership role in interreligious meetings and organizations sponsored by the World Council of Churches, the National Council of Churches, the Vatican, and the Inter-Religious Peace Colloquium (of which he was vice-president from 1977 to 1982) made him the most visible and prolific Muslim contributor to the dialogue of world religions. His writings and presentations set out the principles and bases for Muslim participation in interreligious dialogue and social action.[20]

As *On Arabism* was the product of his study and lecturing in Cairo at Al-Azhar and the Institute of Higher Arabic Studies at Cairo University, so too his experience at McGill University's Institute of Islamic Studies resulted in his first major ecumenical work, *Christian Ethics*. A Muslim study of Christianity, it was an ambitious two-year project. He read widely in the history of Christian thought and Christian theology and had the opportunity to enter into extended conversation and debate with colleagues such as Wilfred Cantwell Smith, then founder and director of McGill's Institute; Charles Adams; and Stanley Brice Frost, then dean of the Faculty of Divinity.

In its time, *Christian Ethics* was a ground-breaking exercise—a modern-trained Muslim's analysis of Christianity. Faruqi combined an impressive breadth of scholarship, voracious intellect, and linguistic skills. While some took issue with his interpretation and conclusions, he could not be faulted for not doing his homework. His ecumenical intentions and desire to proceed as a historian of religions were evident at the outset. The extensive introduction outlined the principles for what he called a metareligious approach, principles that transcended the boundaries of specific traditions. This was followed by an assessment of Muslim–Christian dialogue and a critical evaluation of several Christian comparativists/theologians: Stephen Neill, Hendrik Kraemer, A. C. Bousquet, and Albert Schweitzer.

Faruqi advocated the need to transcend an apologetic or polemic approach to the study of comparative religions and to engage in what he regarded to be a more objective, scholarly study. He indicted much of past scholarship as proceeding from the biases of past confrontations and conflicts as well as missionary polemics and Orientalist distortions. In their place he proposed a methodology to transcend dogmatic theologies and get back to a "theology-free metareligion" by basing the analysis of religions on a set of self-evident principles.

The difficulties of this undertaking were clear from the outset. Faruqi spoke of his desire to contribute to the task of identifying the spiritual principles of the future unity of humankind and, more specifically, to bring about a rapproachment between Christianity and Islam by uncovering their deeper common ground. However, his claim to the right to reconstruct Christianity and to show Christians "where they have complacently allowed their ethical doctrine to run *ad absurdum*" was one that many found unacceptable.

Al-Faruqi decried the study of Islam by Christians. Moreover, he maintained that the majority of books written on the religions of other peoples by nonbelievers have been the products of the authors' subjecting a religion to standards taken from their own tradition. He concluded: "We do not know of any analytical book on Islam, for instance, written by a Christian, which does not reveal such judgement of Islam by Christian or Western standards."[21] Yet Faruqi's analysis and critique of Christianity provided a reverse case in point, often reflecting judgements informed by his Muslim faith.

Methodological Principles of Interpretation

The foundation of Faruqi's approach to interreligious dalogue was the identification of "higher principles which are to serve as the basis for the comparison of various systems of meanings, of cultural patterns, of moralities, and of religions; the principles by reference to which the meanings of such systems and patterns may be understgood, conceptualized, and systematized."[22]

The first principle was internal coherence, that is, that "the elements of which (something) is constituted are not contradictory to one another."[23] Thus, in the case of the doctrine of the Trinity, Muslims would maintain that there is in it an inherent contradiction. Similarly, Faruqi stated unequivocally that internal coherence excludes recourse to paradox as a theological principle. He felt little need to respond to critics who might question the universal basis for his elevation of an assertion to the status of a self-evident truth.

While Faruqi's third principle maintained that God's commands can not contradict one another, he did not indicate by what criteria competing truth claims and contradictory statements are to be reconciled or resolved. He does state that "after the rules of understanding religious systems (the theoretical and principles of internal and external coherence) have been scrupulously applied to a religion, we may expect that the internal contradictions of a religion have been removed."[24] However, he never seemed concerned with the practical issues that such an approach raises, such as who is to make this judgment and on whose authority, how others would regard this assumption of authority, or how one would counter the charge that one person's principles are another's presuppositions.

What are the bases for assuming the validity of these principles? The answer to this question seems to be reason or rationality. Faruqi used reason to explain or critique Christianity. Jesus' resurrection from the dead is sympathetically but psychologically explained by an underlying assumption that this is the only "rational" explanation. Other Christian doctrines, such as the divinity of Christ, are denied or refuted because they do not make sense. Al-Faruqi characterized his methodology as solely based on reason: "the analysis is rational, critical; and the only argument that may be brought against its principles is an error of reasoning."[25] He maintained that this was an objective, indeed "absolute," critique, saying that "this work is neither a 'Muslim's' nor an 'Islamic' critique, but a human critique of Christian ethics."[26]

He justified the seeming contradiction of this statement by asserting that his study embodied the Islamic spirit, which he identified with rationality itself, maintaining that "in Islam faith (*iman*) means conviction based upon certainty of evidence . . . whatever is oppugn to reason must *ipso facto* be repugnant to Allah."[27]

While some might be tempted to simply see the influence of the early Mutazilah rationalist thought here, it is more accurate to note that Faruqi was an Arab Muslim trained in Western philosophy writing for a Western audience. Thus he employed the canons of modern Western scholarship (reason and empiricism) as the sole instruments for credible study and argumentation. In the process, the historic tension between faith and reason in Islamic history and thought, as witnessed in the debates between the Asharites and the Mutazilah or the theologians and the philosophers, was bypassed or seemingly transcended. Longstanding theological positions and differences not only between Islam and other religions but also within Islam itself were transcended in order to focus on what he regarded as primary—ethics: "Let us drop our old questions regarding the nature of God, which have brought nothing but deadlocks; and let us turn to man, to his duties and responsibilities which are, in fact, none other than God's will. Let God be whom He may; is it not possible—nay, necessary—that all men agree to establish divine will first?"[28]

Ethics

Faruqi believed that emphasis on the will of God as seen in terms of human responsibility and accountability was the key to transcending theological differences and realization of the one brotherhood of humankind. Yet even this noble belief and intention had hidden presuppositions. He presumed that believers would more or less agree on divinely revealed ethical principles, failing to acknowledge that though the three Abrahamic faiths have much in common, there are also important differences with regard to such issues as marriage (the permissibility of polygamy), divorce, alcohol consumption, birth control, and abortion.

Faruqi's analysis of Judaism and Christianity is remarkable both for its scholarship and for its evaluative judgments. He studiously avoided the pitfall of those Christian comparativists whom he faulted for having relied on secondary and tertiary writings rather than working with primary sources. He demonstrated a broad knowledge of biblical texts and scholarship, Christian history, theology, and ethics. Yet, ironically, although he maintained that the world religious community had little to gain from the work of missionaries and those who engage in the scientific study of religion, some of the conclusions that follow from his metareligious critique are little different from those that might be found in the writings of a missionary or a historian of religion. Thus, for example, his conclusion that Genesis's priestly tradition (editing) should more correctly be called forgeries proceeds from Islamic beliefs and values about the nature of revelation and the community as well as metareligious principles grounded in reason.

Faruqi's judgment that Jesus' revolution was betrayed by Christianity, and thus his distinction between Christianism and true Christianity, struck many Christians as resulting from an analysis that used reason to arrive at Muslim conclusions rooted in Islamic revelation and belief. While his methodology may be different, missionary diatribe having been replaced by a sophisticated rationalist polemic, the results were the same. One can see this merger, as it were, in Al-Faruqi's characterization of Jews as falling into two categories. On the one hand, there are those who rejected understanding Hebrew scriptures in racial terms, whom he calls "un-Jewish," or truly Mosaic, Jews. They "stand fundamentally, in our camp from which that which is called Hebrew Scripture is regarded as a heavily edited, oft-changed version of that divine Torah which God had entrusted to Moses." And on the other hand are the Jews who "are regarded as those who gave up that divinely inspired pattern for the sake of tribalist self-seeking and assertion and preservation of their race."[29]

Faruqi's call for Christians and Muslims to join together in producing a new theology often seemed a call to jettison much of belief and tradition and accept Islam's corrective vision of religious history. He maintained that a second reformation was required, which, though not rejecting all of the past, liberated itself from the authority and ambiguities of the cumulative tradition, from the Gospels and St. Paul to Barth and Tillich. Many Jews and Christians would wonder what is left.[30]

As in many other areas, Faruqi served as an example to other Muslim scholars of the importance of studying other faiths seriously. This belief was institutionalized at Temple University, where he insisted that Muslim students seriously study other faiths and write dissertations in comparative religions. He provided many observations and insights that challenged and forced others to appreciate and respond to an intelligent Muslim's perception and criticism of Christianity or Judaism. Faruqi's analysis of the two poles, or "pulls," in Christianity—renunciation on the one hand and worldliness on the other—critiqued the ambivalence in much of Christianity toward money and power. He argued that Christian tradition celebrated the poverty and suffering of the crucified Christ and at the same time found it necessary to morally justify self-assertion and worldliness, the pursuit of power through conquest and colonialism, as sacrifice and altruism. This understanding could be applied to the role of imperial Christianity and the papacy in Christian history as well as modern Christian apologias for European colonialism, neocolonialism, and Western capitalism.

Stanley Brice Frost, dean of Divinity during Faruqi's years at the Institute of Islamic Studies at McGill University, summarized his position well: "He became a man of two worlds, intelligently at ease in both and at peace with neither."[31] This grappling with his two worlds was no doubt responsible for the writing of *Urubah* and *Christian Ethics*. Arabism, Islam, and Western Christian culture were Faruqi's religious, historical, and cultural baggage.

Conclusion

The twentieth century has made enormous demands on Muslims throughout the world, swept along by the realities of rapid political, economic, and social change. It has brought the rise of nationalist movements, the emergence of modern states, increased modernization and Westernization, the creation of the state of Israel and with it a series of Arab–Israeli wars, the Arab socialist revolutions in the 1950s and early 1960s, civil and regional wars, and the resurgence of Islam in private and public life. Throughout this period, a series of influential Muslims, such as Muhammad Abduh, Muhammad Iqbal, Hasan al-Banna, and Mawlana Mawdudi, to name but a few, have attempted to address critical issues of religious faith and identity. In recent decades, the world of Islam has had a number of prominent intellectuals who have combined the best of educations in Western universities and their Islamic heritage and attempted both to explain Islam to non-Muslim audiences and to contribute to the contemporary interpretation and understanding of Islam among Muslims. The growing importance of a Muslim presence in America is reflected by the fact that the United States has also provided a context for this endeavor. Faruqi was among its most prominent representatives not only in the process of knowing (religious reinterpretation and reform) but also of doing. In his publications, scholarly colloquia, classroom teaching, ecumenical dialogues, and other activities, he wrote, spoke, and acted with the clarity and conviction of one who has a vision and mission. He was among the vanguard of Muslim intellectuals who settled in America but then reversed the process of knowledge transformation (from Muslim countries to the West). His vision, ideas, and impact were multilayered. They were transmitted through his writings, his Muslim students (as well as non-Muslim students) who returned to teach and work in government ministries throughout the Muslim world, and the organizations and institutions he founded and led. He provided an important intellectual foundation for both the scholar-activists of the 1970s and 1980s and the emerging intellectual generation at the beginning of the twenty-first century. Ismail al-Faruqi was indeed a maker of contemporary Islam.

2
KHURSHID AHMAD
Muslim Activist-Economist

The Islamic resurgence has put Islam in the headlines and drawn a great deal of scholarly as well as media coverage. While one man, the Ayatollah Khomeini, has come to be equated with the resurgence of Islam in the popular mind and imagination, in fact the reassertion of Islam in Muslim life is a broad-based, complex, multifaceted phenomenon that has embraced Muslim societies from Sudan to Sumatra. Its leaders and organizations are as varied as its manifestations.

Contemporary Islamic revivalism has included a greater emphasis on religious identity and values in private and public life. As a result, organizations like the Muslim Brotherhood and the Jamaat-i-Islami, that combine both the private and public emphases, best reflect the dynamism and leadership of contemporary Islam. Khurshid Ahmad of Pakistan is among the dominant figures in this select group. An early follower of Mawlana Mawdudi (1903–1979), the founder of the Jamaat-i-Islami, and a trained economist, Khurshid has been a leader of the Jamaat, a member of the cabinet and senate of Pakistan, a father of modern Islamic economics, and an internationally recognized Islamic activist.

The economic dimension of the Islamic resurgence, while not in the headlines as a part of the Islamic revolution, is an important part of contemporary Islam. Islamic economics involves both conceptual developments and active concrete programs. During the past decade Islamic economic institutions (banks, finance houses, insurance) and taxes have been introduced in many countries. As in other areas of the resurgence, the interrelated emphasis on theory and practice has required leaders who are both theorists and activists. Khurshid Ahmad has been one of the leading figures in the emergence of Islamic economics as an intellectual discipline and as a foundation for new institutions and programs. He has combined an active commitment and participation in one of the major Islamic movements of the modern era with a career as an economist, working both in academia and with governments and financial institutions in developing economic theory and practice within an Islamic framework.

Khurshid Ahmad reflects in his life and thought the basic themes and dynamics of the emergence of contemporary Islamic economics. It is important, then, to know his basic biography, since he is an activist as well as a theorist and his life is as important as his thought in reflecting the nature of Islamic economics. It is equally important to situate Khurshid Ahmad within the context of the Jamaat-i-Islami, a movement that has shaped his life and thought and thus informed his understanding and formulation of Islamic economics. This essay will examine Khurshid Ahmad's life, the Jammat-i-Islami and his connections with it, and the fundamental ideas of Islamic economics as he sees them.

Biography

Khurshid Ahmad was born in Delhi, India, in 1932. His father, Nazir Ahmad, was a well-to-do businessman who was very active in Delhi society, involved in financing projects such as magazines and a student of political science and Marxism. He was also active in Muslim politics during the preindependence period, serving as counselor to the Muslim League in Delhi. Among Nazir Ahmad's friends was Abul Ala Mawdudi, a journalist and writer on religious topics, who would later found the Jamaat-i-Islami (the Islamic Society), which come to play a central role in Khurshid's life and development.

Khurshid had a traditional Islamic education as a young boy; he was at the top of his class in the fourth grade and remained so throughout his later studies. He attended the Anglo-Arabic higher secondary school in Delhi. He was an excellent student and already showed an inclination to political activism. Influenced by his father, who was active in the Pakistan movement, he was elected president of the Children's League in Delhi in 1946. As a student leader he led demonstrations for Pakistan's independence regularly in the final months before partition. In 1948, after the partition of the Indian subcontinent and the creation of Pakistan, Nazir Ahmad and his family emigrated, with millions of Muslims, to West Pakistan, traveling first to Lahore for a few months. Mawlana Mawdudi, the founder of the Jamaat-i-Islami, was also in Lahore and was a regular visitor at the Ahmad home in the Muslimtown section of Lahore.

The family moved on to Karachi and settled there. Khurshid enrolled at Government College of Commerce and Economics. It was here that he would seriously encounter economics and the Jamaat, the twin passions of much of his life's work. In 1949 he wrote his first article, on Pakistan's budget, which was published in the *Muslim Economist*. This was also the time when he discovered Mawlana Mawdudi. He had known Mawdudi the man as a frequent visitor in his father's house; in 1949 he encountered

Mawdudi the religious scholar for the first time. In particular, he was impressed with Mawdudi's discussion of both Islamic and Western thought and the conflict between Western civilization and Islam. Khurshid had been exposed to Western thought through his father's interest in political science and his schooling. In fact, he had written his first article in English. The young student was drawn to the writings of two other great Muslim thinkers who were schooled in both Western and Islamic thought and wrote about the contemporary relevance of Islam. Muhammad Asad (formerly Leopold Weiss), an Austrian Jewish convert to Islam, had moved to Pakistan and written *Islam at the Crossroads*, which greatly impressed him. Muhammad Iqbal (1876–1938), the poet-philosopher and cofounder of Pakistan, who had earned a doctorate and a law degree in Europe, had dominated the first decades of the twentieth century subcontinent as a great poet of India-Pakistan. Although Khurshid, like most South Asians, had memorized his poetry as a child, it was only now, as a college student, that he discovered Iqbal the prolific Islamic modernist thinker and author who used both poetry and prose to explore such themes as the relationship of Islam to Western science and philosophy, the relevance of Islam as a comprehensive way of life, and the need for reinterpretation and reform to renew Islam to and revitalize the Muslim community. The latter themes were synthesized in Iqbal's *Reconstruction of Religious Thought in Islam.*

Khurshid Ahmad's years at Government College in Karachi proved to be a significant turning point, setting him on a path he would pursue for the remainder of his life, for here he combined the intellectual and the religious, embarking on the path of a scholar-activist. While he excelled as a student, he also became active in the Islami Jamiat-i-Talaba (IJT; Islamic Student Association), the student wing of Mawdudi's Jamaat-i-Islami. Three fellow students were particularly influential in attracting him to the IJT: a fellow student of economics, Zafar Ishaque al-Ansari, who would later earn a doctorate in Islamic studies at McGill University and teach at the University of Petroleum and Mining Engineering in Dhahran, Saudi Arabia, and who is now director of the Islamic Research Institute in Islamabad; Khurram Murad, who would train in science, write on Islam, and succeed Khurshid as director of the Islamic Foundation in Leicester, England, and who is currently deputy *amir* (leader) of the Jamaat in Pakistan; and Khurshid's older brother, Zamir, who studied science and then rose to the rank of vice-admiral in Pakistan's navy, prior to his death in 1985. Reflecting back on this early exposure to the IJT, Khurshid Ahmad has remarked that it "determined the future course of my life."[1] In the fellowship of the IJT, Khurshid deepened his understanding of Islam and formulated his future activist orientation through his reading and discussion of Mawlana Mawdudi's writings, in particular *Let Us Be Muslims*. The experience moved him emotionally as well as intellectually: "It covers the fundamentals of Islam (faith, prayer, worship) in a manner which moves the soul and the consciousness that to be a Muslim is something different. That is, that it is not just belief (*aqida*) and prayer but also to play a new role in life, to have a mission to change the world."[2]

In December 1949, he officially became a member of the IJT. The IJT were serious-minded students who held training programs in religious beliefs, prayer, discipline, social etiquette. As he excelled as a student, so, too, he emerged as a gifted leader. In 1950, he was elected head of the IJT in Karachi. From 1953 to 1955, he served as president of the All-Pakistan Islamic Student Association. He introduced two major changes. A biweekly student newspaper, *The Students' Voice*, addressed current issues such as whether Islam could provide the basis for Pakistan's constitution and student concerns; shortly after it published an open letter to the prime minister on student problems, student riots broke out in Pakistan. Between 1952 and 1956, he wrote a series of articles on Islam, capitalism, socialism, secularism, and Western civilization. As with other Muslim intellectuals of the time, such as Egypt's Sayyid Qutb, who would become a principal ideologue of the Muslim Brotherhood, Khurshid Ahmad's analysis of Islam and socialism explored the relationship of his religiocultural upbringing, Islam, to social justice. In particular, he emphasized the rights of labor and the poor in an attempt to demonstrate that Islam possessed its own notions of social justice and thus its own alternative to capitalism and the social ills of society. The second change, conducting weekly meetings at the university instead of private homes or mosques, gave the IJT a higher profile and reinforced its image as a student-based and student rights organization. The IJT became a center of campus politics with a reputation for excellent organization and dedication. It recruited students from the first day of class by replacing a British-inspired freshmen orientation, which emphasized drinking and hazing, with an "Introduction Day" when members of the IJT received new students and brought them to their classes and the library. New students were assisted with books and given other means of support as well as offered opportunities to become involved in campus study groups, debates, and publications. Their recruitment and organization techniques paid off. In 1953, the IJT won its first campus-wide election at the Urdu College. By 1960, Islamic Student Associations in Pakistan were winning from 60 to 80 percent of the student elections.

The 1950s and early 1960s were a long formative period of development, both academically and Islamically, for Khurshid Ahmad. He earned his B.A. in commerce (First Class) in 1953, M.A. in economics in 1955, L.L.B. (First Class) in 1958, and M.A. in Islamic studies (First Class) in 1964. During that period, after serving as national president of the Islamic Student Association from 1953 to 1955, he formally joined the Jamaat-i-Islami as a full member in 1956. In addition to serving as editor of *Students' Voice* (1952–1955), he was the editor of three other Islamically oriented publications, *New Era* (1955–1956), *Voice of Islam* (1957–1964) and *Chiragh-e-Rah* (1957–1968), as well as associate editor of the *Iqbal Review* (1960–1964). From 1955 to 1977, Khurshid taught economics in the Faculties of Economics and Commerce at the Urdu College and in the Department of Economics at Karachi University. Increasingly, in the late 1960s and 1970s, as a member of the Jamaat, he combined teaching and writing as an economist with *dawa*, the spread of Islam nationally and internationally. Understanding his life, thought, and activities requires an appreciation of the nature and ideological outlook of the Jamaat-i-Islami, which has provided the inspiration, motivation and context for his life's work.

The Jammat-i-Islami Experience

The Jamaat-i-Islami was founded in Lahore, Pakistan, in 1941 by Mawlana Mawdudi as an ideological rather than a political party. Mawdudi, who had moved to Lahore in 1938, believed that Islam was a universal and comprehensive way of life that should govern state and society. Critical of Muslim dependence on the West, he advocated an Islamic revolution—a gradual Islamization of all aspects of Muslim life: politics, law, economics, education, and social life. He had for a number of years been developing and disseminating his interpretation of Islam in his journal *Tarjuman al-Quran* (Exegesis of the Quran). Now, gathering around him seventy-five faithful followers, he set about realizing that vision. His goal was to train and produce a dynamic nucleus, a vanguard of true believers who would constitute a new elite prepared to lead and implement a true Islamic society in the subcontinent.

Formation, indoctrination, discipline, and religious propagation were cornerstones of the Jamaat. Its ideology and program came directly from the prolific writings of their leader, which were based on two principles—the unity and sovereignty of God: "The belief in the Unity and sovereignty of Allah is the foundation of the social and moral system propounded by the Prophets."[3] That system was delineated and preserved in Islamic law (the Shariah), a sacred law based on God's revelation (the Quran) and the example (Sunnah) of the Prophet Muhammad. Thus, Islam is an integrated way of life. Mawdudi believed that imitation of Western secularism (the separation of religion and the state), nationalism, capitalism, and Marxism were among the major causes of the decline of Muslim societies. The health, vitality, and power of the Islamic community (ummah) would only be restored by recognition that Muslims have their own divinely revealed and mandated Islamic alternative and a return to true Islam.

The Jamaat recruited its members from schools, universities, and mosques. It attracted the urban middle class in particular: students, merchants, professionals. Modern learning and religious commitment were combined in an effort to produce a new educated elite that would be represented in every sector of society. The organization's message was propagated through student groups, worker organizations, research institutes, publications (newspapers, magazines, journals), preaching, social services, and youth centers. As a result, the impressive impact and legacy of Maw-dudi has been twofold: first, it has provided the common understanding of Islam that has informed the training and activities of the Jamaat; second, Mawdudi's systematic presentation of Islam has had a broad impact on Muslims within the subcontinent and, through translation, the greater Islamic world. In Pakistan, he is among the most widely read authors, providing middle-class Muslims with an intelligent, coherent explanation of Islam that speaks to modern concerns and issues. Internationally, Mawdudi and the Jamaat have long been formative influences ideologically and organizationally. He is commonly regarded as among the most significant Islamic ideologues (along with Hasan al-Banna and Sayyid Qutb of Egypt's Muslim Brotherhood) whose writings may be found from Morocco to Indonesia and beyond.

From Khurshid Ahmad's early days as a youth leader, editor, and professor of economics, as well as editor and translator of Mawlana Mawdudi's works, to the present, he has attempted to realize and extend the message of Mawlana Mawdudi and the Jammat. He has authored or edited some twenty-four books in English, written sixteen books in Urdu, translated and edited ten works of Mawdudi, authored many chapters and articles. He has often averaged three to six months a year lecturing at universities, participating in international ecumenical gatherings, speaking to Muslim audiences, and helping Muslims in Europe, Africa, Asia, and America organize their communities.[4]

Like his mentor, Khurshid Ahmad believes that Islam is a divinely revealed code of life. The comprehensive guidance of Islam and its integral relationship to all aspects of life are rooted in the doctrine of tawhid, the unity or oneness of God. Absolute monotheism is the essence of Islam. Belief that there is one omnipotent, omnipresent Lord of the universe, creator and sustainer of the world, "points to the supremacy of the law in the cosmos, the all pervading unity behind the manifest diversity. . . . It presents a unified view of the world and offers the vision of an integrated universe. . . . It is a dynamic belief and a revolutionary doctrine. It means that all men are the creatures of God—they are all equal."[5]

The vocation of humanity is to serve as God's vicegerent, representative (khilafa), on earth, and to fulfill God's will by establishing a new order of equity and justice, peace and prosperity. This duty is encumbent on both the individual and the Muslim community. Thus, according to Khurshid, individual rights are counterbalanced by Islam's emphasis on social responsibility. Similarly, Islam establishes an equilibrium between the material and spiritual aspects of life. Avoiding the Western pitfall of separation of the sacred and the secular, Islam is a complete way of life; "Islam provides guidance for all walks of life—individual and social, material and moral, economic and political, legal and cultural, national and international."[6] It is this holistic vision of the world that undergirds the multifaceted yet religiously motivated and integrated career of Khurshid Ahmad. It also accounts for his intellectual and ecumenical dialogue with the West, despite his deep criticism of it.

One of the characteristics of contemporary Islamic revivalism is its criticism of the West and its assertion of the self-sufficiency of Islam. Mawdudi, who had been self-educated in English and Western literature, had tended to cite Western sources in constructing his indictment of the West and its values, its hostility to Islam and decadence. In contrast, Islam held the answers to the failures of the West and Muslim decline. Khurshid Ahmad shared this indictment of the West. However, he represented the next generation, which had far more exposure to and mastery of Western education. Though critical, he also appreciated the importance of science and technology and that Muslim societies were part of an international political and economic system. For Khurshid Ahmad, knowledge of the past was necessary not only to understand the hostility and mistrust but also to inform efforts to develop better relations and cooperation with the West. His writing of *Islam and the West* in 1958 signaled the acceptance of this important distinction by Mawlana Mawdudi, who wrote in his foreword: "The call of our times is that, with a view to achieving world peace and international amity, mutual relationship among different nations be reconstructed. . . . [T]he need for the establishment of a relationship of the people of Europe and America with the Islamic fraternity, on new foundations of good will and good-cheer, stands out as of paramount significance."[7]

While Khurshid critically reviewed the history of confrontation between Islam and the West, the vilification of Islam and the Prophet Muhammad, and the impact of European colonialism (economic exploitation, political and cultural dominance, the imposition of Western education and Christianity, the attacks on Islam perpetrated by missionaries and Western scholars of Islam), these were now presented as the causes for Muslim distrust, which must be understood as a prerequisite for the new task at hand, mutual cooperation. In contrast to radical militants, Khurshid Ahmad did not call for a total rejection of the West. He had spent a major portion of his time mastering Western knowledge, from history and religion to science and economics. Instead, he argued self-confidently that the basis for better relations was a redefining of the relationship of the West to the Muslim world from that of master and servant to that of equal partners. This would enable the two parties to coexist and interact without Muslims having to pay the price of domination and assimilation: "If the only practical ground of cooperation is the assimilation of the Western culture and rejection of Islam as we understand it, then there is no ground for any meeting. But if the cooperation is to be achieved on equal footing, then it is most welcomed."[8]

Khurshid Ahmad's activities from 1966 to the present have reflected this opening to the West. While retaining his position as a member of the foreign relations department of the Jamaat, he moved to Great Britain in

1968, where he resided until 1978. During that time, his assignment was to engage "in worldwide dawa," that is, propagation of Islam in Europe, Africa, and America.[9] He helped organize and served on the executive council of the Islamic Council of Europe, was a research scholar at the University of Leicester (1969–1972), and established the Islamic Foundation in Leicester. The Foundation, though legally not affiliated with the Jamaat, is, nevertheless, inspired by its outlook and ideals. It publishes and distributes Islamic books (including new translations of Mawdudi's writings), publishes journals and bibliographies of Western and Muslim materials on Islam, conducts conferences, and engages in ecumenical programs. Khurshid often traveled six months out of the year establishing and/or serving as a trustee of Islamic centers in Europe and Africa, lecturing at universities and to Muslim organizations in Europe, America, and Africa, and initiating and participating in international ecumenical dialogues. The breadth and diversity of his activities are reflected in the offices he held during that time, among them director general of the Islamic Foundation in Leicester, England, member of the advisory council of the Centre for the Study of Islam and Christian-Muslim Relations, and vice-president of the Standing Conference on Jews, Christians, and Muslims in Europe.

Events in Pakistan led to his return in 1978 to serve in the cabinet of General Zia ul-Haq, who in July 1977 had seized power from prime minister Zulfikar Ali Bhutto (1971–1977). Bhutto, as prime minister, had increasingly appealed to Islam to attract Arab oil money and enhance the legitimacy of his socialist policies. At the same time, a coalition of opposition forces, representing a spectrum of religious and more secular-oriented parties, had joined together in the Pakistan National Alliance (PNA). Placing themselves under the umbrella of Islam, they rejected Bhutto's Islamic socialism and promised an Islamic system of government.

When Zia ul-Haq seized power, he used Islam to legitimate his rule, promising an Islamic system (*nizam-i-Islam*) and invited members of the PNA, and in particular those associated with religious organizations like the Jamaat-i-Islami, to join his government. The PNA components that joined the government included the Muslim League, the Pakistan Democratic party, Jamiat-Ulema-i-Islami, and the Jamaat-i-Islami. Khurshid Ahmad, along with three other Jamaat members, became a government minister. He was federal minister (planning, development, and statistics) and deputy chairman of the Planning Commission in August 1978. Although the other members of the PNA resigned in April 1979, Khurshid (and the Jamaat) remained actively involved, both as an advisor to the government and as a leader of the Jamaat, in Pakistan's experiment in introducing a more Islamically oriented system of governemnt.

Khurshid was, at the same time, increasingly involved internationally in the Islamic revivalist tide that swept across much of the Muslim world. Because of his particular expertise, a primary focus of his activities was the development of Islamic economics and the implementation of Islamic reforms. While a professor at Urdu College and Karachi University, teaching basic courses in economics and comparative economic systems, he had begun to introduce Islamic perspectives on economic problems and eventually to speak of an Islamic economic system. While Islamic universities such as al-Azhar in Cairo and Umm al-Qura in Mecca taught about the economic teachings of Islam, he undertook a a systematic effort to develop Islamic economics. He had served as vice-president of the First International Conference on Islamic Economics in Mecca in 1976. Now he lectured and wrote on Islamic economics, created and became chairman of a think tank, the Institute of Policy Studies, in Islamabad, chaired the Second International Conference on Islamic Economics in Islamabad, became chairman of the International Institute of Islamic Economics at the International Islamic University, Islamabad, served as a member of the Supreme Advisory Board of the International Centre for Research in Islamic Economics in Saudi Arabia, and lectured and published books and articles on Islamic economics. International recognition for his contribution to Islamic economics and to the Muslim world has been given in many contexts. He was elected the first president of the International Association of Islamic Economics, which was founded in 1986, a position he continues to retain. In 1988 he was awarded the first Islamic Development Bank prize for distinguished contribution to Islamic Economics. And in 1990 he was awarded the prestigious King Faisal award for service to Islam.

Fundamental Ideas of Contemporary Islamic Economics

In his full life of religious and political involvement, Khurshid Ahmad has participated in the creation of the contemporary discipline of Islamic economics. This has not been done *in addition* to his other activities but as a direct part of his active involvement in the Islamic movement. Like other contemporary Islamic activist thinkers, Khurshid combines theory and practice, not because he believes that this is the most efficient or effective way of operating but because he believes that it is the only way for a Muslim professional. His life as a believer, as a member of the Jamaat-i-Islami, and as an economist are combined in many important ways.

As an economist, Khurshid has played an imprtant role in the evolution of economic thought and programs in the Muslim world. He has himself described the major lines of transition:

Initially the emphasis was on explaining the economic teachings of Islam and offering Islamic critique of the Western contemporary theory and policy. During this phase most of the work was done by the Ulama, the leftists and Muslim social thinkers and reformers. Gradually the Muslim economists and other professionals became involved

in this challenging enterprise. Perhaps the First International Conference on Islamic Economics [held in 1976] . . . represents the wa-
tershed in the history of the evolution of Muslim thinking on Economics, representing the transition from "economic teachings of
Islam" to the emergence of "Islamic Economics."[10]

This statement provides both a description of the changes taking place
in the intellectual world of Islam and also an insight into Khurshid's perceptions of those changes. It is clear that this transformation is something
he approved and that it came to constitute the program and challenge to
which he devoted his future activities as a Muslim economist.

Khurshid Ahmad and other contemporary Muslim economists would
maintain that the fundamental values and message of Islam are no different than they have been since the days of the Prophet Muhammad. What
is new is the approach and method; the different approach can be seen
clearly in Khurshid's works.

The more traditional approach concentrates on "the economic teachings of Islam." There is an effort to search out all of the verses of the Quran
that have specific economic implications. This is supported by a similar collecting of the Traditions (hadith) of the Prophet Muhammad that have an
economic message. The description of the plans for a conference, "The
Place of Economics in Islam," held in New Jersey, in 1968, provides an example of the more traditional approach. Planners said there was to be "a
classified presentation of relevant verses from the Quran and selections
from the Hadith literature on the subject." In this way it was hoped that
prior to entering into the details of specific issues and practices, participants in the conference would be reminded of the basic sources on which
Muslim economic thought is based.[11]

This approach has as its foundation a vast aggregation of separate
propositions and specific cases that are then used to provide the legitimizing proof for particular positions. From the perspective of many Muslim intellectuals in the decades since World War II, this methodology had the advantage of grounding the presentation in explicitly Islamic sources and
fundamentals. It emphasizes the effort to go beyond apologetically trying
to show that Islamic teachings and some Western concepts are compatible.

At the same time, this approach has some problems. It tended to result
in a collection of discussions rather than a more holistic and integrated
analysis. In addition, the traditional approach involves the scholar in many
of the traditional debates of Quranic study and hadith analysis. For example, old arguments about abrogation (naskh) of one hadith by another or of
one Quranic verse by another become the necessary starting points for
analysis.[12] These debates are regarded as of critical importance in presentations of "the economic teachings of Islam."

Islamic economics, however, is a more holistic enterprise. Muslim
economists like Khurshid Ahmad are aware of specific Quranic verses

and traditions, but this is the foundation for their perspective rather than the starting point for their analysis. Khurshid makes this distinction clear in his definition of the "first premise" of Islamic development economics: "The first premise which we want to establish is that economic development is an Islamic framework and Islamic development economics are rooted in *the value-pattern embodied in the Quran and the Sunnah*" (emphasis added).[13] In Islamic economics, Khurshid speaks of the broader Quranic "value-patterns" rather than the specific provisions of particular verses. This enables him to present a more broadly integrated model of Islamic economics rather than a list of Islamic characteristics and teachings.

Certain basic themes and beliefs provide the foundation for the approach of Khurshid Ahmad as an Islamic economist. These are often consciously distinguished from basic assumptions of Western economics. However, Khurshid's perspective is not simply apologetic or defensive; it is an attempt to create an intellectual discipline on an Islamic basis so that it can provide guidance for operational programs and activities.

The first principle of Islamic economics is that it is not a separate system describing a distinct aspect of human experience. Islam is seen as a comprehensive system and a total way of life. In this framework, economics as a discipline is only part of the picture and must be integrated into other aspects of analysis from the very beginning of the process.

The comprehensive nature of Islam was one of the major keystones of the teachings of Mawdudi, and Khurshid maintains this principle. The implications of this comprehensiveness were clearly spelled out in essays by Mawdudi that Khurshid edited and published recently. It is clear that Khurshid shares these views. In an address entitled "The Economic Problem of Man and Its Islamic Solution," Mawdudi says:

[T]he economic problem of man which was, indeed, part of the larger problem of human life, has been separated from the whole and looked at as if it were an independent problem by itself. And gradually this attitude has taken such a firm root that the economic problem has come to be regarded as the sole problem of life. This . . . has made its evolution infinitely difficult.[14]

The human economic problem is defined, in simple terms that are similar to those in any economic system, as,

with a view to sustain and advance human civilization[,] how to arrange economic distribution so as to keep all men supplied with the necessities of existence and to see that every individual in society is provided with opportunities adequate to the development of his personality and the attainment of the highest possible perfection according to his capacity and the aptitude.[15]

Within this perspective, economic problems arise when the economic dimension of life is separated from the rest. Problems of distribution arise not from inefficiencies but from immorl acts by humans.

The basis and position of Islamic economics is defined by Khurshid:

> Islam does not admit any separation between "material" and "moral," "mundane" and "spiritual" life, and enjoins man to devote all his energies to the reconstruction of life on healthy foundations. It teaches him that moral and material powers must be welded together and spiritual salvation can be achieved by using the material resources for the good of man, and not by living a life of asceticism.[16]

In this broad perspective, two key concepts set the basic framework for analysis. One is the unity and sovereignty of God, or *tawhid*, and the other is the stewardship, or *khilafah*, of humans operating in God's creation. The delineation of the economic implications of *tawhid* and *khilafah* represent the primary focus of thinking and analysis in contemporary Islamic economics.

Tawhid means that there can be no other source of authority than God and that there can be no other focus for ultimate human loyalty than God. These are implications accepted by all Muslims. However, people involved in the contemporary Islamic resurgence have drawn more limiting conclusions from *tawhid* analysis than the more general, inclusive Islamic modernist thinkers of the 1960s did. In political terms, people like Khurshid emphasize that while state institutions are necessary and national communities legitimately exist, loyalties to states or nationalisms must be subordinated to allegiance to God and the global community of Muslims.

In more economic terms, Khurshid's discussion of economic development in Islamic economics shows that *tawhid* sets the goals of development: "The development effort, in an Islamic framework, is directed towards the development of a God-conscious human being, a balanced personality committed to and capable of acting as the witness of Truth to mankind."[17] In concrete policy terms, this means, for Khurshid, that human resource development—education, vocational training, improvement of the quality of life—is the objective of development policy.

In this perspective, while industrialization programs are not rejected, policies that regard industrialization as the leading element in development are seen as unsuitable. The development of the industrial sector must be placed in the broader context of creating conditions of social and economic justice for all citizens in the society. Property can be possessed and used for investment but, in the Islamic model, may not be used to gain advantage over or exploit others who may be in need. In this way, the emphasis is on "God-conscious" planning.

The economic role of human beings is also seen in this way. In Islamic economic analysis, the basic operating unit is not "economic man." Instead, humans are seen as the direct agents or representatives of God in God's creation. The concept of Muslims as God's *khalifahs* (or "human khalifah-ship," for which the term is *khilafah*) is an important part of Khurshid's presentation of Islamic economics. For him, khilafah is the "unique Islamic concept of man's trusteeship" in moral, political, and economic terms.[18] It is the source of the Muslim vocation and mission: "This exalts man to the noble and dignified position of being God's deputy on earth and endows his life with a lofty purpose: to fulfill the Will of God on earth. This will solve the perplexing problems of human society and establish a new order wherein equity and justice and peace and prosperity will reign supreme."[19]

The concept of khilafah provides the basis for the creation of an economic system in which cooperation and mutual obligations replace competition as the dominant feature of human economic interaction. Thus, Islamic economics, as defined by Mawdudi and Khurshid, affirms private property as part of the human agent's management responsibilities. Both scholar-activists also recognize and accept that there can be competition and differing successes in obtaining material goods.

In this framework, Khurshid rejects the concept of private ownership that allows an absolute right of an owner to manage property in any way. (He also sees a socialist system where all means of production are nationalized as a threat to human initiative.) Instead, he argues that "Islam's most important contribution in the field of economics lies in changing the *concept* of ownership. No one has the right to destroy property. If misused it can be taken away. If it is not needed it must be passed on to others."[20] Ownership is, in other words, stewardship of God's property rather than an absolute right of the individual human. The concept of stewardship means that those who succeed in gaining wealth must do so without harming others and then must use that wealth to help other human beings.

Some of the more familiar aspects of Islamic economics, such as Islam's alms tax ot tithe (*zakat*) and the banning of usury (*riba*), are part of these religious obligations or duties. One of the Five Pillars of Islam is the giving of charitable support to the less fortunate. *Zakat* is a "compulsory levy . . . on accumulated wealth, trade goods, various forms of business, agricultural produce, and cattle. Its purpose is to create a fund for the support of economically depressed classes."[21]

Similarly, the well-known Islamic prohibition against usury, which traditionally has included banking interest, is based on the overall obligation of Muslims to help one another. Mawdudi and Khurshid both argue that interest has damaging effects: "Usury develops miserliness, selfishness, callousness, inhumanity and financial greed in the character of man. . . . It increases a tendency among the people to hoard money and spend it to promote their private interest only. It blocks the free circulation of wealth in the society, and diverts the flow of money from the poor to the rich."[22]

In this way, it undermines the function of human stewardship of God's resources.

Another major characteristic of Islamic economics, as it has developed in recent years, is that it has been consciously programmatic. Past discussions that aimed at presenting the "economic teachings of Islam" tended to remain in the realm of theory. Much of the scholarship was in the hands of the traditionally oriented ulama, who were not practicing businessmen or government officials. With the growing involvement of professional economists like Khurshid Ahmad in the debates, there was an increased emphasis on actual projects rather than doctrine. Khurshid was, for example, one of the early advocates of Islamic banks and financial institutions and has played an important role in their establishment and rapid growth. In the past decade, more than one hundred Islamic banks or investment groups have been created in many different parts of the world, with some relatively high degrees of success and profitability.[23] This programmatic activism is an important part of the emergence of Islamic economics.

A final major characteristic of Islamic economics as developed in the work of Khurshid Ahmad is that it is a self-consciously value-oriented discipline. Khurshid, like many other Muslim social scientists, rejects the idea that economic analysis can take place in "a climate of positivistic objectivity and of complete value-neutrality. Most of the economic thinking that masquerades as value-neutral turns out, on closer scrutiny, to be otherwise."[24] The experience of many Muslims with Western economic planners and analysts over the past few decades has tended to confirm this belief. The value commitment of so-called value-free Western economic analysis becomes apparent when it is applied in non-Western contexts.

Muslim economists like Khurshid firmly believe that economics is not a value-free academic discipline. The effort to develop a value-free system of analysis is seen as, at best, being counterproductive and, at worst, satanic. Instead, they believe, economists have a moral responsibility to work for economic justice and the betterment of humanity. This, then, points to a positive characteristic of Islamic economics: "The major contribution of Islam lies in making human life and effort purposive and value-oriented. The transformation it seeks to bring about in human attitudes and *pari passu* in that of the social sciences is to move them from a stance of pseudo-value-neutrality towards open and manifest value-commitment and value-fulfillment."[25]

In this way, the emergence of Islamic economics reflects a rejection of some of the basic assumptions of traditional Western scholarship, just as it represents a move away from the traditional Muslim approaches to economic subjects. Khurshid views his work as a mission, that of bringing a more effective programmatic awareness to Muslims and a recognition of the importance of value-commitment to economists in all societies. His contributions to Islam and to the field of Islamic economics were recognized in the late 1980s when he received the Islamic Development Bank's first award in economics and the Faisal Award for Service to Islam.

The fundamental ideas of contemporary Islamic economics lead Khurshid Ahmad to the position of being a Muslim activist-economist. Islam, for him and in Islamic economics, is a comprehensive system in which no sector can be viewed as autonomous. Its basic concepts of tawhid and khilafah provide an effective conceptual foundation for a programmatic and value-committed discipline that represents an important part of contemporary intellectual life and policy-making in the Muslim world.

3
MARYAM JAMEELAH
A Voice of Conservative Islam

In recent years, it has become more common to hear Muslim women's voices in the public arena. However, if we look at twentieth-century Islam, Muslim discourse has been overwhelmingly dominated by male voices, from the Islamic modernism of Muhammad Abduh and his Salafiyya movement in the early twentieth century to the writings and activism of contemporary Islamic activists and movements; from the writings and speeches of the ulama to those of the many educated Muslim professionals who have increasingly employed Islamic rhetoric and symbolism to critique their societies and to plan a more indigenously rooted future. Maryam Jameelah is among the very few women who have crossed the gender gap. For several decades she has been a prolific voice in defense of traditional Islam. Her many books and articles have been translated into Urdu, Arabic, Persian, Turkish, Bengali, and Bahasa Indonesia. At first glance, Maryam Jameelah would appear to be the most unlikely of Islamic voices, a New York–born American Jew.

Maryam Jameelah was born Margaret Marcus on May 23, 1934, in New Rochelle, New York. Her great-grandparents emigrated to America from Germany in the nineteenth century. She grew up in Westchester, New York. Her parents were nominal, nonobservant Jews who in later life broke their formal ties with Judaism and joined the Ethical Culture Society and finally a Unitarian church.

Margaret, or as she was called, Peggy, was an unusual child in many ways, one whose personality and intellectual/religious orientation often ran counter to her culture's norms and expectations. Margaret was psychologically and socially ill at ease and at odds with many aspects of her culture. Although regarded as a bright and talented child, from an early age she experienced difficulty fitting in socially: at school, at summer camps, and in other social settings. Although she had friends in her early school years and at summer camp, she never seemed to fit in or to sustain any of her early friendships. Her teachers often took exception to her personality and interests. When she expressed an interest in returning to a camp where she had been particularly happy, the director rejected her application, noting her "eccentric habits" and need for an excessive amount of supervision.[1] As a result, Margaret felt alienated from society and often experienced social rejection. In a letter written to Margaret years later, her mother described her daughter as attractive and exceptionally bright but also "very nervous, sensitive, high-strung and demanding."[2] These characteristics and problems would continue to play a pivotal role in Margaret's life, her personal, intellectual, and religious development.

From her earliest school years, Margaret Marcus seemed fascinated with the "Orient" and was increasingly critical of Western culture. Her paintings, reading in history and politics, and taste in music were more global than Western: China, the Middle East, South Asia. Jewish in background, she nevertheless developed a particular interest and affinity for Arabs and Muslims, from their politics to their culture. Her early enjoyment of opera and Western classical music gave way in her teenage years to a fascination with Arabic music, Arab and Muslim history, and politics. Raised in a society, culture, and family that generally supported the establishment of Israel and often denigrated Arabs and Islam, she nevertheless was shocked by Zionism and was very sympathetic to the plight of the Arabs and Palestinians. At twelve, she began to write her first novel, a story about Ahmad Khalil, a young displaced Palestinian boy. When she encountered condemnation of the Arabs for atrocities against Israelis in Hebron, she countered with reports of the massacre of Arabs at Deir Yasein. As a twelve-year-old, she wrote: "But the trouble is, most of the books I read in the public library about the Arabs and Islam are written by Zionists and Christian missionaries are prejudiced against them in the same way."[3]

Margaret's sensitivity and nervousness proved a stumbling block throughout her early life. Despite her high school principal's characterization of Margaret as an above average student and a "good citizen," she continued to have problems adjusting. When she first arrived at the University of Rochester, she wrote to her parents: "The girls in my dormitory are the finest, nicest, friendliest, and most wholesome people one could ever want to meet. There is the warm glow of friendship beginning to bloom which is the most happy event I have ever experienced." Yet, before classes even began, she was sent to the infirmary and informed that she could not begin classes unless her parents agreed to place her under intensive psychiatric treatment. She was subsequently forced to withdraw from the university before she even began classes.

Margaret entered New York University in 1953. It was during this period of her life that her search for her identity and religious quest would come to a head. Her identity crisis manifested itself in many ways. As a first-year student, her studies were accompanied by a brief attempt to reclaim her Jewish heritage and embrace orthodox Judaism. She also joined a Zionist youth organization—only to conclude: "What had I in common with them? Nothing! Absolutely nothing!" Margaret then had a brief fling with the Bahai movement. In the end it was a Bahai leader's sympathy for Zionism and charge, "You are among those renegades who hate your own people more than the goyim [gentiles]," that caused her to leave. His denunciation triggered a final break with her Jewish identity and her observation in a letter to her sister: "No people I have ever encountered are more intolerant, bigoted and narrow-minded than the disagreeable Jews I have had the misfortune to meet and that is why I find it impossible to identify myself as one of them."[4]

In the summer of 1953, Margaret suffered a nervous breakdown. It was very difficult time in her life:

> Although I had just entered my nineteenth year, it seemed to me as if my life had already come to an end. I was discouraged, exhausted, depressed, and in despair at having met with nothing but one rebuff after another whenever I tried to find my place in society. I was simply adrift at sea, not knowing what to do next or where to go? Neither reformed Judaism, Orthodox Judaism, Ethical Culture or Bahai consoled me in my plight.[5]

It was at this juncture that she turned again to Islam, immersing herself in reading and studying the Quran. Ironically, two Jewish intellectuals had a profound effect on Margaret's turn to Islam in 1955; Muhammad Asad, an Austrian convert to Islam, and Professor Abraham Katsh, a rabbi who taught at New York University. Asad (Leopold Weiss) was a respected Muslim intellectual and adviser to Muslim governments. Margaret discovered the story of his conversion, *The Road to Mecca*, which proved a great source of inspiration and resolve to become a Muslim. Ironically, Abraham Katsh's course on Judaism in Islam, which explored Jewish influence on the Quran and the development of early Islam, did not persuade her of the validity of the course's theme but instead had the opposite effect: "Although Professor Katsh has tried to prove to his students why Judaism is superior to Islam, paradoxically, he has converted me to the opposite position." She would conclude: "And here am I still a Jew—or at least everybody considers me as such—but I am no longer a Jew in my heart."[6] Her resolve to become a Muslim would not be fulfilled until 1961. Margaret's health grew worse; she became more withdrawn and was finally institutionalized for schizophrenia from 1957 to 1959.

After her release, Margaret became very involved with the Islamic Mission and associations in New York and corresponded with Muslim leaders abroad, in particular Mawlana Abul Ala Mawdudi, leader of Pakistan's Jamaat-i-Islami (Islamic Society). Her decision to formally embrace Islam and her correspondence with Mawdudi mark a turning point that would determine the singular direction of her life and work.

On May 24, 1961, Margaret Marcus became a Muslim, with her recitation of the confession of faith, taking the name Maryam Jameelah. She regarded her conversion as less a rejection of Judaism than a turn to Islam, where she found the fulfillment of Abraham's mission and message. Reflecting on her conversion, she saw herself as leaving modern Judaism, whose modern secularism and materialism had eclipsed its religious aspects, for Islam's more revolutionary, universal message: "I did not embrace Islam out of any hatred for my ancestral heritage or my people. It was not a desire so much to reject as to fulfil. To me, it meant a transition from a moribund and parochial to a dynamic and revolutionary faith content with nothing less than universal supremacy."[7] During the next year, events in her life seemed to coalesce and lead to a resolution of her sense of alienation and anxiety over her future. Maryam Jameelah's conversion and continued inability to obtain a job and to fit into American society, as well as the impending retirement of her father and therefore loss of financial support, moved her in 1962 to finally accept the invitation of Mawlana Mawdudi to emigrate to Pakistan: "I did not have the courage to break my ties with my past life but now that my situation here has become intolerable and I have found that I will never be able to function in this society, I am now convinced that my only salvation is to go and live in a Muslim country."[8] In this decision she was supported by her many Muslim friends in New York as well as prominent Muslim leaders internationally, such as Mawdudi, with whom she had corresponded from 1960 to 1962, and Dr. Said Ramadan, the son-in-law of Hassan al-Banna, founder of Egypt's Muslim Brotherhood. Thus began the second stage of her life in Pakistan.

Both her conversion and decision to emigrate to Pakistan entailed sacrifice. Though somewhat reluctant to do so, when Mawlana Mawdudi told her that drawing was un-Islamic, she abandoned her art work and turned solely to literature, in particular writing, to promote as well as defend Islam.

Pakistan

Maryam Jameelah arrived in Pakistan in 1962 and initially lived with Mawlana Mawdudi and his family. She would come to see these early days as "the most decisive and important period of my life (1962–1964). During this time, after an unnaturally prolonged period of adolescence, I matured into full adulthood, grew completely independent of my parents, developed my literary career, married and finally became a mother."[9]

As the Prophet Muhammad had emigrated (*hijra*) from Mecca to Medina to establish an Islamic society/state, Maryam Jameelah emulated his example in search of an "orthodox Islamic society" in which to live and realize God's will. This belief is embodied in the Quranic passage that she chose for the beginning of her memoirs from this period, which says that anyone who has "migrated for the cause of Allah will find much refuge and abundance in the earth and [anyone] who forsaketh his home to migrate towards Allah and His messenger and death overtake him on the way, his reward is then incumbent on Allah. Allah is ever forgiving and Merciful" (Quran 4:100). It was to Pakistan that she came in her "quest for absolutes."[10]

In 1963, she married Mohammed Yusuf Khan, a full-time worker in Mawdudi's Jamaat-i-Islami. She became his second wife and bore him four children. Living with his cowife in a family compound that included the extended family, Maryam Jameelah embarked on a career as a Muslim apologist, speaking both to the Muslim world and to the West. Her books, articles, and reviews, written in English but often translated into Muslim languages, present a traditionalist interpretation of Islam and polemical response to the West that is representative of an important segment of Muslims and has found many admirers in the Muslim world.

Major Themes in Maryam Jameelah's Writings

Islam and Modernization/Western Society

Much of Maryam Jameelah's writing has been directed against the impact and influence of the West on Muslim societies and the issue of Islamic reform. Her reaction to modern Western life deeply affected her attitude toward any form of religious reform. At heart she was a romantic, a traditionalist staunchly opposed to those who would tamper with her view of "classical Islam" or, perhaps more accurately, the "Islamic tradition." (She tended to take the same position with regard to other religions as well.) For Jameelah, the past is not to be criticized or modified in any substantive way but fully embraced. She believes that the entire Islamic tradition is a whole piece of cloth that can not be touched or altered:

> I agree with Maulana Maudoodi that it is imperative to accept the whole of Islam, not only the Quran, Hadith and Sunna but the four Imams and their traditional orthodox interpreters, the heritage of Tasawwaf [Sufism, mysticism], along with all the arts and sciences developed under Islamic civilization, the entire aesthetic and cultural heritage of that culture, and Islamic history down to 1924 when Ataturk abolished the Khilafat and made his country a thoroughly secular state.[11]

Jameelah is critical of premodern and modern reformers alike. However much she may admire eighteenth-century Islamic revivalist leaders and movements, who claimed a right to set aside traditional interpretations of Islam and go back directly to revelation, she has been a consistent critic of their attempt to reject or reform traditional Islamic institutions or interpretations/teachings. Thus, for example, despite her respect and admiration for Muhammad Ibn Abd al-Wahhab, the great premodern Islamic reformer and cofounder of a movement that was the forerunner of what would later become Saudi Arabia, she could not accept his rejection of aspects of Islamic tradition and suppression of Sufism (Islamic mysticism) as the cause of Muslim backwardness. Similarly, although moved by the Islamic modernist Muhammad Asad's conversion experience and influenced by his writings, Jameelah criticized his attempt to deny the authority of "traditional orthodox interpretations by the `medieval scholars'" and return directly to Islam's revealed sources in order to interpret them to respond to present day needs and realities. Indeed, she rejected all Islamic modernists, their usual explanations for the backwardness and stagnancy of Islam, and their reformist correctives, namely, their rejection of the uncritical following (taqlid) of past teachings and call for a reinterpretation (ijtihad) or reform of Islam, their criticism of the rigid orthodoxy of the ulama, and so on.

The bulk of Jameelah's criticisms are directed at both secular and Islamic modernists alike, all of whom are guilty of "West-worshipping."[12] While the former separate religion from public life, the latter are rejected for having Westernized Islam and Muslims by modernizing Islam, that is, interpreting Islam in light of Western criteria.

Jameelah's *Islam and Modernism* is a critique of many of the major names associated with Muslim modernism; all are denounced and condemned both as heretics and as allies of Christian and foreign imperialists: "our indigenous modernists who want to force Islam into the rigid mold of modern secularism and materialism are in alliance with the Christian missions and and foreign imperialisms. Indeed, they are the most effective agents for accomplishing their work."[13] Jameelah's disdain for Islamic modernists in particular can be seen in her treatment of Ameer Ali and Muhammad Abduh. The former was a Shii Indian Muslim whose book, *The Spirit of Islam*, was probably the most widely read English language book on Islam by a Muslim from the late nineteenth to the mid–twentieth century, enjoying a wide readership in the Muslim world and the West. Jameelah's title, "The Spirit of Unbelief—A Critical Analysis of *The Spirit of Islam* by Ameer Ali," reflects her judgment that the book presents "a thoroughly distorted conception of Islam" and should have been declared heretical by the ulama.[14] However, her strongest judgment is reserved for Muhammad Abduh, the man often regarded as the "Father of Islamic Modernism." Abduh, an early protege of Jalal al-Din al-Afghani, was a prominent member of the ulama, a professor at al-Azhar University, and later the mufti of Egypt. He fathered a school of thought that maintained that Islam and modernity were compatible. Abduh criticized the blind adherence to traditional doctrines and called for a reinterpretation (ijtihad) of Islam to apply Islam to the needs of modern Muslim societies. Through his writings, modernist reform of al-Azhar's curriculum, and (fatwas) as mufti of Egypt, he fostered Islamic modernist reforms that impacted education, law, and social issues such as the status of women. For Jameelah, for whom traditional Islam was totally self-sufficient and adequate, Abduh became a tool of European imperialism who opened the floodgates of assimilation of Western thought and culture: "The consequences of Shaikh Muhammad Abduh's willingness to cooperate with the aims of British imperialism and to compromise Islam with modern life proved nothing short of disasterous. He opened the door wide for all the Westernizers who came after him."[15]

Jameelah lumps all reformers (secular and Islamic modernists) together, those who call for the separation of church and state (Ali Abd al-Raziq and Mustafa Kamel, Ataturk) with those like Muhammad Abduh and Sayyid Ahmad Khan who called for a process of Islamic reform rather than secularization. All are

pioneers of westernization in the Muslim world—Sir Sayyid Ahmad Khan, Shaikh Muhammad Abduh, Qassim Amin, Shaikh Ali Abd ar-Raziq, Dr. Taha Hussein, Ziya Gokalp, and Mustafa Kamel Ataturk. . . . [A]ll of these men were merely the mediocre end-product of their circumstances and more specifically, the result of an over-whelming sense of inferiority which engulfed the East after its humiliating capitulation under the feet of the imperialist West.[16]

Modernization and Westernization

For Maryam Jameelah, the issue of modernization and change, the new idolatry, strikes at the very heart of Islam: "The worship of Allah and submission to His will through wholehearted obedience to Divine revelation, is rapidly giving way to a new idolatry of the crudest sort, as more and more of us prostrate ourselves before the contemporary deities of Change, Modernization, Development, and "Progress."[17] She believes that modernization means Westernization and with it evolution, relativism, and secularism. The relationship of Islam to modernization and development is not merely an intellectual or theological issue but, for Muslims, a matter of life and death that challenges and threatens the very core of Islamic faith.

For Maryam Jameelah, modern Western civilization was born of the union of the secular ideology of post-Reformation Christianity ("Christian secularism") and the "parochial nationalism of Jewish tradition.[18] Her understanding and analysis of modernization is based on a presupposition that historic Christianity and Western cultural and political imperialism are inseparable.[19] Its excessive emphasis on the value of change, innovation, newness, and youth as the ultimate good means a corresponding contempt for the past and tradition. Thus, modernization is a path that leads not to greater development and success but to the destruction of indigenous culture, to "cultural suicide." It produces a "crushing feeling of inferiority" and a generation of passive receptors rather than givers. Lacking initiative, they tend to imitate rather than to create and contribute anything original.[20] Modernization's impact on individuals and societies induces a cultural schizophrenia, a profound identity crisis in which the modernized live in two worlds while belonging to none. Here Jameelah cites with approval the observation of the eminent Oxford's historian Albert Hourani:

> To be a Levantine is to live in two different worlds or more at once without belonging to either; to be able to go through the external forms which indicate the possession of a certain nationality, religion or culture without actually possessing it. It is no longer to have standard values of one's own, not to be able to create but only to be able to imitate. It means to belong to no community and to possess nothing of one's own. It reveals itself in lostness, cynicism and despair.[21]

The evils of modernization and Westernization, of its cultural imperialism, are witnessed not only in the Muslim world but also throughout the non-European world. The Westernization of Asia, Africa, and Latin America has produced unprecented intellectual sterility and cultural identity. In contrast to Islam, contemporary culture demonstrates a complete lack of universal moral and spiritual values.

Jameelah believes that Westernization is the most pernicious and destructive force in the Muslim world, a legacy of European colonialism and a universal process repeated throughout the non-Western world: "The reaction to defeat at the hands of Western imperialism, the development of Westernization . . . are the same story, repeated with sad monotony everywhere among all non-European peoples."[22]

Jameelah tends to equate modernization with Westernization. Modernity, modernization, and modernism are not simply universal, global phenomena but, she believes, inherently Western and thus "the same old Western imperialism under a new and far more deceptive guise," a direct threat to the very life, faith, and cultural values of the Muslim community, spawning inferiority complexes and self-hatred (religious, cultural, and historical).[23]

Like many Muslims in the recent past, Jameelah addresses major twentieth-century Islamic issues. "Why were Muslims so easily overcome and subdued by the West and why do they continue in a subordinate position? Is it Islam that is inherently inadequate?" To begin with, she identifies a twofold cause: European colonialism and exploitation but first and foremost Muslims themselves:

Our present plight is the direct and inevitable result of prolonged colonial exploitation. The Muslims must be held primarily responsible for their decline and downfall, but the imperialist powers set about the task of deculturizing us in a methodical, scientific manner to ensure that we should not ever be able to recover and reorganize ourselves into a vital force. A liberal elite was created who regarded their own faith, historical and cultural heritage with indifference which quickly developed into unconcealed contempt.[24]

Jameelah distinguishes between the "Straight Path of Islam" and the lives of Muslims, between the ideal and the reality, and concludes sadly that "most Muslims are virtually indistinguishable in their conduct and behavior from non-Muslims."[25] Similarly, Muslim countries have betrayed their identity and become vassals of the West: "The history of the Muslim-majority countries . . . no longer has any vital connection to Islam but is merely an extension of the West and its total domination."[26]

Jameelah's view of history is that of a ten-centuries-long struggle between European Christendom and Islam for world supremacy, followed by the triumph and threat of European colonialism and with it, Westernization. Modernity is the defeat of non-European peoples and the imposition of Westernization. It is a process that robs Muslims of their identity and faith, creating in its victims acute feelings of inferiority and self-hatred.[27] Jameelah draws on both the black American experience and Pakistan to support her conclusions. She cites Malcolm X's comments on conking his hair to look "white" and her own inability to find a Pakistani rather than a blond, blue-eyed English-dressed doll for her daughter because, as a merchant assured her, no one would buy it.[28] This "West-worshipping" led modernizers to "wage a violent campaign against polygamy, purdah [segregation of the sexes] and the extended family, their brain-washed minds unable to comprehend that the only thing wrong with these practices is that they are not approved by the modern West."[29]

For Jameelah, like the majority of Islamic activists today, the cultural penetration of the West is far more pernicious and destructive than its political domination. She characterizes Muslim cultural dependence on the West as a form of cultural slavery intimately linked to political dependence:

Although there is no doubt that from the standpoint of our faith in Islam and the survival of our unique identity as a people, cultural slavery on principle is indeed for more harmful than mere foreign political domination, yet in practice, cultural slavery is not only intimately linked to political slavery but, to all intents and purposes, they are virtually inseparable.[30]

Jameelah is able to find ample justification or supportive evidence for her claims in the writings of colonial officials and their consultants. She cites a study commissioned by the British government in which Dr. William Hunter recommended educational reform as a method to make Muslims more civilized and tolerant and thus better subjects: "We should instead develop a rising generation of Muhammadans no longer learned in their own narrow learning nor imbued . . . with the bitter doctrines of their medieval law but tinctured with the sober and genial knowledge of the West."[31] A similar prescription for development was offered by Lord Cromer, viceroy of Egypt and architect of Britain's policy in the Arab world: "It is absurd to suppose that Europe will look on as a passive spectator whilst a retrograde government based on purely Muhammadan principles and oriental ideas, is established in Egypt. The material interests at stake are too important . . . the new generation of Egyptians has to be persuaded or forced into imbibing the true spirit of Western civilization."[32]

Jameelah supports her indictment of the West and its inner decadence and decline by employing Islamic sources as well as Western sources very selectively, restricting herself to Western critics of the process of modernization and its impact on religion and society. However, despite her staunch and seemingly unyielding approach, she claims an openness to outside influences in the process of change: "What is condemned is not normal cultural exchange accomplished in an open, confident, critical and independent mind, but blind, indiscriminate, sterile imitation which results in cultural desolation, social and moral anarchy, defeatism, inferiority-complexes an abject slavery of the soul."[33] However, Jameelah does not give examples of such acceptable changes.

When searching for the causes of the West's ascendancy, Jameelah locates it in superior organization, technology, and energy. She counters the colonialist rationale of the "white man's burden" or "mission to civilize" by denying that the West has produced any religion, philosophy, morality, law, or culture that is superior to that of Asian civilizations. At the same time, Jameelah does find the conduct of Muslims wanting. Employing her distinction between Islam and Muslims, she sometimes describes or characterizes Muslims in the stereotypical language of the West. They are lazy ("do much talking but little doing"), do not complete projects, and fail to collaborate and cooperate with one another. However, the ultimate reason for the stagnation of Muslims is "prolonged colonial exploitation."[34] Thus, Jameelah rejects not only the notion that the West is more advanced but also that there is any reason for Muslims to accept this logic and follow the advice of Westerners and of Westernized Muslim elites who speak of the need for Islamic reform and Westernization.

Minorities

Though critical of Judaism and Christianity, Maryam Jameelah consistently asserts that Jews and Christians are People of the Book and therefore enjoy a special status in Islam. By extension all religious minorities are entitled to live safely and securely in their religious communities. However, the status she subscribes to is that of classical Islamic law: "protected" people (*dhimmi*). Thus, while they can practice their religion, educate their children, and be governed in religious affairs by their religious leaders and law, minorities would be prohibited from holding strategic positions in government.[35]

If Islamic modernists argued that Islam and modernization were compatible, Jameelah countered that Islam and Western culture are incompatible. She believes that one can not adopt the Western mode of life without violating, if not altogether abandoning, obedience to Islamic injunctions.[36]

Ulama and the Intelligentsia

In contrast to many reformers who have placed a good deal of the blame for the plight of Islam and Muslims at the feet of the ulama, Maryam Jameelah is among their staunchest defenders. She upholds their historic role as scholars of Islam and defenders of the faith and rejects their critics—both secular and Islamic reformers. Jameelah paints a picture of the ulama as not only the pious scholars who delineated and interpret the law but also as the defenders of Islam who often patiently endured the persecution of impious Muslim rulers. Reformers, secular and Islamic, have often critiqued the teachings of the ulama as stagnant and retrogressive, emanating from a religious elite whose education and worldview is ill equipped to address the demonds of contemporary Muslim life, and attempted to circumscribe the powers of the ulama. They have asserted their own right to interpret or reinterpret Islam. However, Jameelah, sounding very much like an alim defending the authority of the clergy, has observed:

> We are faced with the tragic situation where we find a group of our people with exclusively English-type education, many of whom received their training in Christian missionary schools and colleges, who refuse to acquire any of the Islamic learning for which they have nothing but contempt, insisting upon their right to reinterpret Islam and its law because they argue that Islam is not the monopoly of any priestly class! If a certain task requires specialized knowledge and training, how can it be properly performed except by those who fulfill the necessary conditions? How then can these people who know nothing about the Shariah, be qualified to exercise Ijtihad?[37]

Jameelah's defense of the ulama, like her presentation of Islam, focuses on the ideal rather than the reality. She remembers the suffering of great Islamic scholars such as Ibn Hanbal and al-Shafii but seems oblivious to the failures of the ulama. She speaks of the reverence in which the ulama are held by people without acknowledging that in many Muslim societies, many people (urban elites as well as her "common Muslims") often hold religious leaders in contempt for their lifestyles and demeanor.

If the intelligentsia are not to meddle in religious matters but leave them to the expertise of the ulama, what then is the task of the intelligentsia? Jameelah's traditional orientation and her perspective on the challenge of modernity is encapsulated in her response to this question:

> Muslim intellecuals had better concentrate their attention on finding a remedy for the most acute malady afflicting ebery Muslim country—the curse of modernism. They must recognize that our indigenous modernist movement, which under the slogan of "changing with the changing times" threatens to destroy every trace of the faith in the Quran and the Sunnah, is even a greater menace than the Zionist occupation of Palestine.[38]

The primary task of Muslim intellectuals is to refute modern post-Enlightenment rationalism and empiricism of Western culture, in particular its prophets—Darwin, Marx, and Freud, all of whom are to be rejected. She sets forth a daunting challenge. The educational system must be transferred from the "hands of atheists and the materialists" to Islamically oriented teachers and reformers who are schooled in Western culture and in Islam. The process to be employed is one of refutation and Islamization. School textbooks that carefully refute Western fallacies in philosophy, psychology, economics, and anthropology and provide an alternative Islamic viewpoint must be produced in indigenous rather than Western languages. Islamic standards should be employed to revise or Islamize the writings of western intellectuals like Keynes, Freud, Jung, Adler, Karen Horney, Margaret Mead, and Carleton Coon.

While Maryam Jameelah would agree with reformers on the need for change, in her view the process should not be one of reinterpretation but rather a return to and reassertion of traditional Islam, that system of Islamic belief, practice, and institutions that, she believes, guided Muslims for thirteen centuries. This then should be the cornerstone or basis for the reform of Muslim societies. As al-Ghazzali and Ibn Taimiya responded to the challenge of the philosophers and rationalists of their times who tried "to concoct a new brand of Islam," so, too, "[w]hat the Muslim world today needs above all is a modern al-Ghazzali and a modern Ibn Taimiya" to refute the "bogey of progress" and change.[39] To those modernists who would distinguish between the letter and the spirit of the law, Jameelah responds that this principle is Christian in origin (Paul's Epistles: "The letter killeth but the spirit giveth life") and "totally foreign to Islamic values," for "the letter of Islam lives in its spirit and the spirit in its letter, the two indivisible and inseparable."[40] This then is the basis for her critique of Islamic and secular modernists and of modern reforms regarding marriage, purdah, divorce, or jihad. Thus she rejects modernist interpretations of Islam that seek to reinterpret or circumvent the letter of the law by arguing that the spirit of Islam would favor monogamy over polygamy or free intermingling of the sexes over segregation or that emphasize that Islam's commitment to peace precludes jihad instead of defining jihad against aggressive unbelievers as a sacred duty. For Jameelah, modernists are engaging in an historical and doctrinal revisionism that has little to do with Islam and more to do with the "westernization of Islam," that is, a reinterpretation of Islam motivated primarily by the effective penetration of Western culture and values.

Women

The issue of Muslim women and their role in society provides a primary example of Maryam Jameelah's concerns and defense of Islam against the influence of the West and Muslim elites alike. The status and role of women have been a central concern and value in Muslim history and society. This significance is reflected in Muslim family law (marriage, divorce, and inheritance), which is the heart of Islamic law (Shariah). In the twentieth century many Muslim countries introduced reform legislation affecting marriage (child marriage and polygamy), divorce, and inheritance. These reforms often legislated or mandated from the top by modern, Western-oriented elites. Although acquiesced to, they were not in fact fully accepted and internalized by more traditional religious leaders and their followers, and in recent years they have been the subject of contention and debate. The Islamic Republic of Iran abrogated the Shah's modern family law reforms and in Pakistan successive governments have been pressured by religious leaders to do the same with Pakistan's Family Laws Ordinance.

Maryam Jameelah's handling of Islam and women has been consistent and persistent. As early as 1976, she was addressing Western feminists as well as Muslim women. Combining faithfulness to her vision of classical Islam and condemnation of modern reform as the product of Muslim Westernizers, Jameelah once again casts herself as the defender of "orthodoxy." Indeed she sets out to prove the inherent superiority of Islamic teachings on polygamy, divorce, and purdah (separation or segregation of the sexes). Charging that family laws have been "mutilated" in many Muslim countries, Jameelah attributes reforms to "mental slavery to the values of Western civilization."[41] She regards these Muslim practices as unalterably rooted in and mandated by the Quran and Sunnah of the Prophet. Western abhorence of purdah, she maintains, is due to the inherent contradiction between Islam and Western secularism and in particular "an exaggerated individualism which dominates modern society to the extent that adultery is regarded as far less abominable."[42] The same modern (Western and Muslim) critics of purdah are similarly dismissed as advocates of reforms that are grounded in "perverted cultural values" that thoroughly confuse the roles of men and women.[43] Jameelah dismisses those who would seek to liberate women by abolishing the veil or who advocate coeducation, enfranchisement, employment outside the home, and women's participation in public life as propagating a modern, Western ideal that ascribes honor and respect not to a woman's fulfillment of her traditional (Islamic) role as wife and mother but to a modern (Western) woman's ability to successfully perform the functions of a man while at the same time displaying her physical beauty. Such ideas, she believes, are contrary to Islam, where "the role of a woman is not the ballot box but maintenance of home and family. . . . While men are the actors on the stage of history, the function of the women is to be their helpers concealed from public gaze behind the scenes."[44] Jameelah surveys the impact of the feminist movement in the West and selectively cites Western commentators such as Max Lerner ("We are living in a Babylonian society") to support her conclusion that the social consequences of the feminist movement and its so-called "emancipation of women" are an "epidemic of crime, lawlessness and universal indulgence in illicit sex as a result of the complete disintegration of the family."[45]

Maryam Jameelah's contributions to Muslim self-understanding spanned the latter half of the twentieth century and the beginning of the new millennium. In a world dominated by male interpreters of Islam, she has been one of a handful of Muslim women who asserted her right to interpret Islam and to criticize Muslim and non-Muslim scholars alike. She has been a conservative voice whose prolific writings spanned many of the major issues facing Muslims. If her "defense" of tradition won her many admirers, her critique and rejection of Islamic and secular reformers alike diminished her impact. Today, in many parts of the Muslim world, women in increasing numbers seek new paths of empowerment, redefining Islam and gender relations. For many, Jameelah represents the very conservatism they seek to supplant, an orientation though that still enjoys broad-based support in many quarters of the Muslim world. Whatever the final outcome, Maryam Jameelah has played a pioneering role as an activist Muslim intellectual which makes her truly one of the makers of contemporary Islam.

4
HASAN HANAFI
The Classic Intellectual

Hasan Hanafi arrived in France in the middle of the Suez Crisis of 1956 with a bag of dry bread, a chunk of cheese, ten Egyptian pounds, and general dreams of returning home to Egypt as a philosopher and musician. For Hanafi, France was "the place of formation and the school for the beginners"[1] where he was to explore the wide ranges of philosophy and establish foundations for his later work. When he returned to Egypt ten years later, he accepted a position in the faculty of the University of Cairo and became an important voice for articulating the new philosophical trends of the day.

Hanafi's position in Egyptian society is almost the pure example of the "intellectual" as defined in the scholarly literature. He did not create his own political organization, nor is he a direct leader in a political movement. His primary goal is to provide a reconstruction of the full range of Islamic thought as it relates to society and the world Islamic community. This would be the basis for a series of transformations of worldviews and social structures which would lead "from dogma to revolution," establishing a proper relationship between "heritage and modernity."[2] Such a position started with a strong critique of existing conditions and worked to develop a theology of revolution for Islam.

This mission placed Hanafi in the position of the intellectual critic of all existing power structures. However, his mode of operation was to speak and work publicly and "above ground" rather than to engage in secret revolutionary actions. He recognized that this shaped his work, and he defined his role in comparison with the leading revolutionary Islamic activist of his time, Sayyid Qutb: "I did not go to prison nor was my body tortured. If I had been imprisoned and tortured, I might have written 'Signposts on the Road' [the revolutionary tract written by Qutb while he was in prison in the early 1960s]. Instead, I continue to follow the path of the early Sayyid Qutb, who wrote *Social Justice in Islam*, *The Struggle between Islam and Capitalism*, and *Islam and World Peace*.[3]

When Hanafi set out to provide a formal summary of his position in the early 1980s, he called it "the Islamic Left."[4] He recognized that even the label would be controversial but noted the problems with any other label as well. The Islamic Left, in Hanafi's definition, was within the great tradition of modern Islamic reform, as a continuation of the Islamic project defined by Jamal al-Din al-Afghani in the late nineteenth century and extended by the work of Muhammad Abduh and the journal *al-Manar*. However, he saw the Islamic Left as going beyond that original project. Hanafi argued that the earlier tradition basically appealed to the elite rather than the whole of the Muslim community and that it idealistically emphasized the unity of Muslims within that community. In contrast, the Islamic Left "stresses the distinctions within the one Islamic community between the rich and the poor, the strong and the weak, the oppressors and the oppressed." The Islamic Left "speaks for the silent oppressed majority within the Muslim masses, supports the weak against the strong, considers people equal like the teeth of a comb, since no difference exists between Arab and Persian except in piety and doing good deeds."[5]

Hanafi undertook this broadly conceived mission in the context of Egypt, and his life interacts with the great transformations taking place in his national homeland. Although Hanafi had important experiences both in the West and as a cosmopolitan public intellectual in the broader world of Islam, his identity remains rooted in his Egyptian homeland.

The Egyptian Context

Egypt in Hanafi's lifetime experienced many major transformations. When he was born in 1935, British military forces were an important presence in the country. During his childhood years, the experience of World War II was shaping the Egyptian nationalist spirit. Egypt was a major military center for the Allied war effort, and British and American forces were highly visible in almost every aspect of urban Egyptian life. The German campaign in North Africa brought the war to Egypt in 1942 and raised the hopes of some younger Egyptians that the British could finally be driven out.

Following World War II, Egypt confronted two major issues. One was the growing nationalist fervor that began to combine longstanding Egyptian nationalist themes of opposition to British occupation with the emerging Pan-Arab enthusiasm. In 1947–1948, a major focus of this new Egyptian-Arab nationalism was the establishment of the state of Israel. Egypt participated in the Arab war against the new state, and the loss in this conflict highlighted the second great issue in postwar Egypt: the increasingly visible corruption and incompetence of the political elite and the state they ran. Added to the dynamics of rising nationalism was a growing feeling that a revolution was necessary.

Nationalism and revolution became the great themes of the late 1940s and early 1950s. Among Egyptian students and the urban educated elites, the two competing visions of an alternative to the existing situation were Communism and a revivalist Islam, most thoroughly articulated by the Muslim Brotherhood. Surprisingly, when "the Revolution" actually came in 1952, it was led by young military officers. Some of these new leaders were Communist, and others had ties to the Brotherhood, but the primary aspirations of the leading members of the new Revolutionary Command Council (RCC) were neither Communist nor Islamist. The emerging ideology and programs of the new revolutionary regime combined Pan-Arabism and the new-style radical socialism that was emerging in the so-called Third World of the 1950s. The chief figure in the development of this "Arab Socialism" in Egypt was Jamal Abd al-Nasir ("Nasser"), who was the heart of the young officers' group from the very beginning and became president of the new revolutionary republic in 1956, leading Egypt until his death in 1970.

The new regime soon came into conflict with both the Communists and the Muslim Brotherhood, and both organizations were suppressed and leaders jailed. Islamic and leftist intransigent militants continued to oppose Nasser, but by the mid-1960s, the Communist Left ceased to be a viable or effective alternative to the Arab socialism of Nasser. This development left the militant Islamists as the only effective source of opposition, but in the 1960s it appeared that they, too, would soon disappear as an effective force in society. The leading radical Islamic ideologue was Sayyid Qutb, who was executed by the government in 1966. However, his writings from the early 1960s, smuggled out of prison by women associated with the Muslim Brotherhood,[6] became the foundation for a revolutionary Islamic ideology. Qutb's book *Milestones* (*Ma'alim fi al-tariq*) is an especially important inspiration for the development of a militantly revolutionary Islamist ideology by the 1970s in a number of different places in the Muslim world.

The overwhelming majority of Egyptians, including most students and people in the urban educated elites, accepted the new Arab socialism with enthusiasm. Former Communists and former members of the Muslim Brotherhood faced the challenge of combining the new nationalist radicalism with the earlier perspectives. Most Communists maintained a Marxist secularism within the congenial framework of the new Arab socialism. The challenge was greater for Islamically oriented intellectuals like Hasan Hanafi. Some, like Muhammad al-Ghazali, remained in a precarious position on the fringes of political life, sometimes in prison. They continued to advocate the positions of the older Muslim Brotherhood while rejecting the militant logic of Sayyid Qutb. Others worked to define an "Islamic Socialism" which would be a complementary part of Nasserism. It is in this context that Hanafi worked to define what he ultimately came to call "the Islamic Left." This position roused opposition both from the more secularist Nasserites and the more conservative and militant Islamists, as well as arousing the suspicions of state security police from time to time.

The major event that shaped many aspects of political life in the Arab world in the late 1960s was the Six Day War in 1967. The crushing defeat of the major Arab states by Israel in this war was a traumatic experience, especially for the generation that had come to maturity in the new revolutionary era of independence. Like many others of his generation, Hasan Hanafi engaged in a profound intellectual and ideological rethinking. For Egypt, the defeat, followed in 1970 by the death of Nasser, led to a period of less conceptually ideological and more "pragmatic" leadership under Sadat. It was also a time of greater emphasis on the Islamic heritage and a withdrawal from the enthusiasms and conceptualizations of the older radical socialism. This provided an opportunity for more public visibility for the Muslim Brotherhood, although the organization itself remained illegal, and an opening for the rise of small extremist Islamist groups inspired by the ideas of Sayyid Qutb and others like him. A number of important intellectuals reflected a more explicitly Islamic orientation in their writings.

The pragmatism of Sadat led to the signing of a peace treaty with Israel, and the rise of the Islamist extremists led to the response to the treaty, which resulted in the militants killing Sadat in 1981. However, the crisis of the assassination of the president did not result in a major extremist Islamic revolution or a significant secularist backlash. Instead, the political mainstream in Egypt became increasingly Islamically oriented, with major moves in the direction of Islamization of laws and a significant Islamization of the public arenas of life.

By the 1990s many of the most popular and influential television stars were theologically conservative Islamic scholars presenting messages that would have resulted in prison sentences, if not executions, in the Egypt of the 1960s. Older luminaries in the Muslim Brotherhood, like Muhammad al-Ghazali, moved from the periphery to the mainstream of Egyptian public life, while the leading secularist intellectuals were marginalized and often threatened with violence by militant Islamists. The Nobel Prize–winning novelist Naguib Mahfouz was stabbed by a fanatic, and Farag Fawda, one of the leading secularist public intellectuals, was murdered in 1992.

Hasan Hanafi's general mission and perspective remained remarkably constant during the second half of the twentieth century. However, the dramatic changes in the context of Egyptian political and intellectual life challenged his work in significantly different ways. Early in his life, as a student and a young intellectual, he saw the major challenge coming from the Communists, and then possibly the secular leftists. By the 1980s, some of his strongest criticism was aimed at the "Islamic fundamentalists" and "ritualists" who represented, from Hanafi's perspective, the forces of repression and obscurantism. In many ways, the changing conditions had an impact on what Hanafi did, and his life reflects the great changes of the second half of the twentieth century.

Life Reflecting the Times

Hasan Hanafi wrote an autobiographical account that provides a clear introduction both to his life and to his self-perception of personal mission. In this autobiography, his life is marked by a series of developments in consciousness. Each of these periods in his life coincides with a major era in contemporary Egyptian history. Despite his global consciousness, Hanafi's autobiographical self-definition remains closely tied to his Egyptian roots. Similarly, this autobiography indirectly mentions his family and its life in Egypt, but the primary arena for activity in this account is Hanafi's participation in national life, not the life of his family. This does not reflect indifference to family, since both in his childhood and as a married adult, family plays an important part in Hanafi's life. Instead this affirms Hanafi's sense of mission within the context of Egypt, the Islamic community, and the world, along with the autonomy of his personal life with his family.

The first consciousness identified by Hanafi was the development of a "national consciousness" when he was in elementary school. The childhood experience of World War II, which involved leaving Cairo to escape from the German bombing raids, created a consciousness of Egypt as a homeland under attack—but the enemy was not the Germans. Rather, the British, whose army had occupied Egypt since 1882, were seen as the real enemy. In the years following the war, Egyptian students at all levels were an important element in the growing nationalist demonstrations. For Hanafi, the "true beginning of national consciousness" came in 1948 with the creation of Israel and the outbreak of the war in Palestine.[7] As a secondary school student, Hanafi volunteered to work in the struggle against Zionism and discovered both the excitement of the cause and the dangers of divisions among Arabs and Muslims. It was only later that he recognized that, at that time, the idealistic students did not comprehend "the extent of the betrayal of the national cause" or that it was "we [the Egyptians] who were destroyed in Palestine."[8] Although Hanafi's analysis of the nature of the Palestine conflict changed and developed, the Palestinian cause remained central to his thinking and his view of world affairs.

In the immediate conditions of Egypt in the early 1950s, Hanafi's schoolboy nationalism developed a more Islamic tone. As the country moved toward the coup that brought young military officers to power in 1952, Hanafi joined the Muslim Brotherhood and entered what he called the "beginning of religious consciousness."[9] He was specially active as a Muslim Brother while he was an undergraduate in the University of Cairo. He took part in demonstrations before the 1952 revolution and was active in student politics in the early days of the new revolutionary era. He was particularly opposed to the Communists, whom he "considered to be corrupted, deviants from the right path, alienated and foreign, possessing inclinations that were far from the truth, and immoral."[10] When Muhammad Naguib came to address the students at the University, Hanafi felt moved by the sense of affirmation of Islamic unity and offended by the Communist students who shouted "Constitution! Constitution!" His feeling was that they "were outside of the trends of the Ummah. What could Constitution mean when compared with Islamic unity?"[11]

Hanafi's thought and vision of what was needed gained a clear Islamic dimension in these years. His political positions reflected those of the Muslim Brotherhood. He took part in demonstrations opposing the 1954 agreement with Great Britain governing evacuation of British troops, which permitted their return in times of war. However, following the nationalization of the Suez Canal in 1956, he felt able to support the government as a leader among liberation movements. The suppression of the Brotherhood by Nasser's government in the mid-1950s created difficulties. Hanafi reports that his "activities were restricted to collecting contributions for the families" of Brothers in prison and that he "was not part of any of the secret activities, since that was contrary to my nature."[12]

Even before the suppression of the Brotherhood, Hanafi had not fit the mold of most of the activists within the organization.[13] He remembers that the first time he participated in discussions following a lecture was when he recommended that if the Brotherhood was to be active as a group in the modern world, it might change the organization's logo symbol from a book and two swords to a book and two cannons. He also was a musician and enjoyed classical Western music and playing the violin. This caused much discussion and sometimes debate with his fellow Brothers, who thought that music might be a diversion from a proper life of prayer and piety. As a university student, Hanafi saw nothing wrong with carrying on conversations in public with female students, and he did not advocate separation of men and women in the classrooms.

In intellectual development, however, Hanafi's experience in the Brotherhood was of great importance. It was through the Brotherhood that he became familiar with the major writers of the contemporary movements within Islam. He found the writings of Brotherhood leaders like Hasan al-Banna, Sayyid Qutb, and Muhammad al-Ghazali and other writers, like Abu al-Ala al-Mawdudi and Abd al-Hasan al-Nadwi, inspiring. Reading them he had a strong sense of the renaissance of Islam and of his own mission. However, as a student in the philosophy classes of the University, he found the method of teaching and the content to be out of touch with the reality which he was living outside of the classroom. He tried to present his own interpretations of major topics in medieval Islamic philosophy and mysticism and soon came into conflict with his professors. By his fourth and final year, he says: "My personal view began to dominate the pages of all my answers from A to Z." In this he was beginning to work for the establishment of "a general Islamic method based on the rationality of good and bad, and the unification of truth, goodness, and beauty."[14] This project of creating a complete and general Islamic method has become the core of Hanafi's life mission.

His completion of university studies was a time of personal crisis that coincided with the Egyptian national crisis of 1956. His conflicts with professors reached a point where he was brought before a disciplinary board for showing disrespect for the dean. He lost his status as an honors student, which meant that he would not be eligible for a place in an educational mission to France. He resolved to go to France to continue his studies regardless of the conditions. The crisis of intellectual life in Egyptian universities, the persecution of the Muslim Brotherhood, and the intellectual crisis of Islamic studies combined, in his view, with his own personal crisis. At this point, he says, he went regularly to the mosque to recite the Quran, and "for the first time I felt its philosophical intuitions, the importance of the world of consciousness and the senses, and the necessity for continuing the struggle."[15] He concentrated on the project of Islamic renewal. "There was no time left for music or playing the violin. The contemporary Islamic idea began to sing in my ear like a melody, but the musical melody was empty without any intellectual meaning. It was not possible to remain in Egypt: what would I learn?"[16] It was under these conditions that he was the last student to leave Egypt for France before the outbreak of the 1956 Suez War, when France joined Israel and Great Britain in attacking Egypt.

In France Hanafi found the beginning of his philosophical consciousness in the last years of the 1950s. By 1960 Paris had become one the major centers of contemporary philosophical thought in the world. Many of the trends of thought that would come to prominence by the early 1970s were being formulated at the time of Hanafi's arrival. He quickly involved himself in the debates, many of which reflected his own special concerns for method. However, he tended to recapitulate the process of the development of modern continental European philosophy in his path to the definition of his own new method. His starting point was German idealism, especially as reflected in his readings of the works of Fichte. He soon immersed himself in reading and contemplating the history of Western philosophy, beginning with Plato and Aristotle. He reports having "a special admiration for great negators like Spinoza and Kierkegaard."[17] His study and his personal experiences as a poor foreign student with the danger of serious health problems combined to create a transformation of his philosophical perspective. (For example, he spent the summer of 1959 in the university hospital when he was suspected of suffering from tuberculosis and malnutrition, and that was where he read Plato and Aristotle.) He left his idealism for an existence-oriented realism.

Hanafi describes this transition: "the two moments of European consciousness: the *cogito* of the rationalist and the *Ego* of the existentialists during four centuries were represented in my life during eight years, rationalist idealism in 1956–1960, life reality and existence in 1961–1966. I kept the optimism of Idealism and I left the pessimism of existentialism. I kept Reason and its role in Idealism and I abandoned the irrational in Existentialism."[18] In this transition, Hanafi's general project of creating a whole new Islamic methodology and theology continued, but the approach changed.

Hanafi's initial research proposal for the doctorate, entitled "The General Islamic Method," expressed his intention to formulate Islam as a general and comprehensive method for individual and social life. However, he had difficulty convincing the faculty to accept this proposal. The Orientalists thought that the project was much too broad and recommended that he study some specific individual or movement, while the Western philosophers urged him to study Kant as the appropriate starting point. He reports: "The problem was as follows: the Orientalists read me and said: this is Western philosophy and we are historians; the philosophers read me and said, This is Islam and we are Western philosophers. I was in need of an Orientalist-philosopher or a philosopher Orientalist of the type of Renan."[19]

One scholar who was in L'Ecole des Hautes Etudes and was such a person was Henri Corbin, but Corbin was concentrating on Shi'i studies at the time. Hanafi had discussions with him but wanted to work on the Sunni Muslim experience rather than Shi'ism. Another major Orientalist scholar of the day, Louis Massignon, helped Hanafi define the specific starting point for his work, which was to be the study of *usul al-fiqh*, the fundamental methods of legal thought. Hanafi worked to create a new methodology that would enable Muslims to choose new fundamental axes on which to build the Islamic consciousness of renaissance.

The scholar Hanafai describes as "my master," responsible for "all my philosophical formation," is Jean Guitton, a professor of philosophy in the Sorbonne and a leading Roman Catholic modernist.[20] Guitton served as Hanafi's guide through much of his reading and study of Western philosophy. He also provided guidance for Hanafi in practical matters like how to give public lectures and methods of research. Guitton had been to Egypt in the 1930s and had at least some familiarity with the Egyptian intellectual scene. Guitton's ecumenical perspectives and methods helped to develop Hanafi's understanding of approaches for the reconciliation of different positions. Hanafi describes himself as building on Guitton's foundations and then going beyond them. He describes this as developing Guitton "from individual consciousness to social consciousness, from Right to Left, from religion to revolution. I used Biblical criticism negatively and he used it positively to preserve the articles of faith. I lay the grounds for Liberation Theology, while he fears that people might switch to Marxism and violence, and that alien elements might infiltrate authentic faith."[21]

In developing his scholarship Hanafi started with the basic methods of sociolegal thought in Islam, utilizing a perspective that combined the Islamic perspectives of *tawil* (esoteric interpretation) and *tafsir* (Quranic exegesis) with contemporary approaches of philosophical analysis. The result was his extended essay "The Methods of Exegesis: Essay on the Science of the Fundamentals of Understanding in the Discipline of Usul al-Fiqh."[22] Hanafi described this work as an attempt to "reconstruct Islamic culture at the level of consciousness in order to discover subjectivity. Instead of being theocentric, it becomes anthropocentric. [It] provides the method for analyzing living experiences and describing the processes of linguistic pseudo-morphology."[23]

Hanafi also had to choose a topic for the complementary dissertation. He decided to provide a study of the development of European philosophical consciousness "through a non-European consciousness in order to see it from a distance with a neutral and objective consciousness. The purpose was to declare the end of the European consciousness and the beginning of the Third World consciousness as represented through the cultures of non-European peoples."[24] Hanafi concentrated on the development of European understanding of religion, especially the emergence and significance of phenomenology. The result was a study entitled "The Exegesis of Phenomenology, the State of the Art of the Phenomenological Method and Its Application to the Phenomenon of Religion."[25]

Hanafi's intellectual projects of the early 1960s were rounded out by a third study, in which he provided a specific case of applying the methodology he was developing. This involved a synthesis of the phenomenological approach with the method of exegetical interpretation of text. He chose the New Testament as a basis for applying his developing theory of three types of consciousness: historical consciousness, speculative consciousness, and active consciousness. He completed this work as the book *The Phenomenology of Exegesis: An Essay in the Existential Hermeneutic of the New Testament.*[26] This work on Christian texts reflects Hanafi's interest in gaining a full understanding of the European cultural traditions. He traveled as much as possible on a student's budget.

Guitton arranged for Hanafi to attend the fourth session of the Vatican II Ecùmenical Council in Rome in 1964. He participated in discussions, and Guitton introduced Hanafi to Pope Paul VI. Hanafi viewed his experiences in Rome as the beginning of his departure from "the West" and his return to Egypt and the East. Similarly, at this time in Paris during his dissertation defense, he began his critique of the West and aroused the ire of the chair of his academic jury. However, he also prepared for his return by beginning an active criticism of the developing Arab socialist regime in Egypt. During a visit to Paris by a major figure in the Egyptian government, field marshall Abd al-Hakim Amer, Hanafi openly asked challenging questions. One result was the organization of delegations of Egyptians studying in Europe to return to Egypt in order to see the realities of the new revolutionary government. Hanafi was a part of the student effort to prepare statements and studies for the delegation before it left.

Hanafi himself returned to Cairo in 1966 and began his career as a teacher at the University of Cairo. He began work on his long-term project, "Tradition and Modernity." His goal in this project was to rejuvenate the Islamic tradition and reconstruct its intellectual sciences, as Husserl had done for European philosophy.[27] He also taught a course on Western thought and Christian philosophy at the university. The lack of appropriate texts led him to prepare an anthology of medieval Christian thought that provided examples of many different types of thought. This became a part of his broader intellectual effort "to get rid of unilateralism in religious thought."[28]

These general activities were interrupted by the trauma of the Six Day War of 1967. Hanafi reports that "the defeat of 1967 fell on me like a thunderstorm. I saw everything collapsing and the dream aborted. The house was burning and it was inconceivable that I would not work to extinguish the fire. How could one prepare for the future while we were without a present?"[29] The "Tradition and Modernity" project was stopped, and the more broadly methodological work was suspended. Hanafi began a career as a more visible public intellectual in addition to his work in the university faculty. The period 1967–1971 became the time of the "beginning of political consciousness" for Hanafi.

Hanafi devoted much of his time and energy to writing for two periodicals, *al-Fikr al-Mu'asir* and *al-Katib*. In the essays he wrote regularly for these magazines and his other activities, Hanafi became an important voice in the public debates about the defeat. Hanafi says, "I became more conscious about my responsibility for the daily battle and direct struggle in order to analyze the cause of the defeat and to strengthen the spirit of resistance."[30] In these activities, Hanafi provides a good example of the functioning of a "public intellectual." He was not part of any political party or defined grouping. Hanafi describes his political consciousness of the time as being "a purely philosophical political consciousness based on the analysis of living experiences and the description of their essences."[31] Although his activities were not part of an organized movement, his positions were identified as oppositional and attracted the attention of the security forces. His lectures were taped and on record with the police. In 1971 the rector of the university spoke with Hanafi and recommended that he should stop lecturing and accept an invitation to be a visiting professor in the United States. The nonactivist but critical intellectual had become a political activist in the classic mode of involvement of intellectuals in the political arena. This period in his life ended when Hanafi took the advice of the rector and left for the United States, where he became a visiting professor at Temple University in Philadelphia.

The demands of regularly writing essays for the journals was intellectually challenging for Hanafi. By 1971 he found that he was repeating himself, "expressing outside more than absorbing inside, writing more than reading."[32] His political problems helped to reinforce the sense that it was time for him to begin a new phase of his work. Hanafi's move to the United States coincides with, and may have made possible, a significant effort to articulate Islam as a revolutionary religion.

During the 1970s and 1980s, Hasan Hanafi emerged as an internationally visible Muslim public intellectual. While maintaining his ties with Cairo University, for most of this period he held visiting professorships at institutions around the world. With increasing frequency, he was a participant in international conferences and invited to give addresses for a wide spectrum of Muslim and non-Muslim audiences.

Before leaving for the United States, Hanafi had already been a visiting lecturer for a short time in 1970 in Louvain University in Belgium, where he had close contact with the developing ideas of Catholic liberation theology. He was especially interested in the works of Camillo Torres, whose picture was posted on university walls by Louvain students.[33] He returned to Cairo with the complete works of Torres and wrote a study of Torres's ideas, concentrating on the ideas of revolution as a religious imperative.[34] This was an important beginning in his efforts to introduce Christian liberation theology to Muslims, as well as to provide a part of the broader conceptual basis for his own efforts to articulate a revolutionary religion in Islamic terms. He thought that the universal issues went beyond national and religious boundaries: "The tragedy of unquestioning acceptance in developing societies is the same regardless of religious identity, while the populist religion is that which unifies all of the religions."[35] An interesting dimension of this ecumenical vision was Hanafi's hope that he could publish an essay on liberation theology that could be "a gift to our brothers, the Copts of Egypt, so that I could share with them knowledge of the latest developments in Christian theology."[36]

During his years in the United States, especially 1971–1975, Hanafi expanded the dimensions of his intellectual venture. In France he had concentrated on philosophy, but in the 1970s he worked to develop his understanding of the social sciences, giving special attention to the sociology of religion. He was active in presenting papers at meetings of American scholarly associations. These papers reflect the broad range of Hanafi's interests and the many different topics and perspectives he was attempting to bring together into his broad project of defining the relationship between tradition and modernism or heritage and modernity. He continued his interest in methodology with studies like "Hermeneutics as Axiomatics" and in analyses of Western thinkers like Joachim of Fiore, and he worked explicitly to define an Islamic model of religion and revolution.[37]

A new dimension of Hanafi's work was a more formal study of Judaism, especially Zionism. These studies continued his involvements from the days of his earliest nationalist awareness. However, he placed them in the context of his articulation of liberation theology. He argued that this subject was "not far away from liberation theology since Zionism is a counter-liberation theology."[38] On the basis of this line of analysis, Hanafi opposed the negotiation of a peace treaty between Egypt and Israel in 1978–1979. He became more actively a part of the opposition to Sadat's policies. Although he did not condone the murder of Sadat in 1981, he made an important effort to ensure that the general public understood the arguments that were presented by his murderers when they were placed on trial.[39]

Hanafi also continued his efforts to analyze and interpret Western society and intellectual traditions. Although he had ignored "Anglo-Saxon," that is, English and American, philosophy previously, he made some effort to study it while he was in the United States. However, his major effort was more in the direction of analysis of society and values. He saw a need to present the aspects of American society that tended to be unknown to Muslims in the Middle East: poverty, crime, corruption, racism, and violence. He later said that if he had not been so involved in working on his major project of articulating a revolutionary Islam, he would have completed a book entitled "America: Truth and Mask," so that "everyone who wants to immigrate to America would know where he is going and in order to return our national allegiance to ourselves rather than having it directed toward the Other."[40]

By the 1980s, his position as a Muslim public intellectual with high international visibility provided many opportunities for Hanafi to present his ideas. As an international intellectual, after his work in the United States, he taught in universities in Kuwait (1979), Morocco (1982–1984), Japan (1984–1985), and the United Arab Emirates (1985). He returned to Japan as an academic consultant at United Nations University in Tokyo in 1985–1987.

A flood of publications, ranging from single articles to multivolume works, began to create a more comprehensive presentation of his views. In this, his life project remained remarkably consistent. He worked to provide both a comprehensive methodology and a broadly inclusive content for a new synthesis of the Islamic heritage and modernity.

In the 1990s, however, he published a major new work that was both within the framework of this project and an important expansion of its boundaries. He had long been interested in the challenge of what he came to call "Occidentalism." This was to be the Muslim response to "Orientalism," the old-style of Western scholarship which studied Islam and Muslim societies. Occidentalism was not to be an apologetic defense of Islam against attack by prejudiced Western scholars; it was to be an informed analysis of the West by Muslim scholars. In a substantial book, he presented the foundations for the ways Western philosophy and epistemology could be examined.[41] The key to his approach is his viewing the Western mode of modernity as one of a number of possible alternatives rather than accepting the Western ethnocentric assumption of its universality.

During the 1990s, Hanafi spent much of his time in Cairo, with visits and lecture tours all over the world. He continues to be an independent intellectual rather than part of a more structured political or ideological movement. Although he has a reputation as an advocate for Islamic positions, his radical views mean that he is not a part of the Islamist political groupings or the more extreme militant underground. At the same time, his radicalism is not in accord with more secularist intellectuals who mistrust his Islamic orientation.

This precarious position made Hanafi vulnerable to attack by the more instransigent Islamic forces. In 1997 he was attacked by an ultraconservative group al-Azhar Scholars' Front, for, in their opinion, contradicting the teachings of the Quran and questioning the views of the Prophet Muhammad. The Front demanded his removal from the faculty of Cairo University, and their actions raised concerns about Hanafi's safety. Farag Fouda, an Egyptian intellectual who had been subjected to similar attacks, was murdered in 1992.[42] Although Hanafi received significant support from government officials and others, the attack continued to be a matter of concern and debate in Egypt.[43] In this sense, his experience had come full circle. At the beginning of his life as an intellectual, he was an activist in the Islamic movement that challenged the more secular political authorities and the Communist opposition. By the late 1990s, he was an intellectual attacked by Islamists in the conservative establishment of al-Azhar University, and he received at least some support from other, more secularist intellectuals who had also been subject to attack, as well as receiving some protection from a relatively Islamically oriented state. This precarious balancing reflects the difficulties of maintaining the position Hanafi represents: bringing together Islamic and leftist traditions of reform and revolution and doing this within the mainstream rather than at the violent fringes of political society.

Basic Themes

Hasan Hanafi has written a library of books since he left as a student for Paris. His works are on many different topics and reflect both his immediate needs and his long-term visions. When he taught medieval European thought, he edited a volume of important texts, because the type of book that he needed for his course did not exist. In the time of crisis following the Six Day War, he wrote shorter popular journalistic essays to meet what he saw as the needs of the time. However, in virtually all of his works the broader visions of his major projects are visible.

In general terms, one might identify three dimensions in his lifetime project. One is the examination of the Islamic heritage and its relationship with renewal and modernity. A second builds on that, using the conceptual and faith resources of the Islamic heritage and transforming them into an Islamic revolutionary theology, going "from dogma to revolution." The third aspect of this life project is to provide a thorough analysis of the Western heritage from a perspective that is not Western in its own origin and, in this way, provides a basis for a more comprehensive understanding of the relationship between Islam and the West, especially in the context of modernity.

Heritage, Renewal, and Modernity

Throughout his autobiography and in other writings, Hasan Hanafi identifies his lifelong project as being the study and development of *al-turath wa al-tajdid*, or "Heritage and Renewal."[44] This project involves a delicate balancing between a strong affirmation of the authenticity and universalism of Islam and a critical condemnation of most forms and articulations of Islam in actual historical experience. In the context of the second half of the twentieth century, Hanafi identifies renewal with modernity and frequently speaks of "heritage and modernity" as well as "heritage and renewal."

Hanafi argues that in any great age of transition and significant transformation, the discussion of the relationship between the heritage and the new conditions is crucial.[45] Muslims in the modern era are, in Hanafi's view, deeply involved in just such a transition. In his analysis of the current situation, he notes that movements of religious reform and renewal generally give greater emphasis to "authenticity" than to "modernity," while the majority of the intellectual tendencies on the side of awakening or renaissance are closer to "modernity" than to "authenticity."[46] He warns, however, that the two are necessarily linked and that "authenticity without modernity" becomes unquestioning repetition of the old, while "modernity without authenticity" becomes a premature radicalism that cannot be sustained.[47]

"Heritage" (*turath*) is a subject of intense debate among intellectuals and scholars in the Muslim world. It is generally understood, at least in arguments in the Arab world, that the term refers to "the Islamic element" in culture and history, even when the writer is not a Muslim.[48] This is clearly the focus of Hanafi's analysis when he examines "heritage." However, in the "authenticity" and "heritage" debates, Hanafi argues for a very open and universalistic definition of what is contained in the Islamic heritage.

In Hanafi's analysis, "heritage" is not a fixed pattern of past behaviors and institutions. Instead, the term is used "to represent a concept of evolving religious tradition prescribing norms but not necessarily reflecting words recorded in archives or practices ingrained in daily life; it is constantly under construction."[49] The foundations for this position were laid in his studies in France on methodologies. In his studies of the science of hermeneutics, Hanafi sees the Islamic case as providing a way for broadening of that science to mean more than simply "the science of interpretation" or the "theory of understanding." Hermeneutics can be "the science of the process of revelation from the letter to the reality or from Logos to Praxis, and also the transformation of revelation from the Divine Mind to human life."[50] In the case of scriptural hermeneutics, "Islamic" does not "necessarily mean religious, but it means the most rigorous form of rationalization and the highest degree of axiomatisation."[51] Heritage in this framework for analysis is not the inheritance of past practices; it is the axioms provided by the Islamic revelation that make it possible to develop the "general Islamic method" that would be a formulation of Islam "as a general and comprehensive method for individual and social life."[52]

Much of this effort involves intellectual analysis of sources and theoretical examinations of philosophical and theological principles. Building on his studies of hermeneutics, Hanafi provides a specific method for the interpretation of the Quran as one important foundation for understanding the heritage. The fundamental axioms and specific norms become the basis for the method of "thematic interpretation."[53] According to Hanafi, most Quranic interpretations view the Quran as a sequence of verses to be understood as separate items in a series. However, such a "longitudinal" approach is segmented and breaks up discussions of major themes. The result is the "absence of a coherent ideology or global worldview linking partial aspects of the theme together in a global view."[54]

Hanafi noted that the "rules of thematic interpretation" involved "[s]ocio-political commitment. The interpreter is not a neutral person. . . . There is no interpreter without a commitment to something. The absence of commitment is a negative commitment, a commitment for nothing, for non-commitment. An interpreter is a committed person for a cause. He is a reformer, a social actor, a revolutionary."[55]

The method of Quran interpretation makes explicit the direct connection between "heritage" and "renewal."[56] The rules of the method note that the interpreter "is looking for a solution of problem," creates a synopsis of verses related to certain basic themes, and subjects them to linguistic analysis and examination of the "factual situation." Then, the interpreter must make a comparison "between the Ideal and the real. After building the structure giving the qualitative theme and analysing the factual situation . . . the interpreter draws the comparison between the ideal structure deduced by content-analysis from the text and the factual situation induced by statistics and social sciences. The interpreter lives between text and reality." Then the final step in the method is that the interpreter must take action.

> Once the distance is seen between the ideal world and the real world, between kingdom of Heavens and kingdom of Earth, action emerges as a new step in the interpretation process. The interpreter himself switches from text to action, from theory to practice. . . . Gradual steps, time and combined efforts are required without jumping the steps or using violence. The complete realization of the Ideal and the idealization of the Real are natural process of Reason and Nature.

In this way, heritage and renewal merge through the actions of the inter-preter of the heritage acting in the reality of modernity.

Although there is an insistence on the necessity of action in much of what Hanafi writes, there is also an emphasis, as indicated in his discussion of the Quranic method, on gradualism and nonviolence. Hanafi did not present explicit political platforms or specific blueprints for institutions like Islamic banks. The Islamic Left as he defined it was more a general alterna-tive perspective than a concrete program.

Hanafi believed in the early 1980s that Egypt was not yet ready for the Islamic Left. In an analysis of the prospects for the future in Egypt that he presented in 1981, Hanafi said that "an Islamic left [is] not a real alterna-tive in Egypt as an organized political power."[57] In terms of the specific political and social policy implications of the Islamic Left, Hanafi tied the perspective very closely to Nasserism. He spoke of it as

the combination of Islam and the Nasserist national project. Islam is the heart of the masses and Nasserism is their need. Islam without Nasserism would fall into formalism like it is the case of Islamic groups. Nasserism without Islam will fall into secularism and will always be threatened by an Islamic movement. . . . Islamic left, when it comes, can be the most durable alternative. The masses can find in it their needs and their heart, their body and their soul.[58]

The Nasserism that is part of Hanafi's vision of the Islamic left is the "popular Nasserism" of the masses. After a decade of de-Nasserization, "the masses began to discover Nasser. Nasser in their hearts is still alive. His name is linked to national dignity, food subsidies, agrarian reform, na-tionalization, socialism, Arab nationalism, etc."[59] This association is not tied to specific programs of the 1960s so much as it reflects a continuation of the hopes aroused by the programs and rhetoric of that era.

The Islamic Left, as a combination of Islamic heritage and Nasserite modernity, "mobilizes its powers to face the main problems of the age, at the head of which are: imperialism, Zionism, and capitalism which under-mine us from without and poverty, oppression, and underdevelopment which undermine us from within."[60] In discussing specifics, Hanafi em-phasizes the dimension of socioeconomic justice as the key.

The mode and tone of the program as a whole can be seen in his discus-sion of how the Islamic Left would respond to the issues of poverty.

Although according to the text of the Qur'an, we are one commu-nity, in reality we are two: a poor community and a rich community, despite what we say in our preaching and our acclaimations of Islam. . . . [In Islam] wealth is the wealth of God with which we are entrusted. We have the right to use, to invest, and to utilize; we do not have the right to exploit, misuse, or monopolize. . . . The mission of the Islamic Left is the redistribution of the wealth of Muslims among all Muslims as Islam prescribes, according to work, effort, and sweat.[61]

The key issues in Hanafi's works relating to "Heritage and Renewal" become a synthesis of method of analysis and visions for programs. The heritage can be interpreted through a specific method to establish the modernity reflected in the ideas and perspectives of Hanafi's Islamic Left. As Hanafi makes clear many times, "Heritage" in this perspective is not the rigid ritualism of the fundamentalists; it is the liberating force that can enable Muslims to reject that fundamentalism in the name of an "authentic" Islam.

From Dogma to Revolution

Although Hanafi often expressed his opposition to violence, he firmly presents Islam as a revolution. In his task of speaking of heritage and its relation to modernity, he also speaks of the necessity of moving from "creed to revolution." This aspect of his thought is directly related to Hanafi's view of the current world context and the needs of Muslim peoples in that context. The analysis of the imperative to move from creed to revolution is viewed within the framework of the needs of developing societies in the modern world. He argues that there are two types of societies in the modern world, those where "tradition" or heritage remain strong sources of inspiration and the "so-called modern society" in which tradition is no longer a source of value or authority. In some "traditional Asian societies such as India and Japan" there is a "parallelism between Tradition and Modernism . . . [but] Tradition and modernization are juxtaposed, one upon the other and are not organically unified, one in the other."[62]

Hanafi does not see that parallelism as a successful continuation of tradition, but he sees "tradition" as a possible basis for modern revolution:

> It is possible to conceive a new model of development in traditional societies. Since nothing happens in reality before it happens in consciousness, the reconstruction of historical consciousness, namely tradition, is the way to development. Since historical consciousness is the recipient of tradition and is based on it, the reconstruction of tradition is a possible way for social change. Since tradition is still used as an argument for authority by the political power in the defense of the power-elite against mass interests, why not utilize the same tradition as a counter-weapon against the power-elite in the defense of mass interests? . . . Nowadays no development is possible without mass mobilization for the defense of mass interests. In this sense a reconstruction of the traditional belief-system

would be undertaken, not to defend political authority, but to defend the interests of the silent majority.[63]

The goal in this effort is a theology of liberation that can be an effective opposition to oppression. This involves a reexamination of the structure of inherited belief systems. In this analysis, Hanafi argues that as they developed, the inherited theological structures reflected the general power structures within Muslim societies and supported the powerful against the weak, the elite against the masses. "Theology as hermeneutics is not a sacred science but a humanly constructed social science. It reflects sociopolitical conflicts. Every social group in a believing society has its own interests and defends them in its belief-system. This is what is known as Theology."[64]

In his analysis, Hanafi blends his early methodological considerations with his more concrete historical interests and contemporary concerns. Frequently, the line of argument starts from a description of an apparent clash or contradiction between two positions or concepts. Hanafi then posits a third alternative that resolves the contradictions and does so in a way that creates an imperative for human action. The resolution is seen as being provided by Islam rightly understood as an imperative for action that resolves contradictions of life.

This approach is illustrated by his discussions of the relationships between reason and revelation and his analysis of the theory of leadership. In a discussion of reason and revelation, Hanafi describes some of the traditional perceptions of the contradictions between them. He presents an analysis that fits within the conceptualizations of Islamic modernism of the past century when he affirms that revelation and reason "are of accord when dealing with the inherent goodness or badness of actions. Revelation would never contradict a rational judgment."[65] The rationality of the sense of good and evil and the lack of contradiction between reason and revelation are important parts of the thinking of major early Islamic modernists like Muhammad Abduh in Egypt.[66] However, he goes beyond this as he places the discussion within the context of a liberation theology: "The traditional polarity between Reason and Revelation fails to include the third element of a tripartite equation: Reason, Revelation, and Reality. Both reason and revelation face one common object which is reality."[67] It is in reality that humans must act and fulfill the demands of both reason and revelation.

A contradictory polarity is similarly resolved in Hanafi's discussion of leadership.[68] Hanafi argues that the doctrine of leadership (the imamate) in the traditional Muslim belief system concentrates on the person of the leader even though the "general conditions of the Imamate as an *impersonal* function are stipulated in revelation."[69] He poses the polarity between the position that leadership is necessary (because humans are bad by nature and need the guidance of an imamate or other leadership) and that leadership is unnecessary (because humans are naturally good and, as a result, do not require leadership). Hanafi poses a third alternative to resolve the contradiction: leadership is "possible since man does not live alone and needs the work of others as others need his work. Leadership is spontaneous and natural parallel to the formation of social groups."[70] The conclusion that can be drawn within this framework is that while righteous leadership is advantageous, bad, oppressive, and authoritarian leadership can legitimately be rejected by the community.

In the historical experience of the Muslim community, Hanafi argues that the established belief system as it was defined supported the ruling elite. "The main doctrine in the belief-system comprising the theory of Essence, Attributes and Acts is conceived to justify absolute power. Absolutist theology, the omniscience and omnipotence of God, is a political tool used to strengthen political absolutism, that is, the absolute power of the Imam."[71]

Because the belief system is rooted in the power struggle, it could also provide the basis for opposition. According to Hanafi, in Muslim history there were three modes of opposition. One was the "secret opposition from within," which was the Shi'ite, which continued the doctrines of political absolutism, and the second was opposition from outside or the periphery of society, which was the Kharijite tradition. There was, however, a third position, which was public opposition from within and was represented by the Mu'tazilites, in whose teachings "God is the universal and Rational Principle" and the "theory of Unity (Tawhid) is based on the theory of justice."[72]

This framework provides the basis for how one can move from creed to revolution. In the contemporary world, according to Hanafi, the

> ruling power uses Absolutist Theology to maintain itself. The Opposition forces however are not using a belief-system of opposition. Instead, they utilize either secular ideologies of opposition such as Marxism, Liberalism, Socialism, Nationalism, etc., or the same Absolutist Theology as the ruling power itself. Each one anathemizes the other, authority against opposition, opposition against authority, and the opposition factions against each other.[73]

In this context, Hanafi proposes that the interests of the masses need to be defended by educating them in the belief systems of opposition. However, secret opposition from within is not effective because of the strength of the apparatuses of control available to the state, and open opposition from the outside "is inefficient due to its peripheral nature (separated from masses and easily accused of working for Foreign powers)."[74]

The implications of this in Hanafi's view are that the only possible effective opposition is that which comes openly from within. "It challenges political power through reason before the masses using legal channels of communication. It operates legally because it utilizes legal religious duties such as advice . . . [and to] order the good and prohibit the evil having recourse to the judiciary against the highest political authority in the state."[75] The result is an "Islamic revolutionary blueprint which can be agreed upon through community consensus, regardless of differences in theoretical frameworks and doctrinal belief systems," and this blueprint "can help all traditional societies switch from dogma to revolution . . . [and] effectuate a process of social change through continuity."[76]

The goal of the reinterpretation is clearly put forward by Hanafi in defining the revolution he seeks:

> The purpose of this new construction of the traditional belief-system is not to obtain eternal life by knowing the truth, but to acquire success in this World by fulfilling the hopes of the Muslim world for liberation, freedom, justice, social equality, reunification, identity, progress, and mass mobilization. Therefore, Theology as a science is of first importance because it is the theoretical analysis of action.[77]

The New Science of Occidentalism

Although the most prominent part of Hanafi's work deals with Islam, his studies of Western civilization also form a vital part of his life project. At the very beginning of his work as a student in Paris, the interaction between the study of Islam and of the West is clearly visible. His first three monographs, written as a part of his doctoral studies, reflect this. One was a study of the methods of understanding in the basic discipline in Islamic studies, what he called the science of usul al-fiqh (fundamentals of legal thought). The second was an analysis of the methods of phenomenology as it related to religion, and the third was an application of these methods in a study of the New Testament.

From the very beginning, Hanafi believed that his approach would provide important insights into understanding the West as well as Islam. When he attended the Vatican Council in Rome in 1964, he reports that he saw "thousands of Cardinals" who were voting on creeds and texts "without knowing how they had been formed or created or written down." At times he felt that they were voting mistakenly, and he recounts arguing with some cardinals, telling them that he would have voted differently. Their response was to tell Hanafi that the Holy Spirit was with them and it was immune from error. However, they told Hanafi that despite his knowledge, he was open to making mistakes. Hanafi's conclusion was that "here I understood the difference between passion and reason, between faith and science. . . . Any time when I feel that there is a contradiction between theology and science, I prefer science."[78]

Hanafi's goal, within this framework, has been to create a science for the understanding of the West. This was to be parallel to Orientalism, which was the West's flawed efforts to understand "the East" in general, including Islam. He calls this new science Occidentalism.[79]

Occidentalism has a place in a number of Hanafi's projects and visions. One consideration is a simple and practical one. Hanafi was interested in the history of the West and often taught courses presenting the West. One aspect of the development of his concept of Occidentalism is the pragmatic one that he needed to understand the materials and work with texts that were necessary for his tasks. He was unsatisfied with a Eurocentric vision of the West, and the development of his own understanding of Western civilization was based on his own extensive studies and work with key texts. For a course he prepared an anthology (in Arabic translation) of medieval Christian thought, with special emphasis on Augustine, Anselm, and Acquinas, and he did translations and analyses of major works by Spinoza, Lessing, Sartre, and other Western thinkers.

A second framework within which Hanafi developed the concept of Occidentalism is as a direct response to Western imperialism and Orientalism. This is the aspect most fully discussed by Hanafi in most of his works on the subject. He argues that Orientalism was basically a vehicle used by the West to express and enforce its power over the rest of the world. It created a sense of an exotic Other in caricature that then made it permissible to take any action against that Other. Parallel to this was the Western image of Self as enlightened and virtuous. "By the power of mass-media and its control by the West, the perpetuation and repetition of this double image was made by the Self to disarm the Other and to arm the Self, to create a permanent relation of superiority-inferiority complex between the Occident and the Orient."[80]

Occidentalism is the response of the colonized to the domination of the West. It develops at a time of the liberation of the colonized and the emergence of a new world context. Independence must, however, in Hanafi's view, be complete.

> Occidentalism is a discipline constituted in Third World countries in order to complete the process of decolonization. Military, economic and political decolonization would be incomplete without scientific and cultural decolonization. As far as colonized countries before or after liberation are objects of study, decolonization will be incomplete. Decolonization will not be completed except after the liberation of the object to become subject and the transformation of the observed to an observer.[81]

Some of this effort is simply to "counter-balance Westernization tendencies in the Third World."[82] Hanafi wants people outside of the West to know the realities of Western society. He is concerned that "modernizers" simply and blindly copy Western lifestyles and reject authentic indigenous traditions simply because they are not Western. He sees a tension in this

 KING-ALFRED'S COLLEGE LIBRARY

between tradition and modernity, which is built on his analysis of "Heritage and Renewal." However, Westernization simply creates a lifestyle for the elite in the Third World, with a growing cultural dependence on the West. "Occidentalism as a science gives priority to the endogenous [over] the exogeneous, to the interior [over] the exterior, to the Self [over] the Other. . . . Occidentalism as a cultural movement aims at transforming developing societies from transfer of knowledge to cultural creativity."[83]

Occidentalism becomes a way of doing two things: providing a critique of Western civilization from a non-Western standpoint and asserting the cultural independence of the formerly dominated "Orient." It is an affirmation of the heterogeneity of global cultures and an assertion that "World Culture is a myth created by the Culture of the Center to dominate the periphery in the name of acculturation. . . . There is no One Culture in capital C but there are only multiple cultures, in small cs."[84] Hanafi sees the world context changing and the new vision as a part of that: "The passage from Orientalism to Occidentalism is in fact a change in the balance of power."[85] In this analysis, it is not clear whether Hanafi is affirming that such a power shift has really taken place, since he still speaks of the power of the "Center," or if Occidentalism is to be another weapon in the decolonization struggle.

A third framework within which Hanafi's view of Occidentalism should be viewed is a more recent development in his thought that speaks of the emergence of a "New Social Science."[86] This is the development of a critique of Western social science perspectives, from both Western and non-Western scholars, and the articulation of a new "world scientific consciousness." The New Social Science has the negative goal of showing the problems with older style Western social sciences and the positive goal of providing new methods and concepts.

This new perspective argues that "Western Social Science is not an innocent science free from bias but ideologically oriented and politically motivated."[87] The critique of Western social science provides also a sense of the basic assumptions of Hanafi's new social science. Western social science affirms objectivity, neutrality, and universalism. In Hanafai's view,

[o]bjectivity is a myth, not only in social science but even in natural science. Since the World is lived, perceived and conceptualized, it is always a subjective world. . . . Neutrality is another myth in Western Social Science. It is another device to hide partiality. . . . Universalism is a third myth. There is no absolute social science. Social science is linked to societies developing in history and tied to cultural pluralism. Any pretension of Universalism is in fact a desire for hegemony.[88]

Hanafi does not discuss, in this analysis, how this relates to his affirmations of the universality of basic Islamic principles in some of his other studies.

Occidentalism becomes a way for Hanafi to discuss the West in the same way that he examines the Islamic tradition. However, it has a tone of simply being the reverse of a technique of oppression. Hanafi himself is aware of this and notes that

> Eurocentricity may generate a counter-Eurocentrcity which is still Eurocentricity put upside down. . . . Creating a whole conceptual world, a new methodology and obtaining new results require the whole process of de-Westernization and the simultaneous initiation of all previous fields of research till the Third World becomes conceptually and methodologically independent. For the time being, if "New Social Science" is only even a reaction to Western Social Science, it helps in the process of self-assertion, the minimization of the oppressive exogeneity and the maximization of the liberating endogeneity.[89]

Occidentalism is not neutral. It fits clearly into Hanafi's distinctive affirmation of "heritage" and his critique of the West. However, it is not simply a declaration of the West as the "Great Satan." It is the affirmation of an intellectual in the classical style of a challenge to the status quo and a presentation of a more ideal alternative.

5
RACHID GHANNOUSHI
Activist in Exile

If God wishes me to become a martyr of the mosques, then let it be. But I tell you that my death will not be in vain, and that from my blood, Islamic flowers will grow.

—*Rachid Ghannoushi*

In 1987, Rachid Ghannoushi defiantly faced the State Security Court in Tunis, knowing full well that President Habib Bourguiba sought to strike a mortal blow against the Islamic movement in Tunisia by having him sentenced to death.[1] Two years later, in April 1989, Tunisians participated in the first democratic elections after the fall of Habib Bourguiba's government in mid-November 1987. To the astonishment of many, Islamic activists did extraordinarily well, capturing 13 percent of the popular vote nationally and between 30 and 40 percent in many major urban areas, in a country long regarded as among the most Westernized secular governments in the Muslim world. The Islamic Tendency Movement (MTI; Mouvement de la Tendance Islamique) and its leader, Rachid al-Ghannoushi, who had been imprisoned and sentenced to life in prison in September 1987 and after the coup granted amnesty in 1988, emerged triumphant, earning their place as the strongest opposition group in Tunisia. By the 1990s Ghannoushi was in exile and his movement driven underground.

Despite the growth and expansion of the Islamic resurgence throughout much of the Muslim world in the 1970s and 1980s, most observers had been convinced that North Africa in general and Tunisia in particular, with its strong Western secular orientation, would not experience the impact of contemporary Islamic revivalism in any significant manner. By the 1990s, Rachid Ghannoushi's movement had proven its effectiveness, emerging as the major voice of political opposition, a voice the government progressively sought to silence.

Tunisia, which gained independence in 1956, had had but one ruler for more than thirty years, Habib Bourguiba (1956–1987), its nationalist hero. More than any other Muslim ruler, except perhaps Turkey's Ataturk, who established a totally secular state, Bourguiba set Tunisia on a path of modernization that was heavily pro-Western and secular and in the process became a valued friend and ally of France and the United States. Tunisia's Arab-Islamic heritage was overshadowed by an official Francophile culture. French rather than Arabic was the official government language, the language of higher education, and the language and culture of elite society. Bourguiba carefully circumscribed the presence and influence of Islam. Shortly after independence, Tunisia passed the Personal Status Law (1957), which went farther than any other Muslim country except secular Turkey in banning polygamy. Even more symbolic of Bourguiba's approach to religion and modernization and his wholehearted acceptance of Western values were the abolition of Shariah courts, the ban on the wearing of the *hijab* (headscarf) by women, and his attempt to get workers to ignore the fast of Ramadan. Drinking a glass of orange juice on national television during the fast of Ramadan and thus publicly violating Islamic law, Bourguiba criticized the deleterious effects of fasting during daylight hours and urged Muslims not to observe the fast, which he claimed affected productivity and economic development. The Zaytouna, a famed center of Islamic learning in North Africa and the Muslim world, was closed. The ulama were debilitated, rather than, as occurred in many Muslim countries, coopted by the government. For Bourguiba, Islam represented the past, and the West Tunisia's only hope for a modern future. That attitude was rigorously challenged to its logical conclusion in the 1980s when Islamic revivalism did emerge as a force to be reckoned with.

While much attention was given during the 1980s to Islamic movements worldwide, comparatively little was known about Tunisia's Islamic Tendency Movement and its leaders. Government attempts to portray MTI as an Iranian-inspired radical revolutionary organization only confused its image at home and abroad. The charge of an Iranian connection was acceptable to many people who believed that revivalism could not be indigenous to Tunisia.

The emergence of MTI and the life of its principal ideologue, Rachid al-Ghannoushi, encompass many of the political and religious currents of the times: Tunisian nationalism, Nasserism, and finally the reassertion of Islam in Muslim public life. Ghannoushi, who has guided MTI (subsequently renamed the Renaissance Party, EnEnnahda, or Hizb al-Ennahda) throughout its history and ideological development, has emerged as one of the most adroit and flexible of Islamic activist leaders. While drawing on the richness of the Islamic tradition as well as Western thought, he has proven to be a creative reformer and interpreter of Islam.

Early Life and Formation

Rachid al-Ghannoushi Khriji was born in 1941 outside of a small village, al-Hama, in the province of Qabis in southern Tunisia. His father was a farmer who relied on his ten children and four wives to assist him in his work. A devout man and the only member of the village to have memorized the entire Quran, he saw to it that all of his ten children, sons and daughters, studied the Quran. Despite the pressures to work the land, Ghannoushi's mother, the youngest of his father's four wives, insisted upon the value of education, an emphasis that would see the family produce a professor, judge, and an Islamic scholar-activist.

Ghannoushi's mother had a major impact on his life and attitude toward women. While his father was a farmer and more locally oriented, his mother came from a merchant family that had had more contact with the outside world. Endowed with a "powerful personality" and believing that education would provide the door to the world for her children, she insisted on and prevailed in getting her children formally educated. The Ghannoushi family was the only family in their rural community to eventually leave agriculture and become part of the modern educated professional community.

Ghannoushi began primary school at the age of ten, attending the village school in al-Hama, where he was taught in Arabic and French. Although he began his formal education later than usual, he could already read and write by the time he attended school. His formal education was interrupted when, after several years, his father withdrew him from the school for both religious and economic reasons. His father objected to Rachid's learning French, the language of Tunisia's colonial masters, whom he also regarded as the enemies of Islam, at the expense of his Arabic mother tongue and Quranic learning. Moreover, Rachid was needed at home to help his aging father and the women of the household.

When Ghannoushi's brothers completed their schooling, the family was able to give up agriculture and move to the village. Rachid, who was no longer needed to work the land, went off in 1956 to study at a Zaytouna school (*madrasa*) in the city of Gabbas, where he earned a diploma in theology prior to its being closed by the government. The Zaytouna school system consisted of a network of religious schools based on a more formally Islamic curriculum that culminated in the major mosque-university of Tunis, Zaytouna. Similar to Egypt's al-Azhar University, the oldest center of Islamic learning, it combined a traditional Islamic curriculum with a modern course of study. Rachid studied the Quran and Islamic law and theology—as well as modern subjects and sciences (in a modern curriculum)—in Arabic rather than French. The approach and presentation of Islam was primarily past-oriented and very traditional. Ghannoushi would later criticize the Zaytouna system as a dead end: first, because the study of Islam at Zaytouna made students feel as if they were "going into a museum." Emphasis was placed on past legal practice rather than on Islam's relevance to the present. Second, given Tunisia's French orientation culturally and educationally, admission to university, except for the faculty of theology, was based on graduation from the French system. Thus, Zaytouna graduates were generally restricted to opportunities and jobs as teachers or religious leaders.

After completing his secondary school education in 1962, Ghannoushi studied religion in the faculty of theology at the Zaytouna University of Tunis. However, his tendency to challenge his teachers with questions drawn from his study of Western philosophy led to his withdrawal from the university in his last year there. He obtained a job as a primary school teacher for two years and toyed with plans to become a journalist.

In 1964, Ghannoushi left Tunis and went to Egypt, where he enrolled at Cairo University, studying agriculture. However, his stay was abruptly cut short when President Bourguiba, fearing the influence of Nasser's Arab socialism, withdrew Tunisian students. Ghannoushi was forced to leave Egypt after only four months and transfer to the University of Damascus in Syria, where he completed a bachelor's degree in philosophy. During his Damascus period, he busied himself with the study of philosophy, mostly Western rather than Islamic. He was an ardent Arab nationalist and joined the Syrian Nationalist Socialist Party (SNSP), a pan-Syrian party influenced by Nasserist ideas. At this stage of his life, like many college students of his generation, despite his early upbringing, he discontinued his practice of Islam, that is, observance of daily prayers.

From Arab Nationalism to Islam: The Making of an Islamic Activist

During his stay in Syria, Ghannoushi made a seven-month trip through Europe, which, like Sayyid Qutb's experience in America, was to have a significant influence on his life, perception of the West, and turn to Islamic activism. He encountered "the other Europe," working at odd jobs (in construction, grape picking, in restaurants) and living in youth hostels. Here for the first time he experienced the West in its own context and diversity. In particular, he was struck by the discovery that people were not as prosperous or happy as he had always envisioned. Disillusioned, he became convinced that Europe was not the model of civilization to be emulated by the Arab world. This European experience, combined with his studies and experience in Damascus, seriously altered his perception and attitude not only toward the West but also toward Arab nationalism. He began to question the ideas and realities behind both Western ideologies and Arab nationalism. What was the meaning of Arab nationalism? What was its underlying ideology? What kind of freedom was Nasser talking about—that which existed (or did not exist) in Egypt? Ghannoushi concluded that Arab nationalism was imported from the West and ultimately "was empty."

In addition to the rivalry between Nasserist and Baathist Arab nationalists, the Islamic movement, in particular the Muslim Brotherhood, was also active on university campuses. It was during this period of his self-doubt and questioning of Arab nationalism that Islamically oriented students showed Ghannoushi another alternative, the way of Islam. He discovered a new kind of Islam, "an Islam that was alive,"[2] the antithesis of the stagnant, passive ("museum") Islam that he had so hated during his studies at the Zaytouna. Like most contemporary Islamic activists, Ghannoushi became exposed to and was influenced by the writings of prominent Islamic reformers and activists of the late nineteenth and early twentieth centuries, pioneers of contemporary Islamic activism. He read Muhammed Iqbal's *Reconstruction of Religious Thought in Islam* and discovered an Islam, informed by a unique synthesis of Islamic belief and Western philosophy, that could argue with the West on its own grounds. He also began to read Muhammad Qutb's *Man between Materialism and Islam* and then was introduced to the writings of Hasan al-Banna, Mawlana Mawdudi, Sayyid Qutb, and Said al-Hawa. Here he encountered a "strong Islam"[3] with arguments that made sense, based not only on belief but also on reason. Ghannoushi found himself drifting toward an Islamic alternative. He became increasingly convinced that Arab nationalism was essentially Western in its origins and ideologically not firmly rooted in Arab/Islamic civilization.

The 1967 Six Day War proved to be a turning point in Rachid Ghannoushi's life. He was in Syria when Israeli planes hit Damascus. The attack occurred at a time when Islamically oriented students and Arab nationalists were locked in a bitter argument regarding the Arab struggle with Israel. The Islamists had countered the latter's conviction that the Arabs could win in a war with Israel, maintaining that the defeat of Israel would require much more than a military victory. Like the Israelis, the Arabs needed a strong ideology and faith. The overwhelming Arab defeat shocked Syria's Baathist (Arab nationalist) government and convinced Ghannoushi and many other disillusioned Muslims that the "only refuge . . . was the Quran."[4]

In 1968, Ghannoushi moved from Syria to Paris to obtain a master's degree at the Sorbonne, since study in France and mastery of French could open the door to a good position when he returned to Tunis. Although he had studied and learned about Islam in Damascus, he had not joined an Islamic movement. In Paris, he became more involved in Islamic activities. For the first time, like many others of his generation studying abroad, Ghannoushi found himself immersed in a foreign culture, struggling to retain his faith and identity. In his search for an environment that would enable him to preserve his identity, he stumbled upon the Tablighi Jamaat, an apolitical Islamic missionary society, which originated in Pakistan, whose itinerant preachers travel throughout the world calling (dawa) Muslims to a religiously observant life. Here he found a religious community that provided a source of spiritual sustenance and a sense of moral purpose. The Tabligh provided Ghannoushi's first experience of organized Islamic work/activism. Members walked the streets and visited the local cafes, inviting Muslims (many of whom knew little of their faith) to come to the mosque to learn more about Islam, study the Quran, and be shown how to pray. Ghannoushi traveled to many parts of France, observing the poor living conditions of North African workers, visiting bars, and trying to bring people back to Islam.

Because he was better educated than most of the North Africans in Paris, Ghannoushi was called on to teach them about Islam. In 1969, with property provided by an Algerian merchant, a small store was transformed into a storefront mosque, and Ghannoushi was asked to serve as the imam (leader) of this private, non-Tabligh, storefront mosque. Ghannoushi remembers this year as the most difficult in his life, even more than the later years spent in prison. Financially and morally, it was a severe trial. Unlike some of his friends, he was unable to find a permanent position and was forced to survive on part-time jobs. At the same time, thrust into a position of religious leadership for which he felt ill prepared, he fought both to retain his own identity in the midst of what he regarded as a "morally alien" culture of individualism and unfettered freedoms (sex, alcohol, etc.) and to minister to North African Muslims in destitute situations. As he later commented, whereas in Tunis the basic need of Muslims was freedom of speech and other human rights, "[i]n Paris, the issue was not freedom but rather to learn the Quran, to have a mosque, to worship, and to find a good Muslim life."[5]

Origins of the Islamic Movement

Tunisia, like much of the Arab world, was reeling after the Arab defeat in the Six Day War of 1967. For many, the defeat of Arab nationalism/socialism as an ideological force was experienced at home as well as abroad. As in many parts of the Muslim world, the defeat of 1967 had led many in Tunisia to a stocktaking of the postindependence period and its failed expectations. In Tunisia, thirteen years after Bourguiba had led his country to independence, experimentation with a planned socialist economy during the 1960s, in particular the collectivization of agricultural lands under his minister of planning, Ahmed Ben Sallah (1962–1969), had resulted in the dismal performance of the economy, unemployment, and strikes. For some, the failure of Bourguiba and his Destourian Socialist Party to provide an effective political ideology and economic development merely underscored the need for a more authentic alternative ideology, a return to Islam. At the same time, the government, anxious to distance itself from the left, embarked on a policy of political and economic liberalization and was more amenable to Islam. Among other things, this new mood led to a greater interest in the revivification of Tunisia's Arab-Islamic identity and heritage. The reassertion of Islamic identity was reflected in the establishment of cultural societies in the 1970s, in particular the Quran Preservation Society at the Zaytouna mosque, and in the growth of Islamically oriented student groups at the universities and secondary schools.

The resurgence of Islam in Tunisia was also strongly influenced ideologically by Egypt's Muslim Brotherhood. Bourguiba himself had little sympathy for the Brotherhood; however, because he disliked and felt threatened by the populist appeal in the Arab world of Egypt's Nasser, he permitted the distribution of Muslim Brotherhood literature. The Brotherhood was an outspoken opponent of Nasser and had experienced government suppression, repression, and the execution of some of its leaders, such as Sayyid Qutb. The writings of Muslim Brothers such as Hasan al-Banna, Sayyid Qutb, his brother Muhammad Qutb, and Muhammad al-Ghazzali were avidly read and had a powerful influence on the nascent Islamic movement in Tunisia. The young, educated members of the movement were particularly attracted to Sayyid Qutb, who, in response to the repression of the Nasser regime, had become progressively more radicalized and preached a more militant antigovernment revolutionary Islamic ideology. Qutb's execution by the Nasser government only increased his popular image and following, earning him the status of a martyr for Islam.

In 1970, Ghannoushi returned home to visit his mother after a five-year absence. His stay in his home village was cut short by his family's concerns over the repercussions of his public criticism of Tunisia's failed socialist economic policies. With the encouragement of his brothers, who now feared his imprisonment and whose own positions in society (judge and professor) were compromised by his public criticism, Rachid Ghannoushi left his family with the intention of returning to Paris. He stopped first in Tunis to visit the Zaytouna mosque. There he again met some Tabligh members, who invited him to preach at another mosque in Laconia, a popular quarter. The responsiveness of the local people to his preaching and his first meeting the next day with Sheikh Abd al-Fatah Morou, a lawyer and Islamic activist, led to his decision to remain in Tunis and work in a small group with Morou and other like-minded, Islamically oriented young men.

Utilizing his training in philosophy and his experience as an Islamic worker among poor workers, Ghannoushi assumed the twin roles of teacher and Islamic preacher-activist. He obtained a position as a philosophy teacher in a large secondary school in Tunis, and he began to preach in many of the local mosques. With Morou and several others, he joined the Quran Preservation Society, which had been founded at the Zaytouna mosque in 1970.

The secondary schools and mosques became major centers of activity, organizing conferences and meetings at the former and offering lessons on

Islam at the latter. Muslim youth, the next generation, was the primary focus of attention, for, as Ghannoushi observed, "[i]n those years it was difficult to find a young man praying, especially if he was from the so-called educated people. . . . The system had taken the precaution of indoctrinating the youth—the materialistic tendency rendered them useless and servile."[6] Ghannoushi proved a popular preacher and teacher, drawing large crowds from among the poor working class to his sermons as he moved from one mosque to another. He attracted many students from his school to the weekly discussions conducted at the Quran Preservation Society, which was dedicated to the promotion of Tunisia's Arab-Islamic heritage and enjoyed government sponsorship. To the extent that it remained an apolitical cultural society, Bourguiba found it useful as a foil against his leftist critics. For Ghannoushi, who was convinced that Tunisia's ills were symptoms of a deep-seated identity crisis, his teaching, preaching, and participation in the Society were interrelated aspects of his mission to restore or revitalize Tunisia's Arab-Islamic roots and civilization. His experience and that of other nonelites reflected that deep-seated identity crisis and the source of its weakness:

> I remember we used to feel like strangers in our own country. We had been educated as Muslims and Arabs, while we could see that the country had been totally molded in the French cultural identity. For us the doors to any further education were closed since the university was completely westernized. At that time, those wanting to continue their studies in Arabic had to go to the Middle East.[7]

Ghannoushi's preaching and writing (in the movement's magazine, *al-Marifa,* and in pamphlets like "What Is the West?" and "Our Path to Civilization") drew heavily on the interpretations and ideological worldview of modern Muslim scholar-activists such as Mawlana Mawdudi, Hasan al-Banna, Sayyid Qutb and his brother Muhammad Qutb, Said Hawwa, Malek Bennabi, and Muhammad Iqbal. The message was one of condemnation of the backwardness (political, social, economic, and cultural) of society, its loss of identity and morals because of dependence on a morally bankrupt and crisis-ridden Western society, and the need for a return to Islam, its civilization and values. The culprits were the West, the Bourguiba government, and Tunisia's Westernized elites, as well as the traditional religious establishment, which had been coopted by the government and preached a stagnant rather than a dynamic Islam. For Ghannoushi, the only hope for Tunisia, the Muslim world, and indeed the Third World, was Islam. However, during the period from 1970 to 1978, the Islamic movement and its message remained primarily concerned with religiocultural change in society. As an officially apolitical religiocultural movement, it posed little direct threat to the government. In fact, the religiocultural discussions and activities of the movement, as epitomized by the Quran Preservation Society, obscured the political consciousness and intellectual politicization that were taking place.

From Cultural Reform to Political Activism

As in much of the Muslim world, the years 1978–1979 proved to be a political turning point in the life of Rachid Ghannoushi and the history of Tunisia's Islamic movement. The late 1970s saw the progressive politicization of the Islamic movement in response to the internal social situation in Tunisia and political events that were taking place in Iran. Bourguiba's use of the military to brutally crush demonstrations in the "food riots" of January 1978 and the subsequent victory of Iran's Islamic revolution in 1979 underscored the failures of Tunisian Westernized secular society and fired the imaginations and enthusiasm of many for a return to Islam—an Islamic alternative. The confrontation between the government and the General Union of Tunisian Workers (UGTT) culminated in a general strike on January 26, 1978, in which many were killed or injured by government forces. Although Tunisia's trade union movement was considered by some to be the strongest in Africa and the Arab world, Ghannoushi and the movement had avoided any involvement, leary of unionism and Communism. The UGTT was controlled by the government's Destour Party and regarded by Ghannoushi as Marxist: "The social confrontation between rich and poor is a Marxist formula that did not correspond to our understanding of life. Later on, we realized that Islam also has a say in the confrontation, and that, as Muslims, we could not stay indifferent to it. Islam gives support to the oppressed."[8] In light of their noninvolvement in the social upheaval of January 1978, the Islamists found themselves forced to rethink their ideas and strategy as they struggled with the question: "How could we be that much out of touch with what was actually going on within our own society so that we did not play any role in society?"[9]

Politicization of the Islamic Movement

The deteriorating conditions in Tunisia and the fact that the Islamic movement was positioned outside the political arena convinced Ghannoushi and other movement leaders of the need to move beyond broad ideological statements. They became convinced of the need to relate Islam directly and specifically to the real, everyday problems (political, economic, and social) of the people. Islam must be seen as a source not only of identity but also of true liberation—of the whole person and society. This new direction placed the Islamists on a collision course with the apolitical stance of the Quran Preservation Society; in 1978 they were expelled, denounced as inflexible reactionaries.[10] The transformation of the movement from a religiocultural force into a sociopolitical movement was formalized with the establishment of the Islamic Association (Jamaah al-Islamiyya) in 1979, one year after the 1978 riots and in the wake of Iran's revolution. Thus a hitherto informally organized group of like-minded people, run by its founders and key leaders and centered around group meetings and discussions, became a more structured, participatory activist organization with rules, guidelines, and a commitment to social action.

The Islamic Association was set up as a national organization guided by its amir (leader), Ghannoushi, and an elected consultative council (*majlis al-shura*). Like many other Islamic activist organizations, such as Egypt's Muslim Brotherhood, the organization had both a public and a private profile. The realities of functioning under an authoritarian regime required that some of its cells be secret or underground. The transformation of the Islamic movement into a sociopolitical organization with its direct involvement in Tunisian political and economic affairs enhanced its attractiveness and popularity. Ghannoushi preached his message of a holistic Islam relevant to issues of political and economic rights in the mosques of Tunisia. Tunisia's mosques became the meeting-places for gatherings of thousands of students and provided platforms from which the struggle for Islam could be equated with the needs and grievances of the poor and the oppressed. The movement also addressed these problems in communiques and conferences and in the movement's publication, *al-Marifa* (established in 1973), which provided religious legitimacy for the movement's sociopolitical message. Students and workers in particular were drawn to the new organization either as members or sympathizers. The movement attracted most of its membership from the urban lower middle and middle classes. Ghannoushi's message of political freedom and social activism in defense of the rights of the poor and the oppressed enabled the Islamic Association to align itself with the UGTT and win support within its ranks. At the same time, it targeted universities and schools. Islamic student organizations grew and proliferated on campuses, attracting young men and women from the science and engineering faculties in particular. Although they clashed with secular nationalists and leftist students, Islamic student organizations eventually dominated student politics.

Ghannoushi and the Islamic Association spoke directly to the issues (workers' rights, jobs, wages, poverty, Westernization versus a more authentic national and cultural identity, political participation) many Tunisians faced, presenting a living Islam, not the "museum Islam" he had encountered and rejected in his student days.

The Islamic Tendency Movement

In April 1981 when the Bourguiba government briefly liberalized Tunisia's one-party political system, the Islamic Association was transformed into a political party, the Islamic Tendency Movement (MTI). Its new name distinguished it from its former, more generic title, Islamic Association or group, which tended to equate its identity solely with the global Muslim community (ummah). MTI indicated more precisely that it was one of a number of trends in Tunisian society, Islamic, secular, leftists, and so on. The phrase "Islamic Trend or Tendency" was already in use by Islamic student groups in the universities, who had borrowed the name from their Sudanese counterparts.

Although Bourguiba refused to issue a license legalizing the party, MTI declared its religiopolitical goals: the reassertion of Tunisia's Islamic way of life and values, reemphasis on moral values and restriction of Tunisia's Westernized (Francophile) profile, democracy and political pluralism, economic and social justice. Bourguiba's authoritarianism and the restrictive policies of his government had increasingly alienated many Tunisians, spawning a religious and secular opposition that had shared grievances and had been equally repressed. As a result, MTI proved effective in attracting many of the disaffected—not only workers and union members but also students and young, middle-class professionals, professors, teachers, engineers, lawyers, scientists, and doctors.

The politicization of the Islamic movement drew the wrath of Habib Bourguiba, who regarded it as a threat to the authority and legitimacy of his government. He had tolerated Islamic organizations as long as they remained apolitical religious movements, for, if anything, they helped offset or counterbalance the charges of his Islamic critics. However, politics was quite another matter. MTI's sociopolitical platform was a double challenge. It echoed the criticisms of other (secular) opposition groups with whom it was willing to work and, even more threateningly, did so in the name of Islam and at a time when many Muslim governments were nervous about the export and impact of the Iranian model (revolution). In 1981, the Bourguiba government cracked down on MTI, arresting and imprisoning Ghannoushi and many of its leaders while others went underground or into self-imposed exile abroad.

Having turned its attention to addressing the problems of Tunisian society and generating its own alternative, MTI was forced to shift its attention, from 1981 to 1983, to survival and the creation of a new generation of leaders, since most of its senior leaders were either in jail or in exile. During this period, a major transformation occurred. More than ever before, MTI was brought to the realization of the limitations of the Muslim Brotherhood's ideology, which was conditioned by its Egyptian origins and experience. There was a growing conviction of the need to confront and to address the particular circumstances and conditions of Tunisia by developing an ideology, program, and solutions more specifically suited to the Tunisian experience. The new leadership initiated a process of reevaluation in order to learn from past mistakes and to set new priorities for Tunisia's Islamic movement.

Ali Laridh is a perfect example of the new generation of leadership that emerged during the crisis of 1981. Born in 1955, he represents the second generation in modern Tunisia, that is, those in the emerging modern-educated elite who have been more influenced by Islam. He epitomizes the impact of Ghannoushi in producing a new generation of Tunisians, an alternative elite, modern-educated but more Arab-Islamically oriented. Laridh attended Tunisian secondary schools and in 1974 joined the Islamic movement as a sympathizer. Among the first students to join the university's marine biology program in 1976, he graduated with a degree in engineering in 1980 and immediately began working with the movement. Like many of his generation, his outlook and ideas as a student were shaped by the broader international Islamic movement and its primary ideologues, Hasan al-Banna, Sayyid Qutb, and Mawlana Mawdudi. Pakistan's Mawdudi, in particular, was among the most important. Laridh and many other students were recruited from the mosques and schools, invited or called (dawa) to reaffirm their Islamic identity, and taught about Islam and how to fight the Communists on campus. Both modern education and Islamic formation and activism were combined to produce a "new man." At the same time that they were exposed to Western ideas in science and technology, these students of Tunisia's postindependence generation were required to read books on Islam as well as books about and against Communism in order to be able to confront and refute the communists. Looking for new solutions, Ali and many others adapted well both to their new Western scientific ideas and to an Islamic orientation. Thus, the Islamic movement provided an alternative to the Communists and the nationalists on campus.

While many of MTI's senior leaders were imprisoned during the 1981 crackdown, Ali avoided capture and went underground, where he functioned as one of the new (younger, second-generation) leadership. While loyal, the youths experienced the first generation or founders of MTI as prone to be like protective parents and thus more resistant to the new ideas that come with each generation. At the same time, they responded to the concerns of the older generation, who feared that the movement had been weakened by ideas and innovations that were not based on "true" Islam (such as those of the Islamic Left, represented by Muslim intellectuals like Egypt's Hasan Hanafi). The younger generation searched their tradition more self-consciously for basic principles of Islam on which to base and legitimate their ideas and strategies.

The release of activists in a 1984 general amnesty saw a new period of vitality and growth as the older and the new generation of MTI leaders worked side by side. The Islamic movement grew exponentially. MTI had attracted the support of opposition groups and the UGTT during its period of suppression. Its message and willingness to make common cause with other opposition groups enhanced its image as a moderate group and attracted followers and sympathizers. However, the political situation continued to deteriorate. Habib Bourguiba, president-for-life, tightened his grip on power and muzzled internal dissent amid growing discontent, especially among the youth of Tunisia, who constituted two-thirds of its population of seven million. The government was plagued by poor economic conditions, charges of government corruption, and financial mismanagement. Key government officials and advisors (including the prime minister, Mohammed Mzali, as well as Bourguiba's wife and son) were banished or shunned. Oppositon newspapers were banned, the UGTT was dismantled and its leader imprisoned, and a nationwide security crackdown targeted "Islamic fundamentalism," which the government increasingly denounced as a radical, violent, antidemocratic revolutionary movement backed by Iran.

Within three years after its leaders had been released from prison in 1984, Habib Bourguiba once again moved against MTI in March 1987, arresting Ghannoushi and setting off street battles and clashes between Islamic activist students and leftists in the universities. When French authorities arrested six expatriate Tunisians for possession of arms, Bourguiba charged MTI with initiating an Iranian-inspired plot to overthrow the Tunisian government. The facts indicated otherwise. France had established no MTI connection and had, in fact, claimed that the six were members of the pro-Iranian Islamic Jihad and Hizbullah. Despite this fact, the Bourguiba government arrested more than three thousand MTI members. Similarly, when Islamic Jihad subsequently claimed responsibility for a series of hotel bombings in Tunisia, ten members of MTI, not Islamic Jihad, were charged, despite the fact that the majority of those accused were already imprisoned at the time of the alleged crime. Although the Bourghiba government tried to discredit MTI as "Khomeinists," an Iranian-backed threat to Tunisia, as Dirk Vanderwalle observed, "[t]he Islamic Tendency Movement . . . posed no threat to the country's rulers or its political system. But the movement's criticism of personal power, economic mismanagement, corruption, and moral laxity allowed it to become a symbol— perceived especially by the younger, educated generation as an alternative in a country void of political alternatives."[11]

Bourguiba was so intent on eradicating his "Islamic threat" that when the courts sentenced Ghannoushi to life imprisonment at hard labor but did not deliver a death sentence, Bourguiba ordered a new trial.

The impact of the 1981 and 1987 repression of MTI put severe strains on its leadership's moderate stance. It exacerbated differences within the movement, radicalizing some members who charged that the only response or defense to regime violence was force or armed struggle (*jihad*). As rumors spread that Bourguiba was intent on Ghannoushi's execution and the eradication of MTI, MTI's members divided over the proper strategy or response. Although Ghannoushi advised against violence, voices were increasingly raised, advocating a tough response to government oppression. As the debate raged and a popular uprising seemed likely, Zeine Abedin Ben Ali, Bourguiba's prime minister, a former military man who had served as interior minister and overseen the suppression of MTI, seized power from the aging dictator in November 1987.

Ben Ali moved quickly to consolidate his power, legitimate his rule, and counter the government's Islamic opposition. He promised political liberalization, democratization and a multiparty political system, precisely what all the opposition parties had been clamoring for. Moreover, Ben Ali undertook a number of steps to enhance his legitimacy and counter the challenge of Islamic activists. In contrast to Bourguiba, he deliberately and self-consciously appealed to Tunisia's Arab/Islamic heritage. Ben Ali went on a much-publicized pilgrimage to Mecca. His speeches incorporated Islamic formulae, television and radio broadcast the call to prayer, the theological faculty at the Zaytouna Mosque was reopened, and the fast of Ramadan was officially observed. Ben Ali promised to allow MTI to again publish its own newspaper or journal and to grant them certification as a legal political party.

MTI responded to the government's political liberalization and movement toward democracy. It offered to work with the new leader and participate in his call for a National Pact in exchange for official recognition as a political party. Moreover, it changed its name to the Renaissance Party (EnEnnahda), signaling its acquiescence to Ben Ali's demand that no political party be allowed to appropriate or monopolize Islam. Although Ben Ali as Bourguiba's minister of internal affairs had overseen the attempt to crush MTI, MTI's leadership took the risk. While most observers anticipated government recognition of the Renaissance Party, it never came. In December 1989, Ben Ali categorically ruled out any political recognition for the Renaissance Party. His justification was based on the claim that his decision emanated ``from our firm belief in the need not to mix religion and politics, as experience has shown that anarchy emerges and the rule of law and institutions is undermined when such a mixing takes place."[12] Like Egypt's Anwar Sadat before him, when faced with a significant Islamic opposition, Ben Ali insisted on the separation of religion and politics. He used this excuse to weaken his chief opposition by outlawing their party.

Two events in particular influenced Ben Ali's "change of heart." The impressive performance of MTI candidates (though they had to run as individuals, since MTI was not a recognized as a political party) in national elections in 1988 demonstrated the appeal and political potential of MTI and validated its claim as Tunisia's leading opposition group. This was followed by the Algerian government's movement toward political liberalization in the wake of riots and its recognition of Islamic political parties. The stunning victory of the newly recognized Islamic Salvation Front in the 1989 municipal elections realized the worst fears of Ben Ali and many Arab rulers (as, indeed, many Western governments) that political liberalization or democratization would enhance the power of political Islam and thus threaten the stability of existing regimes.

The confrontation between the government and the Renaissance Party escalated. Though Ennahda had been cooperative during the early years of Ben Ali's rule, his postponement and then refusal to recognize Ennahda as a legal political party and growing use of force to intimidate MTI members contributed to confrontational politics. MTI denounced government authoritarianism and, it claimed, the influence of the "secular left."[13] The government responded with greater force. Student demonstrations and strikes were crushed; Renaissance Party leaders were imprisoned or harassed. The deterioration of Tunisia's human rights record drew criticisms from human rights organizations. Ben Ali's so-called political liberalization program proved far from democratic: "His party, the Constitutional Democratic Rally, rigged the poll in the 1989 general election and took every seat in parliament. Far from legalizing the leading opposition group, the Islamic party, Ennahda, the president has sought to crush it. . . . There is no real democracy and no press freedom."[14]

The Gulf War marked a turning point, as Ben Ali moved against the Renaissance Party in a "transparent effort to discredit it."[15] It ushered in a period that would intensify the clash between the government and the Renaissance Party, a reputed coup attempt, and a split in the Party's leadership with the defection of Abdel Fatah Mourou. In May 1991, shortly after security forces had killed several students at a university demonstration, the Ben Ali government charged that it had uncovered a Ennahda plot, which included members of the Tunisian military, to seize power and establish a theocratic state. More than one-third of those arrested were members of the Tunisian military reputed to be members of the Renaissance Party's secret military wing. Ben Ali called for unity in the face of a fundamentalist threat.[16] Tunisia's Ennahda provides an example of the cycle of violence and the radicalization of movements that often occur when authoritarian regimes manipulate the political system and employ suppression or violence to control Islamic movements.

Ghannoushi's Ideological Worldview

Though MTI/Ennahda has had many voices, Rachid Ghannoushi has remained both its main leader and principal ideologue. An intellectual trained in Western philosophy and self-consciously rooted in Islamic thought, he draws on many sources in formulating his own distinctive perception of the world and of Islam. In the life and thought of Ghannoushi, Islam emerges as both a reaffirmation of faith in the absolute unity of God (tawhid) and a source of liberation. The Islamic movement is a reform movement that targets the individual and society; it seeks to rebuild, to re-vitalize, to re-Islamize Muslim societies. At the same time, it is a movement of liberation from cultural alienation/Westernization, economic exploitation, and moral corruption, based on Islamic principles of equality, equity, and social justice.

Ghannoushi's paradigm is a dynamic process of change informed both by the logic of a long tradition of Islamic revivalism and the realities of the modern world. More proximately and specifically, he has been influenced by and draws heavily on the example and teachings of twentieth-century Islamic movements, both ideologically and organizationally. For Ghannoushi, as for all contemporary revivalists, the problems of the Muslim world are rooted in the European (Western) colonial experience and its legacy, perpetuated by most governments and modern Westernized elites in the Muslim world. As a result, Ghannoushi believes that the identity, unity, and development of Muslim nations have been undermined. The Western secular orientation of modern Muslim states has ignored the traditional Islamic culture of the masses, alienated the nation, and attempted to cut off its people from their indigenous identity and values. Tunisia is a prime example of this process, a deviation that requires the restoration or redefinition of Tunisia's Arab/Islamic identity.

> We need to define our identity. Tunisians are not tourists who live in a hotel. They have a history and background that form their identity. The rules on which they live should come from that background. One of the biggest problems that Tunisians had during the rule of Bourghiba was that he tried to link them with the West and make them forget their Arab-Islamic identity. He believed that Islam was an obstacle to change and modernization. He tried to interpret Islam in a way that would make Islam serve his purposes, his government and his program of Westernization. In effect, he tried to destroy Tunisian-Arab-Islamic identity.[17]

Ghannoushi maintains that Tunisia and most Muslim societies are doomed to failure because Western models of development by themselves are in essence solutions derived from the experience of the West—Western answers to Western problems. He counters that Muslims must develop their own models, based on their faith and experience. Just as Western civilization takes many forms (French, Italian, British), so too Islam, which is a universal religion, has many applications. The implementation of Islam in many contexts generates diverse orientations or frameworks; Arab nationalism is merely one expression of this identity.

Islam and Change

For Ghannoushi, the process of modern change or development is one of synthesis. While it may borrow freely from other cultures, it must be ultimately rooted in Tunisia's indigenous, Arab-Islamic heritage:

> While we should try to keep this [Tunisia's Islamic civilization] identity, we do not refuse to interact and learn from other civilizations. We should do this while also keeping our own identity. The way to civilization is not to completely follow the Western way or become completely Westernized. We have our identity and we learn from modern life and science and try to improve within the framework of Islamic civilization.[18]

Thus the restoration of Muslim identity and power can only come from a process of change that incorporates modern change (in particular science and technology) within an Islamic framework. For Ghannoushi, Muslims have their own paradigm or worldview, an Islamic framework of principles and values that provide a sense of history, identity, and values and a means to resolve their problems. Therefore, they do not need to blindly follow the West for solutions: "we have a distinct culture that can offer its own solutions to its own problems."[19]

In contrast to Sayyid Qutb and more militant activists, Ghannoushi's quest for a more indigenous (Islamic) cultural model does not require a wholesale rejection of the West but rather a reevaluation and redefinition of the relationship of the Muslim community to the West and to Islam. Muslims need to be more self-consciously independent. They must avoid political, economic, and cultural dependence on the West, be more self-consciously Islamic, and reaffirm the relevance of Islam to all aspects of life.

Unlike some Islamic activists, Ghannoushi is able to simultaneously emphasize the self-sufficiency of Islam while acknowledging the accomplishments of the West. Ghannoushi tends to speak from a position of relative personal security and independence, a position that enables him to avoid the reverse cultural arrogance of those Islamic activists who simply contrast the decadence of the West with the perfection of Islam: "The West is neither superior nor inferior to Islam."[20] Both intellectually and politically, Ghannoushi can accept the need for Muslims to accept and work with the West but stipulates that this cooperation must proceed from a new position of equity rather than dependence and must be critical and selective.

The reconstruction of Muslim society requires, according to Ghannoushi, a social transformation based on a reapplication of Islamic principles and values to the needs of Muslim society. However, this re-Islamization of society is not simply a traditionalist reinstitution of a past idealized model. Echoing nineteenth- and twentieth-century Islamic reformers in the Middle East and South Asia such as Afghani, Abduh, Iqbal, and others, Ghannoushi calls for a process of reinterpretation (ijtihad) to develop an Islamically informed framework for modern Muslim life. Renewal is a process not simply of restoration of a past ideal but of reformation or reconstruction. Islamic principles and values must be reinterpreted and reapplied to the present and, often, new conditions of Muslim societies.

The ideological principles of Ghannoushi's Islamic alternative or worldview are: (1) the perfection and comprehensiveness of Islam as witnessed in the Quran and the example of the Prophet Muhammad; (2) the totality of Islam, its guidance for personal and public life, faith and politics, and economic and social life; (3) the egalitarian nature of the Islamic community, which is a populist social movement of the masses not of classes and elites; (4) the self-sufficiency of Islam, which, though not dependent on the West, can be open to the West; (5) the unity and cohesiveness of the Muslim community, which can only be achieved through the reestablishment of the Islamic state, a goal to be pursued; (6) the acceptance of nationalism as a component of Islamic universalism rather than, as some Islamic leaders have maintained, its antithesis; and (7) recognition of freedom and democracy as necessary prerequisites of the new Islamic order.

However, principles are not enough, nor are external scapegoats. Seeing the world as continuing to be dominated by unbelief (kufr) rather than faith, Ghannoushi attributes this weakness not only to the dominance of the West and to the authoritarianism of Muslim regimes but also to the tendency of Islamic movements to fail to appreciate the dynamics of change. He echoes critics of Islamic movements who have often charged that they tend to be long on general principles or ideals and short on specifics (programs and policies). For Ghannoushi, the problem has been the tendency of some Islamic movements to present a monolithic ideal rather than appreciate the reality or diversity of the Islamic world. Though Islam is rooted in belief in the one God and the divine will for all humanity, Islamic ideology varies according to time and context. Too often, Ghannoushi notes, the Islamic alternative is the same, despite quite diverse social and cultural contexts. This approach renders it "empty and vacuous . . . a stereotype with no basis in actual facts and where the time factor has no weight or value."[21] Such idealism ignores the real problems of Muslim society and unwittingly contributes to the decline of Muslim power and fortunes. The challenge is to recognize and bridge the gap between ideal and reality, Islam and the condition of Muslim societies. Islamic principles and values must be applied to the realities of Muslim life. Thus, Ghannoushi declared: "What we need is a realistic fundamentalism (Usuliyah Waqiyah), or if you like, an authenticated realism (Waqiyah Muasalah)."[22]

This understanding of Islam as not only a transcendent, unchanging ideal but also as a multidimensional faith that expresses itself in diverse ways in different historical and cultural contexts made Ghannoushi more critical of blind dependence on the example and interpretations of previous generations. He, like others before him, believed that Islamic movements had to develop responses to their own local and national as well as regional contexts. Though acknowledging his substantial indebtedness to the previous generation of Islamic reformers and activists, Ghannoushi believed that failure to realize the context-specific nature of reform and thus too much dependency on the past had inhibited the development of Islamic civilization and of Muslim societies: "The Islamists of Tunisia and other countries ought to stop repeating a bundle of ideas worked out by the former generation of men of Islamic *dawa*. . . . We must achieve our goals . . . to do that we must be contemporaneous and live in our time."[23] There must be a perpetual interaction between three dimensions: the Muslim mind, the propositions and dicta of Shariah, and the actual state of affairs. Thus, Ghannoushi felt free to reject the tendency of many to uncritically rather than selectively follow the beliefs of the previous generation in their rejection of trade unionism, political parties, the liberation of women, and democracy: "This way of thinking proceeds as if . . . the former generation of Muslims have actually mastered every detail of Islamic knowledge, and have elevated themselves above time."[24]

This insistence on diversity, adaptation, and change enabled both Ghannoushi and Ennahda, while drawing on predecessors, to both respond directly to the particularities of the Tunisian experience and maintain an ideological outlook that is capable of dynamic and creative change. Thus, for example, while strongly influenced by the thought of the Egyptian Muslim Brotherhood and particularly Sayyid Qutb in his early development and Islamic activism, Ghannoushi came to realize that though Qutb was a great man, he is "not the spokesman of Islam."[25] He would say the same for Khomeini and other Islamic leaders with whom he can both identify and differ. Moreover, Ghannoushi in retrospect emphasized that Sayyid Qutb's ideology was heavily influenced by the context in which it was developed, in particular Nasser's secular nationalism and his suppression of the Muslim Brotherhood. Thus Ghannoushi could state that Qutb's prescriptions for his time and place may have been correct but that it was not necessarily suitable ("Sayyid Qutb was wrong") to apply it in other Muslim societies, in particular in North Africa. This position is rooted in Ghannoushi's belief that while Islam is one, when applied in different regions it gives rise to diverse interpretations and applications: "The approaches of individuals to practicing their religion can change from nation to nation and from time to time."[26]

Ghannoushi, therefore, sees a necessary transition today from the earlier days of Hassan al-Banna and Sayyid Qutb or Mawlana Mawdudi. These founders of modern Islamic movements were primarily concerned in the early decades of their organizations with formation and education to prepare the way for the future implementation of Islam or re-Islamization of society. In contrast, today "new practical efforts have transferred the Islamic ideology to the level of everyday struggle in the life of Muslims."[27] Among the pioneers of this practical school of political and social change are Iran's Ayatollah Khomeini, Sudan's Hasan al-Turabi, and Algeria's Abbasi Madani, who have identified the Islamic movement with broader sociopolitical issues of society such as economic exploitation and neoimperialism. It is, according to Ghannoushi, this mission to provide Islamic solutions to the problems of the masses that is the mandate and agenda for contemporary Islamic movements.

Islam and Power

Islamic reform and power are interconnected. The extent to which the Islamic movement has not succeeded in coming to power is due to internal and external causes. Ghannoushi does not shy away from criticizing Islamic movements for their failures and deficiencies. The weakness of the Islamic movement is in direct relationship to its failure to establish Islam as "a way of life beyond the mosque," to make it part of the everyday life of the people, and thus "to liberate all the powers and strengths of Islam so that it becomes the driving force of the people, gives energy to the people."[28] Thus he could conclude: "The problem is that societies have evolved while the Islamists have not."[29]

Despite the successes of Islamic movements, Ghannoushi sees the greatest responsibility for their failures as springing from their continued inability to move beyond the models of the past,

> models from the age of decline [whose] only connection to reality is through texts whose understanding became petrified, whose concepts crystallized centuries ago under circumstances quite different from our time. Thus a Muslim of this mentality is afflicted with what resembles paralysis in understanding reality and in appropriating the strategies and energy necessary to progress.[30]

For Ghannoushi the two clearest examples of the failure of the Islamic movement to develop apace with its society are its failure to adequately identify and speak directly to the problems of the working class and to the degradation of women. Islamists too often failed to move beyond the language and slogans of faith and morality and to address the real everyday lives of people and their political and social problems. Thus he has called for Islamists to move from the lofty high ground of rhetoric and preaching about social justice to acting within the working-class sector of society. The call to Islam can only be effective if its message resonates with the lives of those to whom it is addressed.

The same can be said regarding the status of Muslim women. For many in the Muslim world and the West, the specter of the Islamic movement raises fears about the oppression and seclusion of women. By contrast, Islamic activists assert that their message of a return to Islam signals the liberation of women and restoration to place of privilege and honor. Yet Ghannoushi has charged that the Islamic movement has failed to adequately appreciate and address the condition of Muslim women. Rather than offering a liberating vision, many Islamists have remained ignorant and insensitive to the "oppression, degradation, abasement, [and] restrictions of their horizons and roles . . . during the long centuries of decline . . . [in which] woman's personality was obliterated and she was transformed into an object of pleasure—in the name of religion!"[31] Thus, Ghannoushi argued, is it any wonder that many women looked to the West, since they "were suffering under the yoke of an oppressive, false Islam, sustained by the silence of 'the men of religion.' . . . it had been inculcated in the minds of women that . . . Islam meant only the veil, seclusion within the house, fulfilling the desires of men, lack of freedom."[32] In contrast, he maintains that Islam's recognition of the equality of men and women means that women like men have not only a right but also a duty to participate in finding solutions for the political, economic, and social problems of their societies.[33]

Freedom is the second driving force or goal (in addition to identity) of the Islamic movement. Freedom provides an atmosphere conducive to the development of ideology (ideas and thinking) and programs essential for the revival of Islam. The absence of freedom, the experience of a cycle of government repression, breeds anger, hatred, and rejection.

Islam and the West

As in the case of most twentieth-century Islamic reformers, the impact and influence of the West are major themes in Rachid Ghannoushi's thinking and writing. Historical memory of the Crusades and of European colonialism are not of a distant past but of an enduring and present reality, perpetuated by the continued dependence of many governments and societies on the West politically, economically, and culturally. The relationship of Islam to the West has been a major theme in Ghannoushi's thought as he has grappled with many of the central issues of Islamic revivalist movements: "Why was Muslim society so easily overtaken by the West? What were the sources of Western progress and power? What was the cause of Muslim malaise and how was the Muslim community to be revitalized?"

The impact and role of the West are central to Rachid Ghannoushi's understanding of the plight of Muslim societies and their future. However, he is not a rigid or uncritical ideologue. He sees a West that in its dark ages turned to Islam (Islamic philosophy and sciences), and subsequently a Muslim world that in seeking to overcome its years of decline has turned to the West and its institutions. He acknowledges the sources of Western superiority, its science and technology, fostering of a sense of personal responsibility, individual rights, and freedoms, and the belief that government is a servant of the people and that people have a right to rebel against a government that denies their rights and independence. However, he also condemns the radical individualism of Western society, which leads to an "enslavement to an earthly paradise of materialism" and the transformation of democracy into a tool of the wealthy.[34] In particular, he has warned against the cultural penetration and domination of the West. The extent to which Muslim governments and elites uncritically imitate the West has produced a dependency and loss of identity that is at the root of the failures of many Muslim societies. For Ghannoushi, the plight of modern Muslim societies in general and Tunisia in particular is rooted in the failure of most governments in the Muslim world and their Westernized elites to provide a modern indigenous cultural paradigm for society. The malaise of Muslims is the direct result of a departure from Arab-Islamic identity and heritage and, at the same time, an uncritical dependence on the West. Tunisian society, like that of much of the Islamic world, looks no longer to its faith for guidance but to Europe.

Ghannoushi has indicted the prevailing secular educational systems in particular in the Muslim world as a major cause of the malaise of Muslim societies. Secular education robs people of a sense of their own cultural identity and history, contributes to their dislocation, makes them dependent on foreign culture/identity, and undermines indigenous cultural and belief systems. In the Maghreb in particular, it produced a Francophile generation alienated from its authentic identity, more at home in the West than in the Arab Muslim world.

Ghannoushi believes that a bifurcated or dual educational system, modern Western versus traditional Islamic schools, has divided rather than united society, producing secular and religious elites who have provided a flawed leadership. The former looked to the West while the latter sought refuge in the past, in a "museum Islam." Both failed to produce a modern culturally authentic society, firmly grounded in its Arab-Islamic identity and heritage. The dominant position of modern elites stood in sharp contrast to the atrophy of the religious establishment: its failure to rise to the challenges facing Muslims in the modern world. Ghannoushi has been equally critical of the failures of secular elites as well as religious scholars (ulama). The former are too often seduced by power and secular materialism, and the latter, in particular the religious establishment, are the debilitated guardians of Islam, controlled and coopted by the government. They are men whose consciences and voices are silent, as much a part of the state's bureaucracy as its civil servants. As such they have failed to provide guidance for the people or to generate a modern Arab-Islamic model or solutions for the Muslim community.

While French colonialism was brought to an end with political independence, French influence and indeed presence continued in the Maghreb in general and Tunisia in particular, as witnessed in everything from dress and intellectual discourse, state institutions (government, education, law), and a Francophile and Francophone elite. Ironically, dependency on the West, Westernization, has also inevitably undermined the democratic tradition in Muslim countries, since an unrepresentative minority has had to resort to dictatorship in order to retain power. Thus the reality of the dictatorship of the ruling elite prevails in most Muslim countries. However, Ghannoushi avoids the pitfall of total polarization; he does not see the choice as Islam or the West, God or the "great Satan." In contrast to many in the Arab and Muslim world, he does not see the choice as simply one of grand emulation or rejection.

Ghannoushi is acutely conscious of the negative impact of colonialism on Muslim societies and rejects dependence on the West. However, he also has acknowledged and expressed admiration for the scientific accomplishments of the West. While many Islamic activists have often countered Western imperialism and triumphalism with an Islamic equivalent, Ghannoushi regards the source of these differences as not so much one of superiority or inferiority but of focus and orientation. Western society is essentially human-centered in its outlook and values, while Muslim societies are God-centered. While the West increasingly celebrates man as master of the universe, Islam reaffirms the centrality of God as its ruler or lord (*rabb*). Thus the ultimate reference point for humanity is not human desire but the divine will. This difference in orientation does not preclude Ghannoushi's appreciation for many of the accomplishments of Western civilization: empiricism and use of reason, modern science and technology, rejection of tyranny and championing of human freedom and responsibilty, and the willingness to rebel against any oppressor, whether it be the church or the state, feudalism or communism.

Islam and Democracy

Despite the portrayal of Islamic movements in general and the Renaissance Party in particular as radicalized organizations bent on the overthrow of governments, Rachid Ghannoushi has challenged that image by being an early and strong proponent of open multiparty elections in practice and in theory. MTI from an early period and subsequently as the Renaissance Party sought recognition as a political party. Though this door was closed, members of the movement did participate in elections in 1988.

Ghannoushi's thought has evolved over the years in response to his own Tunisian experience as well as events in the broader Muslim world. He acknowledges democracy as among the positive contributions or accomplishments of the West. As in the case of a number of Muslim intellectuals and leaders, Ghannoushi sees no necessary contradiction between democracy and the traditional Islamic tenets such as ijtihad, *ijma* (consensus), *baya* (oath of allegiance), and *shura* (consultation), which governs the relationship between the political authority and the people. In an attempt to find a historical link between the development of Western democracy and Islam, Ghannoushi maintains that democratic notions and liberal democratic values were derived from medieval Europe, which in turn was influenced by Islamic civilizations. Democracy offers the means to implement the Islamic ideal today: "Islam, which enjoins the recourse to Shura (consultation) . . . finds in democracy the appropriate instruments (elections, parliamentary system, separation of powers, etc.) to implement the Shura."[35] Consensus (ijma) provides the basis for participatory government or democracy in Islam. Ghannoushi believes that democracy in the Muslim world as in the West can take many forms. He himself favors a multiparty system of government.[36]

For Ghannoushi the rule of law, freedom, and human rights are essential components of civilization. Believing that they often exist in the West today more than in the Muslim world, he maintains that it is preferable to live in a secular state where there is freedom than in a country where the Shariah is the official law but where freedom does not exist. Similarly, when discussing whether a Muslim can live in a non-Muslim state such as in Europe or America, he argues that any secular democratic state where religious freedom exists is a *dar al-Islam* (Islamic territory or abode) rather than a *dar al-harb* (abode of war).[37]

In the wake of the Iranian revolution, Iran, or perhaps the specter of other Irans, has often affected Western (and Muslim governments') assessments and fears of Islamic movements coming to power. This fear often equates Islamic government with theocracy or "the rule of the mullahs." Ghannoushi categorically rejects theocracy, maintaining that "[g]overnment in Islam embodies a civilian authority whose political behaviour is answerable to public opinion."[38] When pressed as to the relationship of democracy to Islam, he maintains that

> [i]f by democracy is meant the liberal model of government prevailing in the West, a system under which the people freely choose their representatives and leaders, and in which there is an alternation of power, as well as all freedoms and human rights for the public, then the Muslims will find nothing in their religion to oppose democracy, and it is not in their interest to do so anyway.[39]

Ghannoushi warned that suspending the democratic process, as in Tunisia and Algeria, where Muslims were poised to come to power through the ballot box, runs the risk of fueling radical politics: "It as if there is a plan to force the Islamic movements to lose faith in democracy and resort to violence."[40] He noted that while in the West modernity is supposed to stand for freedom, equal rights, political pluralism, and the rotation of power, "[n]one of the self-proclaimed modernist elite, neither in our country nor in any other Muslim nation, have proven to be democratically inclined, let alone instruments of civil, industrial and scientific progress on a scale even marginally near that of the West."[41]

His acceptance of democracy is not uncritical. Despite its strengths, Western democracies did not give women the right to vote until relatively recently. Moreover, a minority of political, business, and media interests and lobbies often manipulate the system and the majority of citizens. Modern democracies have often been undermined by nationalism and racism. Thus, perceived national interest caused two great democracies like Britain and France to become major colonial powers and the United States to adopt a double standard in its promotion (or more accurately, lack of promotion) of democracy in the Muslim world.

Islam both defines and sets limits upon ruler and ruled. Ghannoushi reinterprets the traditional concepts of leadership (*imamah*), consultation, and consensus to support the belief that rulers have a contract with the community (ummah); the community chooses its ruler, who is accountable to it. The precise mechanism may vary; however, Ghannoushi acknowledges that Islamic states may indeed benefit from Western liberal traditions in redefining and institutionalizing forms of consultation (shura) such as those of elected parliaments or councils, plebiscites, and Western values of freedom and the rule of law.

Though a Muslim democracy is based on equality and freedom, its Islamic character does set limits and influence its institutions. Citizenship in the modern state, according to Ghannoushi, should be one in which all, Muslims and non-Muslims, are equal, possessing a common nationality. These rights, Ghannoushi believes, are guaranteed by Islam (the Quran, Sunnah, and Islamic jurisprudence). Although he believes that all are equal regardless of race, creed, ethnic origin, with equal rights and freedoms, he nevertheless continues, as in the traditional Islamic notion of non-Muslims as "protected" people, to postulate two categories of citizenship. Muslims enjoy unqualified citizenship (*muwatanah ammah*), and non-Muslims possess qualified citizenship (*muwatanah khasah*). While the latter enjoy full citizenship, the majority of citizens may choose to have their faith influence public life, and thus the state may prohibit non-Muslims from holding senior positions in government.

The Shariah, Islamic law, sets the limits or boundaries of society. However, since the Shariah provides general principles and does not answer all the problems and needs of modern life, ongoing temporal legislation is necessary. Through a process of interpretation (ijtihad), elected representatives of the people have to right to interpret and legislate for the community. Similarly, individuals' social and economic rights, such as the right to private property and wealth, are subject to limitation in light of Islamic principles of social justice and community welfare. However, Ghannoushi is content to remain at the ideological or normative level rather than delineate a specific concrete Islamic model.

Pluralism and civil society have become the source of major debate and reform in many Muslim societies. Ghannoushi acknowledges that in Islamic thought, pluralism is the subject of acceptance and rejection. He aligns himself with those Muslim intellectuals today who argue the Islamic acceptability of pluralism. Historically, like many, he cites the example of Andalusia (Muslim Spain) where under Muslim rule, non-Muslims were able to live, worship, write and function. More contemporaneously, modern pluralism is seen as a constitutional mechanism for promoting consultation (shura), an effective means by which popular sovereignty is expressed and exercised. It is a source for principles of equality, majority rule and minority opposition, and freedom of expression.

While many Muslims and the Islamic movement may debate the acceptability of modern notions of pluralism, civil society (voluntary, nongovernmental organizations) is seen as a less contested or divisive area. Contemporary Islamic movements have in fact developed an Islamic alternative as they seek to reconstruct civil society through the creation of educational, legal, and social services and economic institutions (Islamic banks and finance houses) and to play leadership roles in professional associations of lawyers, physicians, teachers, journalists. Ghannoushi believes that, ironically, many modern Muslim states have limited or suppressed civil society (by the governments attempt to monopolize power): "The state of pseudo-modernity has taken over the remaining institutions of civil society. Mosques, endowments, courts, religious institutes, trade unions, parties, charities and the press have all been seized."[42]

The Islamic movement that has attempted to resurrect or reconstruct civil society. Muslim governments like those of Tunisia, modernized economically and militarily but, in fact, not politically. Ironically, in their hands, modernization destroyed civil society as the state took control of the administration of education and religious endowments (waqf, pl. awqaf) and absorbed or eliminated religious (Shariah) courts. At the same time, the modernization programs of autocratic regimes did not promote democracy, the rule of law, and Western values of freedom, including freedom of assembly and association.[43]

While Ghannoushi accepts the ability of Muslims to borrow aspects of Western liberal notions of civil society, he is careful to emphasize that civil society should not be based on a secularism that marginalizes or suppresses religion. He distinguishes between different forms or concepts of secularism: those that seek to separate religion and politics and those that seek to control or exclude religion from public life. He charges that governments in North Africa have practiced a pseudosecularism by which they have sought to control religious symbols and institutions, to monopolize the right to interpret and implement Islam. Ghannoushi distinguishes between Anglo-Saxon notions of secularism, which do not see a necessary conflict between the religious and the civil, and the French Revolution's legacy, influential in North Africa, in which secularism becomes an absolute that marginalizes religion and desacralizes the world.

Rachid Ghannoushi and Tunisia's Ennahda movement reflect the extent to which the growth and development of Islamic movements and Islamist thought can be conditioned by political and social contexts. Ghannoushi's thought has been conditioned and transformed by multiple influences: Islamic traditions, the experiences of the failures of Arab nationalism and socialism, life under an authoritarian government, the influences of leaders, movements, and events in other Muslim countries, and the experience of exile in the West.

6
HASAN AL-TURABI
The Mahdi-Lawyer

As young Sudanese intellectual returning to his country in 1964 after completing his doctoral studies at the Sorbonne in Paris, Hasan al-Turabi seemed about to begin a career as a distinguished academic. Instead, he became one of the world's most visible and well-known Muslim activist intellectuals.

Hasan al-Turabi had an important appointment in the Faculty of Law at the University of Khartoum when he returned from Paris and was poised to become a member of the Sudanese intellectual establishment. Instead he gave a stirring oration at a political rally that helped to crystallize opposition to the existing Sudanese military regime of Ibrahim Abboud. Turabi was catapulted into the center of the Sudanese political maelstrom, and he has remained there ever since. He has been an important actor in every major political development in Sudan since 1964. Turabi is reported by most observers to have been the leading ideologue in the regime that came to power in Sudan in 1989 under the banner of establishing an authentically Islamic political system and social order, and even when he was relieved of his positions in 1999 he remained a major political figure.

The ways religious revivalism is understood have changed in the 1970s and 1980s, as has the sociopolitical context, in Sudan, and these changes are reflected in Turabi's career. In the late 1970s, before the Islamic revolution in Iran and before the attempt to implement Islamic law in Sudan was undertaken by Ja'far Numayri, the establishment of an explicitly Islamic state was a less emotional and dramatic issue. Turabi played a significant role in the political transition from the acceptance of the call to implement Islam as a pious (and usually innocuous) slogan to its development into a major political program that many view as threatening.

This transition took place in Sudan at the same time that the scholarly understanding of movements of religious resurgence and renewal was also changing. Many scholars still assumed throughout the 1970s that one important dimension of the dynamics of modern history was the inevitable "decline of religion" as a major historic and societal force. However, during the 1980s, the broader understanding of new social movements and a greater recognition of the continuing vitality of the major world religions created a context in which people like Hasan al-Turabi were recognized as significant actors in the sociopolitical arena.

Turabi's life and work reflect many important trends in Sudanese history, African history, Islamic history, and global postmodern history. The great danger in viewing Turabi in such contexts is that the real person can get lost in the construction of ideal types and stereotypes. The flesh-and-blood personality should not get lost in global and analytical constructs. Journalistic coverage often utilizes stereotypical labels that obscure the distinctive individuality of people like Hasan al-Turabi. It is useful to examine Turabi as an individual, then look at him in connection with the movement that he has been a part of, and, finally, put both into a broader framework.

Turabi as an Individual

Hasan al-Turabi can be viewed from many different perspectives, but an important starting point is to recognize that he is a distinctive individual human being. To understand him within this perspective, there are three personal frameworks of identity that are important: his sense of family tradition, the formative influence of his father, and his distinctive mode of leadership. In addition, it is important for understanding Turabi as an individual to see him within the specific context of his contemporaries in Sudan.

Family Tradition

First, Turabi's personality is framed by his perception of the family tradition of which he is a part. His family is a well-known family of "religious notables" with an important tradition of recognized piety. This family has a well-established religious center south of Khartoum where the tomb of a famous ancestor, Hamad al-Nahlan (known as "Wad al-Turab"),[1] has long been a center for local religious education and pious visitation. Turabi is acutely aware that he is a part of this long tradition. In interviews describing the history of his family, he presents a portrait that is similar to many of the established "holy families" in Sudanese history.[2]

The family was historically distinguished from neighboring groups as being somehow more religious, and their piety was widely recognized. The general group of which Turabi's family is a part is the Bedayriyyah, a group famous for its "holy men." The "Turabis" began their history as a recognized family with the career of Hasan al-Turabi's eighteenth-century ancestor Wad al-Turab.

Wad al-Turab is identified first as one of the ulama, a scholar and teacher. He was a scholar of jurisprudence (*faqih*) who taught the standard text of Maliki law, the book called *Khalil* in the old historical accounts.[3] He had appropriate scholarly credentials; however, he was also "a reformist-jihadist," in the descriptive terminology used by Hasan al-Turabi. It is clearly an important part of the remembered family identity that the first Sudanese person to identify himself as a mahdi ("divinely-guided leader") was Wad al-Turab in the eighteenth century. This ancestor is reported to have made the proclamation of his mission in the manner regarded as correct by traditions, in Mecca.

In the words of Hasan al-Turabi, " 'In those days, if you were a reformer, you could not make claims against the establishment unless you had a strong legitimacy, and the only legitimacy that you could invoke to challenge authority and the establishment in the eighteenth century was to be a mahdi.' So, Turabi says, Wad al-Turab was probably the first mahdi in the Sudan, and most scholars agree."[4]

In this broad framework, the family's prestige is founded on the activities and reputation of a pious person who combined the roles of a scholar-teacher and jihadist-mahdist. Then late in his life, Wad al-Turab developed Sufi tendencies, and in his description of the family Hasan al-Turabi says that Wad al-Turab was much more like al-Ghazali than the more inflammatory or less properly Islamic kinds of Sufis. In this description, Wad al-Turab and the family tradition evoke every major leadership style involved in the processes of Islamization in Sudan. There is the Sufi tradition and the tradition of the ulama/scholars, as well as the jihadist tradition, which manifested itself in mahdist modes of presentation. These are the traditions at the core of the Islamization of the Sudan, and the Turabi family tradition identifies itself with all of them. It is possible to argue that this is the basic matrix into which Hasan al-Turabi fits himself as well. He sees himself as essentially involved in the Sudanese Islamic framework or paradigm of the triangle of the Sufi, the alim, and the mahdi.

Immediate Family

Hasan al-Turabi's father was a formative influence on his personality and way of thinking. Hasan's father was raised in Wad al-Turab near the family tomb center, so he was identified with the established family tradition. As a young student he went to Omdurman in the early part of the twentieth century and was one of the early graduates of the Omdurman Religious Studies Institute, *al-ma'had al-ilmi*. This was a training center that had been established by the British to provide a relatively formally structured and regulated education in the basic Islamic disciplines. Most of the graduates became teachers in local Quran schools or mosque imams, and a few were employed in the Shariah courts.

Hasan al-Turabi's father worked in the Islamic court system and eventually became a judge in the Shariah courts in the British administration. Turabi describes his father as not being very easy to get along with and very jealous in protecting his jurisdiction from encroachments by British administrators. As a result, he was moved from post to post around Sudan, never staying for an extended period in any one place.[5] In these moves, his family traveled with him.

Hasan was born in Kassala in 1932 and lived in a number of places in different regions of the Sudan. He was the youngest son, and shortly after he was born, his mother died. This meant that Hasan as a young boy lived with his Shariah-judge father as he moved around the country. Hasan al-Turabi's description of what this meant for his education is vivid: "I went to school in each of the local places, but I would look forward after vacations to going back to school," because in the evenings and during school vacations, his father worked diligently to ensure that his son received a proper education. By the time he was in sixth form, Turabi remembers having memorized, under his father's guidance, the *alfiyyah* of Ibn Malik, and once he had memorized that he went on to Ibn Malik's *Lamiyyat al-'af'al*. These were important books for the traditional study of grammar and were important in older scholarship as a basis for being able to interpret the language of the Quran. Turabi progressed through the study of the traditional disciplines of Islamic studies under his father's guidance. Although this education was not as systematic as studying at a major Islamic university like al-Azhar in Cairo, Turabi received a basic training in the traditional Islamic disciplines.

By the time Turabi had completed his secondary education and was ready to enter the university in 1950, he was a person shaped by a family tradition of piety and Islamic learning as well as a product of a modern school system. His vocabulary was importantly shaped by a basic, memorized Islamic awareness. When he arrived at the University in Khartoum his basic knowledge was significantly reoriented. He says that "the [Islamic] movement which I met at the university was quite an experience for me. All of the dead literature that I had learned by heart became alive. I saw everything in a different light."[6] He did not see himself as having been particularly Islamically oriented before he went to the university, but rather, that he simply had a good Islamic education. While he was in secondary school, he did not join the newly organized Islamic student group, thinking that "it had little to offer to someone like him who had received an advanced home education in religious sciences."[7] Becoming a part of the early Islamist movement in the 1950s was the way he came to see different meanings for all of what he had memorized as a child.

In the Muslim Brotherhood

When Turabi arrived as a student in the university he was in an unusual position within the emerging movement. Many of the participants had a longer record of active involvement. However, although for many of them Islam was a general ideal and something to defend, they were not very familiar with the traditional sources, concepts, and vocabularies. In many different kinds of social movements, those who can actually articulate the ideology in a knowledgeable way are a small minority. These people may not be the actual organizational leaders, but they become the people who provide the words for the manifestos and programs, and by that path they may come to leadership positions in the movement.

The environment of the student movements in Sudan in the late 1940s and early 1950s was such that there were students who would be eager to support an "Islamic movement" but would know little about Islam. There was a sense that the Communist movement was developing rapidly among the students, at the secondary level as well as at the university. To some it appeared that the Communists might emerge as the only really effective student political organization. However, there were students who not only did not want to join the Communist groups but viewed the Communists as a threat.

For some of the more activist students, the real alternative to the Communists was not to join the nationalists but rather to establish an activist Islamic movement[8] that would not be identified with the conservative elite in the country. The most readily available model was the Muslim Brotherhood in Egypt, and Brotherhood-style groups began to be established by 1950. It was in this context that Turabi became a part of the early Islamic movement. Someone like him, who would have a proper vocabulary and some knowledge of basic sources, would not necessarily yet be a leader but would certainly be recognized as an important addition to the movement. Turabi as a student was not a major organizational leader, but he had already begun to have some visibility by the middle of the 1950s. His name was associated with a document "redefining the movement's ideology" in contrast to some earlier radical pronouncements.[9]

When he completed his studies in Khartoum, he left Sudan for studies in London and Paris. Although he returned to Sudan for short visits, he was effectively removed from any real influence in the movement. He completed his studies for a master's degree in law in London in 1957 and then received his doctorate from the Sorbonne; he returned to Sudan in 1964.

Turabi returned to Sudan in the middle of the growing unrest that led to the ousting of the military regime of Ibrahim Abboud, who had ruled Sudan since 1958, when he had led a military coup that took control of the government from the political parties supported by the older mass Muslim organizations. The regime faced growing economic problems and a serious civil war in the southern Sudan. The older political parties and the professional associations and the more radical political groups like the Communist Party and the Muslim Brotherhood were all able to agree on opposition to the Abboud government. One of Turabi's first acts when he returned to Sudan in the summer of 1964 was to make a direct attack on the military rulers in a widely publicized policy debate held at the University of Khartoum. This placed the Sudanese Muslim Brotherhood in a highly visible position at the center of the growing demonstrations that ultimately led to the downfall of Abboud in October 1964.

The experience of Turabi and the Muslim Brotherhood in the October Revolution is a good example of Turabi's mode of operation. His visibility came as a result not of his putting forward a distinctively Islamist position or program but because he effectively articulated broader concerns that were not exclusively part of his own religiopolitical agenda. Within that context, he was able to give visibility to more explicitly Islamist expressions of common concerns. In many ways, Turabi's approach was the classical "United Front" approach utilized more typically by Communists in Europe. By the late 1960s, Turabi was the most visible and influential figure in the Islamic movement in Sudan, and he was operating within the framework of his distinctive personal mode of leadership.

Turabi's Generation in Sudanese Life

Turabi as an individual was part of an important generation of thinkers and leaders in Sudan, and the interaction of these people for the last forty years has been an important dimension of the development of modern Sudan. In the contemporary Islamic world, Sudan produced a remarkable generation of intellectuals and political leaders who have engaged in innovative and significant thinking within the paradigm of Islam and within the paradigm of other ideological constructs in Islamic contexts. This is true across the political spectrum, from radical leftist and Communist positions to the rearticulation of traditional positions.

In the 1930s a group of individuals was born who would, by the 1960s, become significant figures in Sudanese life. In their activities and rivalries they created a remarkable body of new Muslim visions and conceptualizations that, in its variety and innovation, was quite distinctive in the Muslim world. It is useful not simply to think in terms of broad institutional rivalries but also to note the personal relationships that are involved. Three of the most important northern political leaders in the final decades of the twentieth century, Sayyid Sadiq al-Mahdi, Sayyid Muhammad Uthman al-Mirghani, and Hasan al-Turabi, were all born within the same decade and are in the same age cohort among the Muslim elite families of Sudan. Sadiq al-Mahdi, the great-grandson of the nineteenth-century Sudanese mahdi, was prime minister in the eras of parliamentary politics in both the 1960s and the 1980s. Muhammad Uthman al-Mirghani became the leader of the Khatmiyyah Tariqah when his father died in 1969. He transformed the role of head of the Khatmiyyah from that of religious leader outside of formal politics into that of head of a major political party. Hasan al-Turabi had already emerged as the leading Islamically identified politician outside the structure of the older parties. The degree of personal interaction among these men is reflected in the fact that Turabi's wife is Wisel al-Mahdi, Sadiq al-Mahdi's sister. These men were and are always aware of each other on a personal basis, as well as in the more general context of the developing political system. The Mirghani family tradition was for less direct involvement in the political arena than the mahdist tradition or Hasan al-Turabi's personal style. However, al-Mirghani had emerged by the late 1960s as a political leader of comparable domestic political visibility, although he was less well known internationally.

The prominence of these clearly Islamically identified leaders in Sudanese politics is remarkable. In other parts of the Arab world and the broader Muslim world, there are few places outside of the more conservative monarchies where people with "religious" credentials similar to those of al-Mahdi, al-Mirghani, and Turabi have such prominent roles. In other areas, leadership tended to come, especially in the 1960s and 1970s, from people with primarily modernizing and possibly secularist credentials. The ideological positions articulated were more often in the tradition of Nasser of Egypt: more leftist, or socialist, in basic tone while giving recognition to general Islamic principles.

The power of the Islamically identified leaders was not the result of an absence of effective articulators of more leftist and secularist positions. The political generation of Turabi, al-Mahdi, and al-Mirghani also included a number of very effective presenters of leftist and secularist perspectives in Sudan. By the late 1960s, the Sudanese Communist Party (SCP) was possibly the largest and most effective Communist party in Africa. This was brought about by strong party leadership, supplied by people like Abd al-Khaliq Mahjub (who was executed by Numayri in 1971) and Ahmad Sulayman (who later worked with Turabi) and by leaders in the Women's Union and the trade union movement like Fatma Ahmad Ibrahim and el-Shafi Ahmed el-Shaykh (also executed by Numayri in 1971). Western-educated and generally secularist intellectuals, like Francis Deng and Mohammed Omer Bashir, had international recognition and political importance. However, this combination of effective intellectuals and political organizers was not able to dominate the Sudanese political arena, where the central position was held by the more clearly Islamically identified intellectuals and political organizations.

The interaction among the Islamically identified political leaders is within the context of their competition with these other political modes. However, the three more established Sudanese Muslim leadership styles— the Sufi "saint," the scholar, and the jihadist—help to define the place of Turabi among his contemporaries as a Muslim activist intellectual. By definition, Sadiq al-Mahdi is the jihadist, the representative of the Mahdist tradition of direct political involvement. At the same time, he clearly presents himself as the scholar and intellectual who works, through his writings, to provide a clear articulation of a modern Islamic perspective. Muhammad Uthman al-Mirghani, by definition, is the Sufi. He is the head of a Sufi brotherhood organization, the Khatmiyyah Tariqah, which was brought to Sudan in the early nineteenth century. His father, Sayyid Ali al-Mirghani, had great political influence but this was always exercised indirectly and shaped by a public posture of noninvolvement in politics. Sayyid Muhammad Uthman, however, became the head of the Democratic Unionist Party and since 1969 has played an important role as a directly involved political leader and, increasingly in the 1990s, presents the mode of the leader of a militant movement of opposition that is functionally jihadist.

Turabi is, by definition, "the scholar." His formal academic credentials are the fullest of the three contemporaries: he has a doctorate and then held a position in the Faculty of Law of the University of Khartoum. His scholarly writings are widely read within the Muslim world. However, by the 1970s, Turabi was also the leader of a significant, if small, political movement whose goals were fundamentally jihadist. Turabi "the scholar" came into direct competition with his contemporaries as each of them worked to create positions of political power. By the mid-1990s, the scholar-become-jihadist (Turabi) was in direct competition with the Sufi-become-jihadist (al-Mirghani) and the jihadist-scholar (al-Mahdi). This competition of personal roles is a significant dimension of modern Sudanese politics and the roles of the activist intellectuals. Each of the leaders competes in a special way, and it is Turabi in particular who overlaps directly with the others' spheres as the Brotherhood is transformed from an elite intellectual group into a mass popular organization.

In the context of the contemporary Muslim world, Turabi clearly is operating in a nontraditional way, and his positions in many ways reflect more radical positions rather than either the more common conservative or the standard Islamist positions. However, he operated successfully in the Sudanese political arena not as a secular intellectual, opposed to what the Sudanese came to call the "sectarian" politics of the Sayyids, but as a *Muslim* opponent of "sectarian" politics.

Earlier a challenge to the Sufi and mahdist political modes from the standpoint of the intellectual class had been made by Ismail al-Azhari, the first prime minister of a self-determining and then independent Sudan in 1953–1956. Al-Azhari was a major leader of the emerging politically conscious educated class in Sudan in the 1940s. "The Graduates," as this class was generally called, provided most of the professional leadership in the government and private sectors, but they were a small minority. In other African nationalist movements and newly independent states, the parties and organizations of this class became the new ruling elite, but not in Sudan. Al-Azhari was forced first to ally himself with the Mirghani family to gain mobilizable mass support outside of the major urban areas, but soon after independence, he came into conflict with Sayyid Ali al-Mirghani. The Khatmiyyah formed its own political party, the People's Democratic Party (PDP), in 1956 and formed a coalition with the mahdists' Ummah Party, forcing al-Azhari out of office soon after independence. By the mid-1960s, al-Azhari and his party, the National Unionist Party (NUP), accommodated itself to the politics of the Sayyids, and in 1969, the PDP and the NUP joined together in the Democratic Unionist Party (DUP) under the leadership of Sayyid Muhammad Uthman al-Mirghani. This reunification and al-Azhari's death in 1969 brought an end to the old-style liberal antisectarian option and left Turabi as the major nonleftist alternative for a new style of politics.

Hasan al-Turabi is an activist intellectual whose life and individual experience is identified with both Islamic and modern themes. His family background provided a distinctive foundation for his ability to interact with his contemporaries in the competition for political power and Islamic influence in the northern Sudan of the twentieth century.

Basic Intellectual Framework: Renewal

Turabi's development as an activist intellectual reflects the changing conditions in Sudan during his long career. At times he was in opposition and at other times associated with the regime in power. Although his commitment to Islamic identified positions remained constant, the implications of those convictions changed depending on circumstances, leading to charges of opportunism. However, his basic ideas about the nature of and need for Islamic renewal are the heart of his intellectual activism.

Definition of Renewal

The foundation of Hasan al-Turabi's perspective is his conviction that effective Islamic renewal is necessary in the modern era. This position combines a pragmatic awareness of the visible weaknesses of Islamic societies in the modern world with a substantive position affirming that Islam requires renewal, or *tajdid*, in every age and it is an obligation for all faithful believers to participate in such renewal. "Tajdid is Turabi's most cherished idea. . . . Tajdid for Turabi takes on a revolutionary and very radical content."[10]

The idea of the necessity of renewal is fundamental to Turabi's understanding of the history of the community of Muslim believers. From the very "first generations," Muslims have, in Turabi's view, advocated that constant renewal in the professing of the faith is an obligation on all believers. In fact, "tajdid is the most necessary of the requirements of the faith of Islam."[11] When subsequent generations ceased to fulfill this obligation, "they bequeathed to us a kind of passive and stagnant profession of the faith."[12] In this situation, "when the enterprise of Muslims becomes stagnant with respect to their being Muslims, their Islam freezes and the history of their life takes a form that is not Islamic."[13] In this way, the history of Islamic civilization is seen as a tension between the forces of renewal (tajdid) and the forces of imitation of the past (taqlid).

Turabi does not argue that the fundamental Islamic principles should change, and he does not advocate abrogation of parts of the Quran in order to adapt to new conditions. The revelation in the Quran is the comprehensive revelation of God's eternal truth. However, the implications of that Quranic message for specific peoples, times, and places *do* change.[14] For Turabi, it is essential for the faithful Muslim to recognize the reality of historical change and accept the responsibility of responding to those changes in an authentically Islamic way—which means to accept the obligation of tajdid. This means that it is an Islamic obligation to cope with change: "God, praised and exalted, does not let us choose our new challenges. Instead, he expects us to choose our responses to those challenges."[15]

Historically, the methodology of renewal involves exercising informed, independent judgment in legal and other areas of interpretation. This effort, called ijtihad, is viewed as the opposite of taqlid, or rigid conformity to past precedents. In the general understanding of tajdid, illustrated by the definition provided by Abu al-Ala Mawdudi, the renewer, or mujaddid, exercises ijtihad "to comprehend the fundamental principles of Religion, judge contemporary culture and its trends from the Islamic viewpoint, and determine the changes to be effected in the existing patterns of social life."[16]

Turabi's view of ijtihad follows this historic definition in general terms. However, in specifics, he advocates much more far-reaching reinterpretations than most of his contemporaries. In his view, ijtihad does not simply open the way "to go to old books to dig out bits and pieces that we hope will help us solve today's problems. What we need is to go back to the roots, and create a revolution at the level of principles."[17]

The degree to which Turabi thinks it is necessary to depart from precedents of earlier Muslims is striking. Most Sunni Muslims, for example, view the Community of the Companions of the Prophet as an ideal and unique model. Sayyid Qutb, the revolutionary Egyptian Islamist ideologue, articulated the common view when he wrote:

There is an historic phenomenon that is appropriate for Islamic advocates in every time and place to consider. . . . The Islamic call brought forth a generation of people, the generation of the Companions of the Prophet, God be pleased with them, which is a unique generation in all of the history of Islam and even in the whole history of humanity. This special type was never brought forth in another time. Some special individuals of this type appeared in the arenas of history, but never again was there the likes of such a large number of people in one place as occurred in the first era of the life of this call to Islam.[18]

In contrast, Turabi argues that although the "prototype community of the Prophet offers us an ideal standard," when we use "that prototype as a basis we may feel obliged to build a new model which unites the eternal principles with the changing reality."[19]

Turabi's departure from historical precedents is also shown in his insistence that renewal, and the necessary ijtihad, is a responsibility of the whole community rather than a small intellectual elite. The foundation for this is Turabi's redefinition of who are the people of knowledge in the contemporary Islamic community. Historically, the "people of knowledge," or the ulama, represented a very small part of the whole community, and as the learned elite they were viewed as speaking for the community of believers as a whole. On the important issue of validation of practices and legal traditions through the consensus (ijma) of the community, for example, it was accepted that this legitimizing consensus was the agreement of the ulama.

Turabi radically expands the definition of the ulama:

> What do I mean by ulama? The word historically has come to mean those versed in the legacy of religious (revealed) knowledge (*ilm*). However, *ilm* does not mean that alone. It means anyone who knows anything well enough to relate it to God. Because all knowledge is divine and religious, a chemist, an engineer, an economist, or a jurist are all ulama. So the ulama in this broad sense, whether they are social or natural scientists, public opinion leaders, or philosophers, should enlighten society.[20]

This broad and inclusive definition of ulama is crucial to the implementation of renewal as conceived by Turabi. It means that professionals in every science and discipline have an Islamic responsibility to use their independent and informed judgement (ijtihad) in the effort of constant Islamic renewal. In the contemporary era, such a renewal must be comprehensive and relate to all aspects of human life and not be solely a spiritual revival and affirmation of old credal statements. In Turabi's perspective, such an effort is inherent in the meaning of the Islamic revelation, and participation in this effort is a requirement for all Muslims.

Renewal and Islamic Law

The renewal of legal systems and interpretations is a vital and central part of Turabi's comprehensive vision. His own professional training was in law, and he served briefly as the dean of the Faculty of Law in the University of Khartoum. When he served in governments, it was usually in some post related to the legal system. Following his acceptance of Numayri's National Reconciliation program, he served as attorney general of Sudan from 1979 to 1982. He then was a presidential advisor on legal and foreign affairs until Numayri suppressed the Muslim Brotherhood in March 1985, and Turabi was jailed. In the third parliamentary era, when National Islamic Front participated briefly in a governmental coalition, Turabi was the attorney general and minister of justice.

Turabi also served on many commissions dealing with legal and constitutional issues. His writing resulting from his work on one of the early special committees provides an important insight into his views on the methods of legal renewal he advocates. While this renewal must be an effective response to contemporary changing conditions, it must be based, in Turabi's view, on the resources found within Islam and should not involve "borrowing" foreign ways of doing things. This position came out clearly in his work on a special committee considering the constitutional crisis resulting from the outlawing of the Sudan Communist Party in 1965.

The Sudan Communist Party (SCP) had been actively involved in the October Revolution (1964), which brought an end to the first period of military rule and marked the beginning of the second parliamentary era. In the elections of 1965, the SCP won eleven of the fifteen seats in the special constituencies for "graduates," and the Brotherhood began an active campaign to exclude Communists from parliament and to outlaw the SCP. The parliament passed a total ban on the SCP in late 1965, and the Supreme Court declared that action to be unconstitutional. In the constitutional and political crisis that followed, the Supreme Council of State, which functioned as the head of state and was separate from the government cabinet, appointed a special committee of three legal specialists to provide advice. This committee was composed of lawyers from the two largest parties in the parliament, Muhammad Ibrahim Khalil (Ummah Party) and Hassan Omar (NUP), and Hasan Turabi. Their report to the Supreme Council affirmed the absolute authority of parliament to make laws without limitations set by other institutions. In a separate publication at the time, Turabi supported the conclusions of the report, although when he wrote: "The Constituent Assembly is the agency entrusted with the exercise of the highest constitutional authority and it is an expression of the sovereignty which the constitutions establish for the Ummah," he added the phase "after God."[21]

Turabi's conclusion went beyond the report and stated that the ultimate cause of this and other constitutional crises was that the Sudanese constitution was simply a collection of "limbs amputated from foreign constitutions" and imposed on the Sudanese people.[22] Effective reform and renewal could not be created from parts borrowed from foreign societies; it would have to be built from the resources within Islam. Legal renewal is, however, an absolute necessity. Turabi presents what he sees as the most effective methods for this renewal in two different areas, the reformulation of the discipline of jurisprudence (*fiqh*) and the implementation of the Shariah (Islamic Law).

The New Fiqh   Historically, Muslims have distinguished between the Shariah, or the actual rules and teachings presented in the Quran and the traditions of the Prophet to guide Muslims in their lives, and the intellectual discipline for analysis and explanation of the Shariah, which is called fiqh. Although the two terms are closely related and sometimes used interchangeably, there is an underlying connotation that fiqh is a human activity, while the Shariah is divine revelation. Turabi utilizes this distinction and calls for a renewal of the whole foundation and perspective of fiqh.

Medieval scholars, Turabi argues, made important contributions to understanding the Shariah, but their contributions were limited by the conditions of their era and their historical context. These early scholars developed a scholastic discipline whose considerations became separated from the conditions of application of Islamic principles in real life. Turabi states that "the issues of the fundamental sources in the fiqh literature were considered abstractly, so that they became sterile speculative discussions which produced absolutely no fiqh at all. Even worse, it produced never-ending controversy."[23] This fiqh tradition is, in Turabi's view, totally inadequate for the needs of the contemporary Islamic movement. "It is clear to the movement that the fiqh which it has in its possession—however specialized its load of deductions and inferences, and however careful in its explorations and consultations—will never be adequate for the needs of the Islamic mission."[24]

Turabi proposes a "new fiqh" that will transcend the limitations of the old, and he is quite specific in defining approaches and methodologies.

> Human knowledge has expanded greatly, while the old fiqh was based on knowledge that was restricted [by the conditions of its historical era.] . . . It becomes imperative for us to adopt a new position in the fiqh of Islam so that we can utilize all knowledge for the service of God. This is a new construction which unites what exists in the transmitted traditional disciplines . . . with the rational sciences which are renewed every day and which are completed by experiment and observation. With that achieved and unified knowledge, we can renew our fiqh for the faith and what challenges it time after time in our contemporary life.[25]

It is within this context that Turabi's concept of the new ulama including experts in all fields becomes essential. Economists and physicists and others are crucial in this process of creating a new and comprehensive fiqh.

In terms of specific methods, Turabi argues for a thorough reexamination of the fundamental sources of the Shariah. In this effort of reinterpretation, Turabi proposes a radical expansion of a traditional method of analysis. In the first centuries of Islam, it was recognized that the basic texts did not deal with all of the specific situations with which Muslims had to deal. As a result, one of the major developments in the study and definition of Islamic law was the utilization of "judicial reasoning by analogy" (*qiyas*).[26] However, scholars developed many rules that narrowed the flexibility of specifically legal reasoning by analogy, and these became a part of the rigid structure that Turabi rejects. He proposed the replacement of the limited qiyas by a new, broad analogical analysis of the fundamental sources.[27] One area where Turabi outlines how this new approach would provide different perspectives is in the redefinition of the meaning of shura (consultation) in the context of the modern world.[28]

Law and Politics These perspectives and methods served Turabi well when he worked on various committees and commissions, operating primarily as a legal scholar. However, as the leader of a political group, he faced the more concrete issues of the actual implementation of Islamic law in an existing society. In these efforts, political and historic contexts played a major role in determining which aspects of the proposed renewal of fiqh would be put into operation. In the 1960s, when Turabi first emerged as a Sudanese political leader, the major issue was simply to get acceptance of the general idea of an Islamic constitution and an Islamic state. Even though the Muslim Brotherhood, and its political organization, the Islamic Charter Front (ICF), were small, they succeeded, under Turabi's leadership, in placing the issue of an Islamic constitution at the center of the political agenda by the late 1960s. However,

> far from working out a comprehensive blueprint or discourse the ICF seemed to have contented itself with the role of a pressure group that reminded influential politicians of the need to return to Islam as the root of "our" identity. In this context the option of an Islamic constitution was viewed as the start of a process of progressive Islamicisation and accordingly details could be worked out in the course of time.[29]

The result was that, while the National Committee for the Constitution, appointed by the parliament, decided that the "Sudanese Constitution should be derived from the principles and spirit of Islam," the draft it presented to parliament[30] "was not particularly Islamic in tone. . . . [A]part from the stipulation of *shari'a* as the primary source of legislation, all references to Islam were rather symbolic and fall short of what could be expected from a constitution based on 'the spirit and guidance of Islam.'"[31] Although the Brotherhood expressed some reservations about specifics, its newspaper called the document "a legal and political weapon in the political struggle of Islam."[32]

This process of gradual Islamization is characteristic of the approach of Turabi when he and his organization were setting their own agenda. Two major events altered this gradualism: Numayri's imposition of Islamic law in September 1983 and the coup led by Umar Hasan al-Bashir in 1989.

The "September Laws" of Numayri Ja'far Numayri's decision in 1983 to institute a comprehensive program of implementing Islamic law in Sudan by presidential decree was a sudden initiative. Although Numayri had been moving in the direction of a more explicitly Islamic policy orientation, the process appeared gradual. His book *Why the Islamic Way?*[33] was a general discussion in the mode of earlier Sudanese political discussions of Islamization. He had also appointed a committee for the examination of laws to make them compatible with the Shariah. The committee began work in 1977 and was headed by Hasan al-Turabi. The committee compiled a number of draft laws, but Numayri "was in no hurry to implement these new bills. Indeed, in the first five years of the committee's work, only the bill regulating the payment of zakat [alms] was approved, probably because it was the least controversial."[34]

This gradual process, which was in line with the approach of the Muslim Brotherhood, was pre-empted with the promulgation of the "September Laws" of 1983. By the summer of 1983, Turabi was no longer attorney general, and he was less directly involved in advising Numayri than previously. The actual proclamations and legal program implemented through the September Laws was the product of a small group of younger lawyers led by Nayal Abu Qurun and Awad al-Jid Ahmad, who had little or no connection with the Muslim Brotherhood. The actual process of drafting the new laws was haphazard and hastily completed by these young lawyers, who were under direct pressure from Numayri to work rapidly.[35] The result was an "Islamization" of laws that did not meet the careful standards of legal scholars like Turabi but that, at the same time, represented a major official acceptance of Islamic law as the law of the land. In this situation, Turabi states that the movement "did not have a free choice between a carefully considered program involving confirmation as it moved toward completion and a sudden program coming unexpectedly from the regime, probably for political reasons."[36] Turabi and most of the Muslim Brotherhood decided to give full support to Numayri's program, assuming that "its deficiencies could be corrected later."[37]

This decision represents a major shift in method and approach for the Brotherhood, whose long-term strategy had been built on the assumption that an Islamic state would be the product of the Islamization of society and the primary effort would be to transform individuals and society. The shift is most clearly seen in criminal law, especially in the distinctive *hudud* punishments of amputation, flogging, and stoning. Turabi and others had long argued that "hudud were applicable only in an ideal Islamic society from which want had been completely banished."[38] However, Numayri's Islamization of law involved the immediate application of the hudud punishments in Sudanese society as it existed in the early 1980s. Retrospectively, Turabi argued that while the movement had accepted the postponement of hudud punishments in the "era of apologetics and defensiveness," the argument had also been used by hypocrites who wanted to block any implementation of Islamic law, and that "the Sharia in its general meaning as a program for life, morality, *hudud*, and judgements is, in reality, the historic *precondition* for the perfection" of society.[39]

The debate following the promulgation of the September Laws involved these issues. No one could argue that the hudud punishments were not prescribed by Islam; it is only possible to debate the conditions in which they are applicable. When Sadiq al-Mahdi challenged the September Laws (and Numayri's regime), an important part of his argument involved whether or not it was appropriate to implement the hudud punishments in Sudan in the 1980s. In his sermon attacking Numayri's policy, Sadiq said, "To cut the hand of a thief in a society based on tyranny and discrimination is like throwing a man into the water, with his hands tied, and saying to him: beware of wetting yourself."[40] Turabi moved away from this position with his support of the Numayri laws.

Turabi's support for Numayri's program of Islamization had both benefits and costs. It provided assistance to a dictatorial regime that was beginning to fail, but it also provided a freedom of operation to the Brotherhood that would not otherwise have been possible. As a part of the opposition movement, the Brotherhood was always a minor partner of the two large sectarian organizations. However, in the context of the last years of the Numayri regime, support for the September Laws provided a way of identifying the Brotherhood clearly with the idea of the Islamization of law in Sudan. The positive dimension of this (from the perspective of the Brotherhood) was that, even after the overthrow of Numayri, his September Laws remained the focus of the debate over the role of Islam in Sudanese society. People opposed to those laws could be charged with opposition to Islamizing Sudanese law. One result of this was that the Brotherhood's political organization, the National Islamic Front (NIF), was able to prevent the formal abrogation of the September Laws in the third parliamentary era, even though Sadiq al-Mahdi, a strong critic of those laws, was prime minister.

In this way, Turabi ended up supporting a process of implementation of Islamic law that involved identification of his movement with an unpopular dictatorship. This experience represented a significant departure from the careful legal scholarly approach and the gradualist Islamization policies that were previously been characteristic of Turabi and the Brotherhood he led. At the same time, from Turabi's perspective, the benefit to be gained was that issues of implementation of Islamic law became more central to Sudanese politics than ever before, and a form of Islamic law, however flawed it might be in scholarly terms, was in place as the law of the land. Rather than having to argue in favor of adopting Shariah, Turabi and the NIF were in the stronger position of defending and working to revise existing laws. In northern Sudanese politics, it is very difficult, as Sadiq al-Mahdi discovered in his period as prime minister (1986–1989), to advocate the revocation of any version of "Islamic law." The NIF used the issue of the Shariah as a means of remaining at the center of the parliamentary political scene, even though this meant that differences over the implementation of Islamic law became a major element in the political instability that plagued the third era of parliamentary politics. The September Laws were not actually repealed until after the end of the third parliamentary era and the government of Umar al-Bashir replaced the Numayri laws in a context where the NIF played a dominant role in defining the legal alternative.

In the Numayri era, Turabi was primarily responding to opportunities presented by changing circumstances. In the 1990s, the situation was significantly different. The military coup of 30 June 1989 brought to power a group of officers willing to follow the advice and guidance of Turabi, and the "Revolution of National Salvation" (RNS) quickly became identified with the NIF. Although there were still practical and policy limitations on the NIF, the 1990s presented an opportunity to an Islamist group to design and implement a full program of social and political reform. The results by the late 1990s were extremely controversial.

The Revolution of National Salvation, after a decade of rule, did not succeed in creating a system that could be utilized as a model by Islamist groups elsewhere in the Muslim world. Despite the fears of policy-makers in the West and leaders of neighboring countries, the NIF was able to provide only minimal support and very little inspiration to movements of Islamic revolution in other countries. In ideological terms, the efforts of the NIF in power were aimed more at the creation of an effective political state system in Sudan than at the reinterpretation of Islamic law. This tendency was further emphasized when Bashir removed Turabi from his official posts in 1999.

This transition in 1989 marked the change from Turabi the challenging activist intellectual to Turabi the ruler involved in maintaining and developing an existing political system. General Muslim renewal and the implementation of the renewed Islamic law were obscured by the demands of the operation of a government that many viewed as oppressive and authoritarian and that was in the midst of a long lasting civil war. In this context, it is important to examine major specific themes in Turabi's thought as they were defined, and redefined, in the changing conditions of the second half of the twentieth century.

Concepts and Programs in Turabi's Thought

Women and Islam

In the early days of the Islamic movement in Sudan, the movement's position with regard to women conformed basically to the traditional view of the status of women. The movement was made up of males and addressed its message primarily to males, under the assumption that "if men were reformed, the whole of society would be reformed" because the women would follow the men.[41] However, following the 1964 revolution and the emergence of Turabi as a major figure in the movement, the Brotherhood began to give more attention to the role of women, both in terms of the broader teachings of Islam and, more specifically, in terms of the movement itself. The basic transformation, in Turabi's account, was that the movement reoriented itself in order to be in accord with the *standards* of religion rather than the existing social norms.[42]

There was a significant effort to reorient the structure and outlook of the movement to give recognition to what Turabi believes is the fundamental equality of men and women in Islam. A critical turning point in the development of this position was the publication in the early 1970s of a small book written by Turabi on "women between the teachings of religion and the customs of society,"[43] which has been described as "the most influential work he ever produced."[44]

In this book, Turabi presents a clearly argued case that starts with a detailed analysis of what women actually did in the early Muslim community during the lifetime of the Prophet and relates that account to the provisions and message of the Quran and the Traditions of the Prophet. The basic position is that "in the religion of Islam, a woman is an independent entity, and thus a fully responsible human being. Islam addresses her directly and does not approach her through the agency of Muslim males."[45] This means that women have the same obligations and rights as men. "The verdict of Islamic jurisprudence is just the practical expression of the dictates of the faith. Women, according to Shariah, are counterparts of men. And in Islamic jurisprudence, there is no separate order of regulations for them. . . . The underlying presumption in the Sharia is that sex is immaterial."[46]

Turabi notes that in the early community, women converted to Islam as individuals, sometimes before the men in their households did, and took an active role in public life, sometimes as warriors in battle, often regularly participating in political affairs. Turabi emphasizes that "public life is no stage where men alone can play. There is no segregation of sexes in public domains which call for joint efforts."[47] These early female paragons of the faith represent appropriate ways of life for all Muslims. This is true also in private life and personal matters, with women having rights to propose and refuse marriage, maintain control over their own property, and not live in isolation from society.

The problem comes from the deviation from the Islamic ideal in the actual history of Muslim societies. After the time of the early community, "women were segregated and isolated, not only from the political process but even from public religion."[48] Turabi places the blame squarely on Muslim males: "Whenever weakness creeps into the faith of Muslim men they tend to treat women oppressively and seek to exploit them. . . . Weak commitment to religion tends to cultivate unjust and hostile treatment of women."[49] This has created a "traditional Muslim Society" in which "the basic religious rights and duties of women have been forsaken and the fundamentals of equity and fairness in the structure of Muslim Society as enshrined in the Sharia have been completely overlooked."[50]

The consequence of this historical development, in Turabi's view, is that a "revolution against the condition of women in the traditional Muslim societies is inevitable" and that it is the task of Islamists to "close the gap between the fallen historical reality and the desired model of ideal Islam."[51] This task is made more complex by the circumstances of the modern world, where modern Western ideals for the role of women constitute "a serious temptation for the downtrodden Muslim women."[52] He advocated that properly Islamic reform be undertaken before the alien trends became fully assimilated, and he opposed simple conservative opposition to Western influences.

> The Islamists should beware of an attitude that seeks refuge from the invading liberating western culture in the indigenous past as a lesser evil that should be preserved with some accommodation. Conservation is a wasted effort. . . . [Islamists] should not leave their society at the mercy of the advocates of westernization who exploit the urgency of reform to deform society. . . . [Islamists should] be the right-guided leaders for the salvation of men and women, emancipating them from the shackles of history and convention.[53]

The result of this new emphasis on the role of women was that the Muslim Brotherhood in Sudan became active in advocating legal and social reforms in general and in the organization itself women came to play an increasingly important part. Women had provided important leadership in the Sudan Communist Party (SCP) already in the 1960s, but by the 1980s, the Brotherhood under Turabi's leadership soon equaled and then surpassed the SCP as the political group receiving support from educated women. One scholar noted that "one of the most striking modernist approaches of the NIF is the open recruitment of women—in Islamic dress only—for political organizing. The Republicans and the SCP are the only other political organizations that have so effectively recruited women."[54] The result is that "women are the nexus of the NIF in a number of ways. They are among the most active and *visible* organizers" and "the only two women elected to the People's Assembly during the 1985–1989 'democratic' era were NIF candidates."[55]

Turabi's assessment in 1992 was that

> in the Islamic movement, I would say that women have played a more important role of late than men. They came with a vengeance because they had been deprived, and so when we allowed them in

the movement, more women voted for us than men because we were the ones who gave them more recognition and a message and place in society. They were definitely more active in our election campaigns than men. Most of our social work and charitable work was done by women. They are now even in the popular defense forces, and nobody raises questions about that. . . . Of course, I don't claim that women have achieved parity . . . but there is no bar to women anywhere, and there is no complex about women being present anywhere.[56]

While many would disagree with the optimistic tone of this assessment, it is clear that the impetus given by Turabi's ideas about women in Islam has had an important influence on political life in Sudan. His book and the experience of the movement under his leadership have also had a significant intellectual impact in the broader Muslim world.

Concepts of the "Islamic State"

There is a direct relationship between Turabi's activities as a political leader in Sudan and the specifics of his evolving definition of an Islamic state. Turabi, like others engaged in efforts to establish an Islamic state, faced the tension between two different approaches. One advocated formal programs of Islamization of laws and society to be initiated and directed by the state itself, while the other saw an Islamic state as the final product of the Islamization of society.

In terms of theory and principle, Turabi was relatively consistent over the years on this issue. His basic position was:

An Islamic state cannot be isolated from society, because Islam is a comprehensive, integrated way of life. The division between private and public, the state and society, which is familiar in Western culture, has not been known in Islam. The state is only the political expression of an Islamic society. You cannot have an Islamic state except insofar as you have an Islamic society. Any attempt at establishing a political order for the establishment of a genuine Islamic society would be the superimposition of laws over a reluctant society.[57]

While this approach provides a theoretically consistent perspective, it may also reflect a mistrust of authoritarian rulers by leaders of movements that are most commonly in opposition. A tension is created when Islamists are presented with the possibility of participating in or controlling governments. Policies of state involvement in or enforcement of Islamization of society, when those policies can be shaped by the Islamists themselves, provide opportunities for the second approach, which involves the establishment of an officially Islamic state before the underlying society itself is fully Islamized. This choice is an important aspect of the debate among Islamists themselves. Some, like Sayyid Qutb in Egypt, argue that existing states (and societies) are irredeemably unbelieving and opposition is obligatory. Others, like the mainstream Muslim Brotherhood in Egypt, argue that participation in political processes can be part of the gradual Islamization of both state and society.

In Sudan, the various organizations that were created by Islamists in the second half of the twentieth century were generally directly involved in the political processes. In every era of parliamentary politics, there was at least one Islamist-style political organization that participated. In many ways, the legal status of such groups was the same as the political parties organized by the major traditional Muslim associations. The Sudanese context was one in which the Islamist groups were not the only Islamically identified political associations and this provided a situation in which working "within the system" was facilitated. It also meant that the issue of whether or not there should be an "Islamic state" was less controversial in northern Sudanese politics than the question of what the nature of such a state would be in Sudan.

Turabi's writings on the nature of an Islamic state reflect the pragmatic opportunities presented by changing political conditions in Sudan. During parliamentary eras, the general approach involved participation in politics and, at the same time, emphasizing the need to Islamize society before the achievement of an Islamic state. However, during periods of authoritarian rule by the military, when the military rulers worked to implement state-imposed Islamization (as happened in the early 1980s under Ja'far Numayri and following the military coup of 1989), these rulers received the active support of Turabi and the Islamist movement.

By the time of the second era of parliamentary politics (1964–1969), a broad consensus emerged among most of the northern Sudanese political parties (with the Communist Party being the major exception) that the Sudanese state and legal system should in some way be Islamically identified. The main lines of this consensus in the late 1960s were presented in the report of a National Committee for the Islamic Constitution, written by a group representing the major northern parties.[58] This position reflects the views of the Muslim Brotherhood at the time, as articulated by Turabi. There is an affirmation that there is no need for "imported positive laws" since Islamic law has long provided the basis for the realization of justice and the foundations for an effective state system.[59] However, the Islamic state defined by the consensus is a modern state, not a traditionally conceived Islamic state. There is no mention, for example, of the historical concept of the "caliphate" in the entire 1967 memorandum. Instead, the committee wrote: "When we call for the establishment of the Islamic constitution and the realization of the principles of the Shari'ah, we are simply calling for the establishment of a modern state with all that is understood by these words. Democracy in all of its forms, political, economic, and social, is known to have been guaranteed by Islam long before it was shaped by the modern state."[60] The committee outlines the basic characteristics of the Islamic state and society, noting the more general requirements of justice and democratic participation, as well as more specifically Islamic requirements involving the economy (prohibitions on interest, monopoly, and gambling) and social life ("combating alcoholic drink and immorality").

The committee also reflected the general consensus of the time that the implementation of an Islamic state and legal system would be gradual. "For the application of any Islamic principle, it is necessary to pave the way for it by creating conditions so that there is no general hardship imposed upon the society of Muslims." Specifically, it is necessary to establish first the general principles and conditions and only then implement punishments defined in the Quran and Sunnah.[61]

The Islamic Constitution, in this consensus, provided for an affirmation of Islamic principles of justice and equity in the format of a modern democratic republic. In this perspective,

the system of rule in Islam stands on the foundation that the state is the land, the people, and the government, just as is the case in its modern form. However, Islam sets up moral foundations and it is required that the state operate within this framework. This leaves open the freedom to build structures in accord with these general foundations, while leaving open the details and secondary matters.[62]

The committee also recognized the importance, in determining the specific laws and institutions, of independent judgment and analysis (ijtihad) rather than simply following past precedents (taqlid).[63]

The second parliamentary era was brought to an end by the military coup lead by Ja'far Numayri in May 1969. The initial ideology and political vision of the new regime was articulated primarily in terms of the radical Third World socialism of the day, and Turabi joined the other political leaders in underground opposition. The situation of non-Muslim southern Sudanese organizations was changed dramatically in 1972 when an agreement between the government and southern opposition brought an end to the civil war that had begun in southern Sudan in 1955 against control by the northern-dominated governments in Khartoum. The result was that by the mid-1970s, the major opposition to Numayri was the old Islamically identified political groups led by Sadiq al-Mahdi, Muhammad Uthman al-Mirghani, and Hasan al-Turabi.

The general northern Sudanese sentiment favoring some Islamic identification for the state, which had been articulated in the consensus regarding an Islamic constitution, remained an important dimension of northern Sudanese politics. This was recognized even in the Permanent Constitution promulgated by Numayri in 1973.[64] Although this constitution was primarily a document reflecting the later "Arab Socialist" perspectives, it gave special attention to religions, noting that "[i]n the Democratic Republic of the Sudan Islam is the religion and the society shall be guided by Islam being the religion of the majority of its people and the State shall endeavour to express its values" (article 16.a). However, special recognition was also given to Christianity as "being professed by a large number of its [the Republic's] citizens" (article 16.b) and, more broadly, "[h]eavenly religions and the noble aspects of spiritual beliefs shall not be insulted or held in contempt" (article 16.c).

Turabi and the other Islamically identified political leaders in opposition did not accept this as an appropriate constitutional recognition of Islam. This was not, however, the primary focus of their anti-Numayri position, which was the call for restoration of civilian parliamentary democracy. During the 1970s, a number of unsuccessful attempts were organized by the old political parties to overthrow Numayri, and by 1978 many were ready to consider seriously Numayri's call for National Reconciliation.

Turabi was the most prominent figure to accept the reconciliation invitation, and he soon became active in the government, as attorney general and in other posts. In this, Turabi illustrated in practice his expressed views about implementing Islamic law gradually within an existing system of state and society. He was head of a committee for the Islamization of laws, which systematically examined the existing legal codes to check for conformity with Islamic law and recommended appropriate amendments or new laws. At the popular level, the Muslim Brotherhood that he led remained formally illegal but had a relatively wide range of freedom to act within the framework of the National Reconciliation policies. The Brotherhood's organizational transition to the National Islamic Front (NIF) involved becoming more active as a public educational and social welfare organization. By the early 1980s, the Brotherhood/NIF had become an increasingly visible political influence group, despite the fact that it remained illegal.

Turabi's position regarding the nature of the state and its role in the Islamization of society was transformed by dramatic changes in the political context during the early 1980s. The promulgation of the controversial September Laws by Numayri in 1983 changed the terms of the debate about an Islamic state in Sudan. Numayri's Islamization program was unsystematic and was not related to the legal review process he had initiated in the late 1970s.

The new "Islamized" political system was defined by a series of hastily produced proclamations that were relatively eclectic collections of materials drawn from standard classical sources (e.g., Ibn Taymiyyah on rules of evidence) and some modern formulations (e.g., the modern Jordanian commercial code).[65] As a result, the terms of debate shifted to whether or not the September Laws represented an "Islamic political system." Most of the northern political opposition leaders took the position that the new laws did not represent an authentic Islamization. The leading spokesperson for this position was Sadiq al-Mahdi. Turabi and the NIF argued that although the specifics of the September Laws were inadequate and inaccurate as a representation of the Shariah, the September Laws represented an official recognition of the necessary Islamic nature of the state. As such, they should be accepted and then amended as the opportunity presented itself. This resulted in a shift toward a state-guided program of Islamization as the basis of Turabi's view of the relationship between the state and Islam.

Following the overthrow of Numayri in 1985 and the initiation of the third era of parliamentary politics (1985–1989), the National Islamic Front under Turabi's leadership emerged as the third largest political party. In the 1986 elections, the NIF won about one-quarter of the votes, the best showing for a nontraditional party in any of the Sudanese elections since independence.

In the third period of party politics, the NIF program was explicitly aimed at preserving the recognition given to Islam in the public sector in the last years of Numayri. Although implementation of the September Laws was suspended, the NIF succeeded in preventing their abrogation without a formally Islamic system being adopted to replace them. In the terms of its organizational constitution, "[t]he Front aims at the sovereignty of Islam in faith and law" within the context of the transformation of society.[66] There was only limited development of the conceptualization of an Islamic state in the context of this high level of direct political involvement in the politics and policies of the time.

In the years since the establishment of the NIF government in 1989 significant efforts have been made to define the NIF ideal of the state. For a decade there was a transition from a simple military command council to the promulgation of a constitution in 1998 and the first steps toward its implementation in 1999. In this it is important to distinguish between the ideal and the actual experience.

From the very beginning of NIF governance, the government faced significant opposition both from those who continued the civil war, especially under the leadership of John Garang and the various groups involved in the Sudan People's Liberation Army (SPLA), and from those northern Muslim political groups like the Ummah Party and the DUP who had been overthrown by the 1989 coup. In dealing with opposition, the early military regime maintained control through means of violent suppression of opposition, and only limited disagreements with policy were expressed or allowed. Well-documented accusations of torture of even political opponents who were not in the militant opposition emphasized the autocratic nature of the political system.

In the following years, although various elections were held, it was clear that there were very narrow limits imposed on expression of views in opposition to those of the NIF or the government of Umar Hasan Bashir, the leader of the original coup. The government continued to be willing to take strong measures to suppress its opponents. In this context, the promulgation of a constitution in 1998 that guaranteed the right of citizens to form political associations (part 2, 26) provided the basis for the development of a multiparty political system. The actual implementation of that feature of the new system was still unsure in early 1999.

The issues of freedom of political expression are related to the whole problem of bringing an end to the civil war, but these represent two different areas of policy and political activity. In the decade following the 1989 coup there was a significant evolution of the formal political structure that was separate from the series of negotiations aimed at bringing an end to the war. It is in the constitutional developments that the NIF's (and primarily Turabi's) concepts of a legitimate state can be seen.

The Constitution of 1998 provides a summation of most of these basic ideas. It is a presidential system, which was gradually defined through a process of the dissolution of the original Revolutionary Command Council (RCC) and its replacement by a primarily NIF civilian regime, which was closely coordinated with the Islamist military leadership of Umar Hasan al-Bashir. Bashir himself began as the commander of the coup and the head of the RCC, and his role was transformed into that of the elected president. The RCC dissolved itself in 1993 in a process that named Bashir as president with a council of ministers and created an appointed Transitional National Assembly (TNA). Between 1992 and 1996 a series of "base level committees" and local and regional congresses were established by a mixed process of election and appointment, leading to national elections in 1996 for a national assembly and the president. The elections were controversial, and virtually no one from any visible opposition group participated. Bashir was elected president, and in the new National Assembly, Turabi was elected the Speaker. This was the first formal office in the government Turabi had held since the 1989 coup.

From the very outset, the new regime had advocated a federal system in which local and provincial institutions would have some special recognition and power. While this was in the context of considering special autonomy in some form for southern Sudan, in the view of Bashir and the NIF, the political system for the whole country should in some meaningful ways be federal in structure. Although strong control continued to be exercised by the central government, state governments were established, and in 1994 the number of states was increased from nine to twenty-six.

In many of these transitions there is little that is explicitly Islamic. However, the emerging system, as defined by the 1998 Constitution, provides an important indication of Turabi's conceptualization of an actual state system built within the framework of his understanding of Islam.

The preamble of this Constitution emphasizes at the very outset Turabi's distinctive definition of continuing renewal (tajdid) that must take note of historical conditions and be continuing adjusting: "In the Name of God. . . . We the people of the Sudan, By the assistance of God, Considering the lessons of history, And by the thrust of the ever evolving National salvation Revolution, Promulgated for ourselves this Constitution."[67] The same conceptual flexibility is in the articles defining amendment procedures. The Constitution can be amended by a two-thirds vote of the National Assembly, with the exception that those parts of the Constitution that represent the "basic provisions and fundamentals" can only be amended by receiving both the two-thirds vote of the assembly and being passed by the people in a referendum (part 9, 139–3). This means that even the fundamental provision that "Islamic law and the legislative consensus of the people by referendum, the Constitution or custom are the prevalent sources of law" is subject to possible amendment.

In general terms, the Constitution tends to define a state of Muslims rather than an Islamic state, although there are distinctively Islamic provisions. The first provision defines the state in relatively inclusive terms: "The State of Sudan is an embracing homeland, wherein races and cultures coalesce and religions conciliate. Islam is the religion of the majority of the population. Christianity and customary creeds have considerable followers" (part 1, 1). There is the old assumption seen in Turabi's early definitions, that a society of properly practicing Muslims will have an Islamic state and that the state is only one part of society rather than being the dominant institution.

The problems arise, of course, in practice and the degree to which the Muslim majority should be able to impose distinctively Islamic provisions on non-Muslims. It is in this context that Turabi emphasizes the importance of the federal system, and the official policy of NIF in the 1990s reflected the principles presented in the NIF charter in 1987. The charter says:

> The effectiveness of some laws shall be subject to territorial limitations, considering the prevalence of certain religions or cultures in the areas at variance with the religion dominant in the country at large. . . . In these matters exclusive local rules can be established in the area based on the local majority mandate. . . . Thus the legislative authority of any region predominantly inhabited by non-Muslims can take exception to the general operation of the national law, with respect to any rule of a criminal or penal nature derived directly and solely from a text in the Sharia contrary to the local culture.[68]

This means that the Shariah-defined punishments for stealing, for example, would not necessarily be enforced in the southern provinces, although they would in the northern. The imposition of these punishments on non-Muslims was a source of strong criticism of the regime during the 1990s.

The distinctively Islamic provisions of the Constitution provide an important guide to Turabi's priorities in defining an Islamic state. There is a specific reference to prevention of usury (part 1, 8), state control of the levying of zakat, the charitable alms payments that are a requirement for Muslims (part 1,10), and the instruction that the state "shall endeavour by law and directive policies to purge society from . . . liquor among Muslims," as well as a number of other more general obligations dealing with "morals and unity of the society" (part 1, 16). All of this is summed up in the more general injunction to faith in government that echoes the articulation of political goals by Turabi in many places:

> Those in service in the State and public life shall envisage the dedication thereof for the worship of God, wherein Muslims stick to the scripture and tradition, and all shall maintain religious motivation and give due regard to such spirit in plans, laws, policies and official business in the political, economic, social and cultural fields in order to prompt public life towards its objectives, and adjust them towards justice and up-rightness to be directed towards the grace of God in The Hereafter. (part 1, 18)

This is a constitutional expression of Turabi's and the NIF's rejection of secularism. The 1987 NIF charter noted explicitly that "Muslims . . . do not espouse secularism. Neither do they accept it politically" and that they "have a legitimate right . . . to practice the values and rules of their religion to their full range—in personal, familial, social or political affairs" (part 1-C).

The Constitution presents a number of basic Islamic political contexts in the definition of this political system. There are regular references to the importance of "consultation," in the description of the system as a whole (part 1, 2), in the duties of citizens (part 2, 2), and in the prescribed oaths of all public officials. There is also emphasis on the importance of "consensus" in the operation of the political system. "The consensus of the nation by referendum" is listed, along with Islamic law, Constitution, and custom as one of the "sources of legislation"(part 4, 1, 65).

The Constitution also reflects a conceptual transformation in line with Turabi's renewalist ideas. This is the definition of the "caliphate" in democratic terms, as a way of reconciling issues of popular and divine sovereignty. The Constitution says: "Supremacy in the State is to God the creator of human beings, and sovereignty is to the vicegerent people of the Sudan who practice it as worship of God, bearing the trust, building up the country and spreading justice, freedom and public consultation" (part 1, 4). In this the people become the "caliph" in a conceptualization of the caliphate that goes far beyond that of the medieval theorists.

The situation created by the 1989 coup created the conditions within which Turabi was able to define an operational Islamic state within the framework of his own conceptualizations of renewal. The Constitution of 1998 is an important milestone in the evolution of his thinking. It contains many themes that have long been present in his writings. However, the multiparty federal system defined by the Constitution is also a new phase, both in the political development of Sudan and in Turabi's thought. As a political document, it has not had as much impact within the Muslim world as Turabi's earlier writings. This is partly because it is specifically devised for Sudan in the 1990s. However, because of the visible policies of suppression of opposition and the continuing civil war, it is also true that Turabi's global impact has been reduced because of the actual record of the state he has guided.

Turabi and Sudanese National Unity

The major problem facing the NIF government in the 1990s was the continuing civil war, primarily in southern Sudan. This issue had been a part of Turabi's political life from the very first. It was his speech in 1964 opposing government policy in the south that gave him his first national political visibility, and it was a major obstacle for the success of the state that he tried to construct in the 1990s.

The development of the conflict parallels the development of both Turabi's ideas about the nature of Muslim society in Sudan and his role in Sudanese affairs. The conflict continually raised the issue of the nature of the Sudanese state and the degree to which Sudan, which has a significant non-Muslim population, can define itself as a Muslim society. The conflict began in the mid-1950s as a revolt by southern non-Muslims against the domination of their region in the newly independent Sudan by "Arab Muslims" from the north. The first parliamentary government (1956–1958) and the first military regime (1958–1964) were unable to reduce southern mistrust and attempted a military solution. Following the reestablishment of civilian parliamentary rule in 1964, northern political leaders attempted to affirm Sudanese national unity in a way that emphasized the Arabic language and Islam. The result was that the war continued, despite many different attempts at negotiation. The affirmations of the importance of an Islamic constitution in which Turabi played a major role at the time helped to confirm in the minds of southern leaders that continuing conflict was inevitable.

The role of the south in Sudan was a difficult issue for Turabi and the Brotherhood. Initially, for members of the Brotherhood, "the south was perceived as a distant, vaguely symbolic place. Like the rest of the educated [in the north], Ikhwan only saw in the south the alienated, lost brother, who had to be retrieved through the spread of Islam, the Arabic language and better communications."[69] In Turabi's words, "the movement, despite its being a manifestation of renewal, was shackled by the limits of its traditional northern Sudanese society."[70] At first, Turabi and others opposed the idea of giving special recognition or autonomy to the southern region. However, when the second military regime, that of Numayri, succeeded in negotiating the Addis Ababa agreement in 1972, the key element in the agreement was recognition of southern autonomy. In that context, the political opponents of Numayri opposed both the agreement and the principle of southern autonomy.

In opposition during the 1970s, the members of the Brotherhood debated what their "southern policy" should be, and two points of view emerged.

> In 1975–76, extensive discussions were held among the Ikhwan in Nimeiri's jails, where most of them were at the time, on future relations with the south. One point of view that emerged called for the separation of the south, since its demands appeared to have become the major obstacle to setting up an Islamic order in Sudan. The opposing view, which won in the end, advocated tackling the problem head-on. If the Sudanese Islamic state were to become a bastion for Islam in Africa, it had to accept the challenge of accommodating a non-Muslim minority.[71]

In Turabi's words, the movement decided to work for the "realization in Sudan of the Islamic project which would bear witness to the humaneness of Islam."[72] Turabi played a major role in the following years in defining the Islamist solution to the issue of the south in Sudan, and increasingly it involved the articulation of some kind of a federalist solution that could provide a special recognition for southern autonomy. The 1998 Constitution provided a summation of that long line of policy development.

The peace that had been achieved by the Addis Ababa agreement of 1972 was broken in the early 1980s as Numayri's arbitrary interference in southern politics violated the prescribed autonomy of the region. Informal opposition groups were brought together early in 1983 in the SPLA under the leadership of John Garang. Garang emphasized that the Sudan Peoples' Liberation Movement (SPLM), the political organization of the SPLA, was not a separatist movement but rather was the instrument of the "protracted revolutionary armed struggle" that was necessary to create "a united Sudan under a socialist system that affords democratic and human rights to all nationalities and guarantees freedom to all religions, beliefs and outlooks."[73] In practice, this resulted in the formulation of a program for the creation of a secularist political system in Sudan. Although the SPLA arose in opposition to Numayri, it continued during the third era of civilian politics. Although Garang engaged in negotiations with Sadiq al-Mahdi's government, his view was that "the government of Sadiq el Mahdi was a sectarian dictatorship" that was far from the "United New Sudan" sought by the SPLA.[74] Savage fighting continued between the SPLA and government forces throughout the third era of civilian government.

These experiences provided the foundation for the development of the NIF approach to national unity during the 1990s. The starting point was the creation of a federal system in which southern autonomy would receive recognition. In a long series of discussions and negotiations, the real differences between the NIF and SPLA positions, reflecting the differing views of Turabi and Garang, came to be most clearly expressed in the sharp contrast between Garang's emphasis on the absolute necessity of establishing a secular state and Turabi's insistence on an Islamic state in which special arrangements could be made for non-Muslim regions.

The clash of views that took place in negotiations in the Abuja II talks in Nigeria in 1993, with the head of Nigeria serving as mediator, shows the impasse.

> The mediator had decided to tackle head-on the issue of religion and state. If that issue could be resolved, then other issues would fall into place; if not, then no accord was possible. That approach lead to fierce debates, in which government delegates accused the SPLM of seeking to abolish religion, and declared that abolishing shari'a and hudud as the law of the land would lead to a Muslim uprising. The SPLM, in turn, rejected religious apartheid and stated starkly that the south could be part of an Islamic state only if it were defeated militarily.[75]

The impasse was further complicated by the development of the military situation in which it became clear that neither side was actually capable of military victory, despite public relations pronouncements by both sides on a regular basis.

The NIF government undertook a major initiative that reflected changing realities and also represented a further development of NIF's vision of an Islamic state in Sudan. A division within the SPLM provided the opportunity for this change of policy. In 1991 a group of high-ranking officers in the SPLA broke with Garang, creating the SPLM/A-United (originally informally called the "Nasir group"). Under the leadership of Lam Akol, Riek Machar, and Gordon Kong Chuol, the group advocated independence for the south. They argued in their manifesto that the differences between the two regions were so great that "Sudan will be condemned to perpetual war unless some drastic action is taken fairly soon. It is evident that the only feasible course of action to bring peace is for all to accept the fact that the North and the South need . . . a period of time of separate existence."[76] This represented a revival of an older theme of southern separatism that had been a part of southern opposition from the very beginning of the conflict in the 1950s. Garang's SPLA and the new group soon began their own destructive war within the broader war.

This division provided an opportunity for the NIF government, which began negotiations with the anti-Garang groups. In April 1996, Machar and others signed a political charter that additional groups accepted during the following year. The result was the signing of a peace agreement in April 1997 by the Sudan government and seven southern opposition groups, with Garang being virtually the only nonsigner. The agreement created a coordinating council for southern political affairs and accepted the principle of multiparty politics. In a major break with policies of previous governments in Khartoum, the peace agreement also affirmed "the right of the people of Southern Sudan to determine their political aspirations and to pursue their economic, social, and cultural development" and that this right would be exercised in a referendum that would allow secession as a choice.[77] The provisions of this agreement were included in the text of the 1998 Constitution as further confirmation of the peace agreement.

Garang and the northern opposition groups rejected the peace agreement, and fighting continued in the south, but the structures defined by the agreement were created, and steps were taken toward greater southern participation in the NIF political system. In addition, movement toward the referendum also was made. Although Garang continued to oppose southern separatism, the government and the SPLA both agreed, in negotiations in Nairobi in May 1998, to accept an internationally supervised self-determination referendum in the south as a part of the continuing conflict.

These developments represent a clear change in the position of Turabi and the NIF, reflecting the gradual recognition of the high costs of the civil war in terms of the ability of the NIF's Islamic state to succeed. In the early 1990s, Turabi still viewed the NIF mission as being to provide a "national" solution to the problem of Sudanese civil conflict. At that time he wrote: "Although the movement had laid out the frameworks responding to the challenges of the immediate political context and the civilizational future, much still remained for it to do in perfecting its regional model and its national authority in order for it to be a national and global example."[78] The vision of a model Islamic society with a significant non-Muslim population came to include allowing the non-Muslims to opt out of that society. The 1996 and 1997 agreements defined this option, which was confirmed by a series of statements by Sudanese leaders. President Bashir, in February 1999, noted that "his government would continue to try to preserve the unity of the mainly Muslim north and the Christian and animist south but that secession was better than war."[79]

These developments after a decade of NIF rule made the priorities of Turabi, Bashir, and the NIF clear. If a choice has to be made between continuing the Islamic experiment and maintaining Sudanese national unity, the NIF would opt for its Islamic rather than its Sudanese national mission. These priorities continued to appear as the government's priorities following Bashir's removal of Turabi from his posts in 1999.

Conclusion

Hasan Turabi has throughout his life been a person of ideas, an intellectual. He has also been, since the completion of his graduate studies in 1964, an active and visible political leader in Sudan. In many ways, he is the prototype, almost the stereotype, of the Muslim activist intellectual. The major significant difference between him and most other Muslim activist intellectuals is that he had a decade in which he had the political power to put his ideas into practice.

His ideas have had an impact on Muslims throughout the world. His writings are widely read. As a political leader, however, his impact has been primarily local. Few people in the Muslim world look to the Sudanese experience since 1989 as a model for how an Islamic state should be. The continuing civil war has made it difficult to judge the effectiveness of the political system created by Turabi, and his removal from official posts in 1999 reduced his direct role in the evolving political system. However, whatever the results of the NIF experience, it is clear that the role of the Muslim activist intellectual has been great in Sudan.

7
ABDOLKARIM SOROUSH
AND CRITICAL
DISCOURSE IN IRAN

Valla Vakili

Abdolkarim Soroush emerged in the late 1980s and early 1990s as the foremost Iranian intellectual operating within the terms of religious discourse.[1] From an initial articulation of a flexible, interpretive understanding of religious texts, Soroush moved on to overt political commentaries on the role of religion in state administration. His writings and speeches alike combine a deep knowledge of Islam with a subtle mastery of Persian poetry, creating an individual style that has appealed strongly to many religiously inclined Iranian university students[2] His training in philosophy of science during the late 1970s in England lends his style an analytical bent that distinguishes him among his university audiences. While these students form Soroush's core following, his critics range across the political spectrum. Soroush's arguments have garnered substantial opposition from the Iranian clergy and from more militant-minded Islamic student groups[3] Unlike secular critics of Iranian politics, Soroush speaks the dominant religious language of political discourse in Iran. His ability to move fluently and innovatively within a domain traditionally dominated by an exclusivist clerical establishment has rendered him a more dangerous critic than many of his contemporaries. Compounding this effect are his revolutionary credentials. Associated both with Ali Shariati and, at a deeper level, Murteza Mutaharri—two architects of the Iranian Revolution's Islamic ideology—Soroush boasts a powerful rhetorical, revolutionary lineage. His appointment by Ayatollah Khomeini to the Advisory Council of the Cultural Revolution in the early years of the Revolution grants him an additional domestic legitimacy.[4] For many years following the advancement of his best known work, "The Theoretical Expansion and Contraction of the Sharia," Soroush dominated the Iranian intellectual and critical scene. He occupied a position disproportionately larger than his contemporaries, dramatized by the wide audience for his lectures and tapes as well as his substantial readership.

In recent years—particularly since the 1997 election of President Mohammad Khatami in Iran—Soroush's position within the critical field has changed. The election dramatically rewrote the boundaries of public political debate in Iran, ushering in a host of powerful, critical concepts: for example, pluralism, democracy, popular will, rule of law, and civil society. President Khatami's vigorous advancement of many of these terms granted them a legitimacy in public discourse on which reformist forces quickly drew. A number of newly inaugurated newspapers and periodicals helped spread this new discourse, positioning it in opposition to a ruling dogma identified as monopolist, authoritarian, antidemocratic, arbitrary, and violent. Soroush's role within this new discursive space proves quite different from his previous position within tighter borders of critical discourse.

Prior to the 1997 election the boundaries of critical discourse, although flexible and at times more open than others, were nevertheless a fraction of what they are now. Soroush proved more capable than other critics at negotiating the ambiguities, uncertainties, and restrictions of this space. His thorough knowledge of the terms of religious discourse, dominance over the language of poetic subtlety, and sensitivity to linguistic equivocation created an individual flair for criticism within restricted space unmatched by his contemporaries. Soroush could speak the unspeakable without ever actually saying it. In the new discursive space marked by President Khatami's ascension, the formerly unspeakable is suddenly common currency. The result is a new style of critique, in which explicitness, directness, and daring have replaced equivocation and subtlety. Whereas the previous limits on critical speech demanded considerable rhetorical talents for critics to distinguish themselves, the new freedom grants individuals distinction through their adoption of the new terms of discourse. Today, state critics increasingly speak the same language—of human rights, civil society, law—and Soroush is no exception. Concepts, not individuals, increasingly dominate, and hence the question of Soroush's future as a foremost critic remains an open one.

I begin here with a review of Soroush's biography, and then I will discuss the development of his political critiques during the pre-Khatami period of less stable, more restricted boundaries of public discourse. These arguments, which earned Soroush his considerable domestic and foreign audience, cover four main areas: the relationship between religion and the study of religion; the role of religion in politics; the Iranian clerical establishment; and relations between Iran and the West. Soroush argues for key reform in these fields. On the basis of the conviction that no understanding of Islam is ever complete or final, he dismisses any attempts to formulate an official Islamic political ideology. He rejects outright the possibility of administering a modern state by religious methods and calls instead for the establishment of a democratic state in Iran. He upholds the dissociation of the clerical establishment from organized political activity and proposes fundamental reforms for the clergy. And he strongly supports the need for continuous and open cultural dialogue between Iran and Western countries. After detailing these arguments, I close with an assessment of the impact of Khatami-era changes on the elaboration of Soroush's thought, and his role within the critical Iranian intellectual scene.

Biography

Soroush is the pen name of Hossein Dabbagh, who was born in Tehran in 1945.[5] Soroush studied at the Alavi secondary school in Tehran, an institution that eventually would graduate several future members of the Islamic Republic's elite. The Alavi school's combination of religious and scientific studies prefigured a trend that would preoccupy Soroush throughout his later studies and writings. He took his first university degree, in pharmacology, in Tehran; and after a two-year period of practical work in this field, he left Iran to continue his studies in England (mid- to late 1970s). He began his graduate studies in London in analytical chemistry (M.Sc., University of London), followed by several years of research in the philosophy of science (Chelsea College, London). Throughout his secondary and higher education, Soroush paralleled his official studies with a deep interest in Persian poetry and with Quranic exegesis. Political events in Iran, particularly the rise of religious activists such as Mutahhari, Bazargan, and Ali Shariati, also influenced him. In particular, Soroush was attracted by these activists' attempts to produce political interpretations of religious texts—an attraction that signaled a later return to the very question of textual interpretation. In terms of his own activism, Soroush emerged in London as a powerful religious critic of Iranian leftist and Marxist discourse. His criticisms of what he saw as dogmatic tendencies in Iranian leftist thought and practice established his initial reputation, both in England and in Iran.[6]

Soroush returned to Iran shortly after the Revolution, and he took up the directorship of the Islamic Culture Group within the Tehran Teacher's Training College. He later participated as a high-ranking member—appointed directly by Ayatollah Khomeini—of the Advisory Council of the Cultural Revolution in Tehran. This particular period of his life marks substantial controversy, owing to the Cultural Revolution's role in the closure of Iran's universities and the restriction of free speech and academic inquiry. Soroush's response to this controversy is that his tenure began after the universities had already been closed, and that the Advisory Council in fact was charged with the reopening, rather than the continued restriction, of Iran's universities. After four years on the Council, Soroush resigned, owing to differences of vision which have yet to receive proper public expression. Consequently, in popular discourse at least, Soroush's involvement with the Cultural Revolution is likely to remain a contested subject for some time.

Soroush's anti-Marxist writings earned him a privileged position as what is often referred to as the Islamic Republic's "premiere ideologue." In time this would pass, drastically so, as any privileges Soroush enjoyed were replaced by restrictions on research and expression. Following his involvement in the Advisory Council, Soroush held research and teaching positions at Tehran University and the Tehran-based Research Institute for Human Sciences. In the late 1980s and early 1990s he began a series of investigations into the process of change in the interpretation of religious texts, which sparked continuous controversy, leading to the closure of the journal in which the investigations first appeared. In 1991 the monthly journal *Kiyan* was formed and has since then acted as the primary outlet for Soroush's critiques. His writings have earned him a mixed audience within the Islamic Republic's elite, where he is both admired and attacked. These attacks stem from Soroush's detailed critiques of the impossibility of any final interpretation of Islam and his forthright criticisms of the Iranian clergy. Soroush, in turn, has been banned from teaching, writing, traveling, and public speaking, and at any given moment one or more of these restrictions may be in place. Finally, Soroush's denial of any practical role for religion in politics has found him a substantial opposition in certain activist student religious groups. This opposition, as well as other critiques, are covered in further detail hereafter.

The Interpretation of Religious Texts

Soroush's argument begins as part of a larger project of Islamic revivalism in the modern Muslim world.[7] Contemporary Muslim thinkers often argue that Islam must be "reconstructed" or "revived" in order to meet the needs of modern Muslims and society. Soroush differs. He accepts the need to reconcile changes in the modern world with the immutability of religion, yet he does not propose the reconstruction or revival of Islam. For Soroush Islam is unchanging, and any attempt to reconstruct Islam is both futile and illusory. Religion need not be changed, but rather the human understanding of it.[8] In this distinction lies the key to reconciling a fixed religion with a dynamic world. To meet the challenges of modernity Muslims should seek not to change their religion but rather to reconcile their understanding of religion with changes in the outside world.[9] This requires a conception of religion that accepts the inevitability of change in the human understanding of religion. Soroush advances such a position, on the basis of an analysis of the development and growth of religious knowledge (*marifat-i dini*).

While religion itself does not change, human understanding and knowledge of it does. Religious knowledge is but one among many branches of human knowledge. It is not divine by virtue of its divine subject matter, and it should not be confused with religion itself.[10] Religious knowledge is the product of scholars engaged in the study of the unchanging core of Shii Islamic texts—the Quran, the hadith, and the teachings of the Shii imams.[11] These scholars interpret the texts differently, depending on their methodology, which may range, for example, from the rules of Arabic grammar to inferential logic, from Aristotelian philosophy to contemporary hermeneutics. Religious knowledge changes then as a function of these methods. But it is also influenced heavily by the worldview that informs each particular scholar's work.[12] In addition to the use of particular methods for the study of religion, a scholar of religion also possesses a distinct understanding of the world, nature, and a muslim's place in both. This is determined not only by his study of religion but also by his understanding of advances in the natural and social sciences.[13] A medieval scholar's worldview, for example, dramatically differs from that of a modern one, resulting in different interpretations of religion and leading to different bodies of religious knowledge.

Religious knowledge changes and evolves over time, as more comprehensive understandings replace previous, more limited interpretations. Yet all interpretations are bound by the era in which a religious scholar lives and by the degree of advancement of the human sciences in general and religious studies in specific within this era. Moreover, it is impossible to study the Quran without certain presuppositions derived from outside the Quran. These presuppositions, determined by a scholar's intellectual worldview (understanding of the other human sciences), ensure that any understanding of religion is time-bound;[14] for religious knowledge is created by the application of the "knowledge of the day" to the study of the core religious texts.[15] Religion on the other hand, is eternal, and the relativity of religious knowledge does not entail the relativity of religion itself.

Nor does the relativity of religious knowledge eliminate the possibility of discerning between "correct" or "incorrect" interpretations of religion.[16] The responsibility for distinguishing between these interpretations falls on the scholarly community. The central issue here is one of methodology.[17] Like scientists, scholars of religion possess a methodology that is both distinct to their field of study and publicly accepted. Soroush holds that knowledge is public—as the creation of new knowledge is always in reference to the overall body of public human knowledge—and so the criteria for judging correct from incorrect knowledge must be public as well.[18] Soroush does not articulate these criteria, for he is not concerned with distinguishing better from worse interpretations but rather with uncovering the means by which religious knowledge (of any quality) is formed and develops.[19]

Explicit within the argument is the total reconcilability between religious and scientific knowledge.[20] There is an intimate connection—a "continuous dialogue"—between religious and nonreligious branches of human knowledge.[21] Hence the parallel growth of all human sciences can occur only in an open and rational intellectual climate. Soroush is committed to freedom of intellectual inquiry and the right to criticize rationally all academic theories, religious or nonreligious.

Soroush's position is fundamentally one of caution: caution against confusing religion itself with the knowledge gained from the study of it. To avoid this error is to understand religious knowledge as a human construct that necessarily and constantly changes. Muslims can then "reconstruct" their religious *interpretations* in accordance with their changing understanding of their world.

Soroush's project is not limited to the articulation of a theory of religious knowledge but extends to the establishment of conditions necessary for the manifestation of this theory. His political critiques stem from this latter concern. In moving from the realm of theory to that of practice, he finds that there are significant social and political obstacles to the proper growth of religious knowledge. In identifying and criticizing these obstacles, he casts fundamental aspects of state and society in a new light. Soroush's comments on religion and politics, the role and structure of the clerical establishment, and relations with the West are three examples of the application of his religious paradigm to practical matters.

Religion and Politics

Should religion act as a political ideology? Can a state base its religious legitimacy on a notion of Islamic ideology? Are religiously derived methods alone sufficient for the governance of a modern state? Soroush's answer to these questions is an emphatic no. He calls for the abandonment of Islamic "ideology" altogether, arguing that it hinders the growth of religious knowledge. And he maintains that religiously derived methods of governance are insufficient for administering a modern state. He rejects, then, any government that claims legitimacy based on the implementation of some notion of Islamic methods of governance. Instead, Soroush considers a democratic government the only kind compatible with his notion of Islam. In fact, it is not only compatible with but essential to this notion. To understand these conclusions, the reasons for Soroush's total rejection of the use of Islam as an ideology must be examined first.

Islam as an Ideology

One of the striking features of the contemporary Muslim world is the emergence and power of Islamic political ideology. "Islamic ideology" has galvanized revolutionaries and legitimized political systems. It has gained acceptance as a political manifestation of Islam, and much of the debate surrounding it regards the form of Islam as an ideology, not the existence of Islamic ideology itself. Soroush too considers Islamic ideology a central issue in the modern Muslim world; yet he is not an Islamic ideologue. Instead, he completely opposes any form of Islamic ideology; indeed, he sees religious ideology as one of the primary obstacles to the growth of religious knowledge. [22]

Soroush defines ideology as a social and political instrument used to determine and direct public behavior. It "consists of a systematized and ordered school of thought . . . that situates itself as [a] guide to action . . . [and acts] as a determining factor in people's political, social, and moral positions."[23] In order to fulfill this guiding role, ideologies provide an interpretation of the world that is easily apprehensible by the public. This interpretation also has to mobilize individuals toward particular ideological ends. Soroush argues that these ends generally are defined in opposition to a competing ideology. This confrontation between rival ideologies leads to an interpretation of the world as divided between two ideological poles. While this interpretation provides a clear object for mass mobilization, it is fundamentally reductionist, as it views the world solely in terms of the prevailing ideological discourse.[24]

Islamic ideology then requires both a religioideological interpretation of the world and an ideological enemy. Revolutionary movements that embrace Islam as an ideology, such as those of the Iranian Revolution (1978–1979), well illustrate these qualities. Possessed of a distinct enemy (the shah), who himself represented an increasingly intolerable ideology (kingship), many among the Iranian revolutionary masses also held a religioideological interpretation of the world. This brand of Islamic ideology, as formulated by Ali Shariati and other thinkers, played a major role in mobilizing the Iranian public against the Pahlavi state.[25] As a revolutionary force Islamic ideology has proven its power, and Soroush does not deny this. Yet he rejects ideology even for revolutionary ends.

The reason for this rejection lies in the characteristics of ideology and their effect on religion. In situating itself in opposition to a particular rival, and interpreting the world based on this rivalry, religious ideology reduces the complexity of religion to a fixed ideological worldview.[26] According to Soroush, it is impossible at any time to defend one understanding of Islam as definitive. All understandings change over time. But to transform religion into an ideology is to cast it in a definitive, unchanging mold. This replaces religion with an ideological version of it, for the permanence of religion is now ascribed to the religious ideology. The use of religion as a political tool also subordinates the depth and complexity of religious understandings to the imperatives of a temporary political struggle.[27]

Ideological governments provide another view of the shortcomings of ideology. A government that rules through an official ideology possesses all the problems of ideology just described. Yet it also manifests additional impediments to the growth of religious knowledge. An ideological government must both develop and maintain an official ideological platform that at once legitimizes the government and acts as an unifying and mobilizing force. To accomplish this it requires an official class of government-allied ideologues, whose sole task is the formulation and defense of the ruling ideology. In a government ruled on the basis of a religious ideology, this official class takes the form of government-allied interpreters of religion.[28] Whereas in a revolutionary movement, religious ideology serves the temporary purpose of overthrowing an established enemy, in an ideological state this ideology assumes an official and permanent form. Here religion becomes the servant of the state, as it is transformed into a legitimizing ideological base.

For Soroush, it is the official nature of this ideology, together with the existence of government-allied religious ideologues, that presents a substantial challenge to the free growth of religious knowledge.[29] One of the conditions for the growth of this knowledge is the acceptance of transformation and evolution in religious understandings. Yet the articulation of an official religious ideology restricts an individual's freedom to interpret religion. By forcibly imposing an ideological vulgarization of religion upon society, state-allied ideologues do not only reduce individual freedom; they also determine the acceptable standards and use of reason in religious inquiry, as any rationality not based on the logic of the prevailing ideology is deemed unacceptable. Since unobstructed reason is necessary for the development of religious knowledge in conjunction with the other human sciences, these restrictive ideological standards substantially threaten this development.[30] In addition, the restricted range of free thought and rational inquiry in a religioideological state impedes not only the natural growth of religious knowledge but also the continued development of the state: "In principle the possibility for the internal growth and development of a [political] system exists only when that system is flexible, and [when] the possibility for new reasoning and change exists within the system, . . . [and] if [this] does not exist, inevitably for reform, the foundation [of the system] must be inverted, and upon this inversion, a new foundation built."[31]

Clearly, then, to Soroush, religious ideology threatens both the proper pursuit of knowledge and the governance of society. A religious society should resist the ascension of an ideological regime and resist being transformed into an ideological society. Profound differences separate these two kinds of society:

> In an ideological society, the government ideologizes the society, whereas in religious societies, the society makes the government religious. In an ideological society, an official interpretation of ideology governs, but in a religious society, [there are] prevailing interpretations but no official interpretations. In an ideological society, the task of [the formulation of] ideology is relegated to the ideologues. In a religious society, however, the issue of religion is too great for it to be relegated solely to the hands of the official interpreters. In a religious

society, no personality and no *fatwa* is beyond criticism. And no understanding of religion is considered the final or most complete understanding.[32]

Soroush argues that religion itself contains all the ideals that religious ideologies manipulate yet is not limited to these ideals alone. A comprehensive understanding of religion includes an appreciation of the religious injunctions to resist oppression, to act justly, and to aid the oppressed that characterize a revolutionary ideology.[33] Unlike religious ideology, this understanding is not limited to the combative and dynamic aspects of religion but also includes the more peaceful, esoteric, and mystical aspects that religious ideology ignores entirely. Religion is "more comprehensive than ideology," and people should aspire to an understanding that includes and exceeds the values enshrined (imperfectly) in ideology.[34] Not to do so is to discard religion for an ideological caricature of it.[35]

Islam and Religious Government

Although Soroush rejects Islam as a political ideology, he does not advocate the simple separation of religion and politics. He argues instead that in a religious society politics inevitably takes a religious form.[36] Individuals in a religious society naturally manifest their commonly held religious sentiments in their politics. If a political system rests on public opinion and participation, then in one form or another it will embody these religious sentiments. The question for Soroush is not whether religion and politics are compatible but what the nature of the interaction between the two should be. In addressing this question, Soroush reveals his fundamental concern that obstacles to the growth of religious knowledge not arise. This leads him ultimately in the direction of democracy. But the path to democracy begins with an analysis and rejection of alternative forms of government.

Soroush approaches the issue of religious government by asking whether in a religious society there is a religious right to governance and which, if any, individuals possess this right.[37] He considers two ways of answering this question: one rooted in fiqh (jurisprudence) and the other in *kalam* (theology). The jurisprudential response emphasizes the need to implement religious justice, and the role of the faqih in interpreting and applying this justice. In a religious society the faqih enjoys the right to govern, and the exercise of this right requires the establishment of a particular type of religious (fiqh-based) government. Soroush rejects this as too limited an interpretation of religious governance. Fiqh is but one dimension of religion, and to understand religion solely in terms of fiqh is reductionist. While fiqh provides answers to strictly legal questions, it does not address deeper issues, such as the meaning of justice and freedom.[38] To address the latter issues, Soroush turns to kalam: "The question of religious justice is a question for *fiqh*, but the question of a just religion is a question for *kalam*."[39]

Soroush maintains that a religious government must be a just government and that justice is a term independent of religion.[40] Religious justice, based on fiqh and understood as the interpretation and application of Quranic law, can be derived directly from the Quran. Yet the concept of justice itself cannot be defined by reference to the Quran alone. Justice includes a conception of humanity, of what it means to be human, and of what rights humans enjoy. This conception must accord with religion, but it cannot be defined on the basis of the religious texts alone: "we do not draw [our conception of] justice from religion, but rather we accept religion because it is just."[41] The relationship between religion and justice can be understood only by entering into a theological debate that makes use of, for example, the combined terms of philosophical, metaphysical, political, and religious discourse.[42] This debate would reveal that humans, by virtue of their humanity, enjoy certain rights that are not defined in the core religious texts. A religious state that reduces its notion of justice to the implementation of fiqh jeopardizes these extrareligious rights.[43]

Beyond the right to govern, there is the question of the values embodied in and the methods employed by government. Soroush argues that a religious government must embody religious values yet necessarily must use methods developed outside of religion to protect these values.[44] There are no specifically religious methods of governance. A government ruling on the basis of fiqh alone not only reduces the range of human rights but also lacks sufficient methodological tools for governance. Soroush holds that religion does not offer a plan for government, and any attempts to derive such a plan from religion are wasted.

Bereft of any blueprint for government, Islam at best contains certain legal commandments.[45] These commandments, interpreted through fiqh, can only respond to a limited range of legal issues. The rational administration of modern society requires more than a highly developed code of religious law. Modern methods of government should be derived instead from the modern sciences—for example, economics, sociology, and public administration.[46] These methods must not violate religious values, but they cannot be derived from religion itself.

Soroush does not exclude the possibility of a religious leader—for example, a faqih—in government, although he maintains that this leader, like all political officials, must be subject to criticism and removal by the people. His primary concern lies with the reduction of government to the implementation of fiqh. As a governmental head, the faqih is responsible for leading the state. The issue of leadership is distinct from that of administration.[47] A faqih, as the lone head of state, may lead the state successfully. Yet the state cannot be administered by fiqh alone. Moreover, a state reduced to fiqh is essentially an ideological state, for in order to legitimize its emphasis on fiqh and the exclusion of other aspects of religion, the state requires an interpretation of religion that accords primary importance to fiqh.[48] This interpretation must be both final and official and hence demands the creation of a class of state allied ideologues. The result is the establishment of an ideological government that blocks the growth of religious knowledge by limiting religion to an ideological notion of fiqh.

This rejection of a government based on fiqh does not amount to a denial of the doctrine of *vilayat-i faqih*, the guardianship of the jurisconsult, which forms the theoretical basis of the Islamic Republic, calling for leadership by the faqih. According to Soroush, vilayat-i faqih as a political theory cannot be derived from fiqh. The theory is based on a consideration of the historical and theological importance of the imamate (*imamat*) and prophecy (*nubuvvat*), and the faqih's relationship to these two. This consideration, then, falls outside the field of fiqh, which is restricted to legal issues alone: "the debate concerning it [vilayat-i faqih] is outside the scope of *fiqh*, because the questions of prophecy and Imamate are theological (*kalami*), not jurisprudential (*fiqhi*), ones. Therefore the theory of "*vilayat-i faqih*" as a theory of governance must be debated in the realm of theology, prior to jurisprudence."[49]

Islam and Democracy

Soroush's criticisms of Islamic ideology and his discussion of religious government reject the use of any religious interpretation as a governing platform. Rather than legitimize a government, Islamic ideology perverts religion and stunts the development of religious knowledge. Instead of defending religious rights and implementing religious justice, a religious government founded on fiqh alone compromises a Muslim's extrareligious rights and lacks the depth to govern properly. Yet Soroush sees a place for Islam in politics. He argues that the only form of religious government that does not transform religion into an ideology or obstruct the growth of religious knowledge is a democratic one. Soroush does not identify democracy with a particular Western culture as a foreign force to be resisted. He considers democracy a form of government that is compatible with multiple political cultures, including Islamic ones.[50]

Soroush maintains that a government in a religious society may claim legitimacy either on the basis of an interpretation of Islam or through representation of the popular will. The first leads to the reduction of Islam to an ideology; the second bypasses this problem and leads to democracy. If a government in a religious society reflects public opinion, then it necessarily will be a religious government. Citizens in such a society are concerned that their government not violate or offend their religious sentiments. A democratically elected government in a religious society cannot be an irreligious government, for irreligious sentiments do not characterize this society.

For a government to be both religious and democratic, according to

Soroush, it must protect the sanctity of religion and the rights of human beings.[51] Yet in defending the sanctity of religion the government must not value a particular conception of religion over human rights. A government that rules by one official interpretation of religion, and demands that its citizens live according to this interpretation, sacrifices human rights for ideological purity.[52] The guiding criteria for governance instead must be human rights.[53] Soroush maintains that a religious society embraces religion in large part because it accords with the society's general sense of justice. Today this sense includes respect for human rights. If a government defends human rights, it also defends religion, as a just understanding of religion incorporates human rights: "observance of human rights . . . not only guarantees a government's democratic, but also its religious, nature."[54]

A government based on the will of the people does not derive its legitimacy from an Islamic ideology. It retains legitimacy so long as it rules in accordance with the desires of its citizens. A religious democratic government loses legitimacy when its actions not only oppose public will but violate the public's sense of religion. In a religious society, a commonly held understanding of religion provides an outer limit on acceptable public actions.[55] This understanding must be allowed to grow over time, in order for it to reflect society's changing needs and beliefs.[56] Unlike an ideological government, a democratic government is rooted in this public understanding and hence does not block the growth of religious understanding and knowledge. A democratic government, as opposed to one reduced to fiqh, does not follow a strict implementation of religious laws. Instead, religious laws, as they appear in the core religious texts, are interpreted and expanded upon, using the tools of religious and nonreligious branches of knowledge.[57] These laws must accord with society's general, yet changing, understanding of religion. Soroush argues that today this understanding includes a notion of human rights that demands individuals be free to choose their own form of government.[58] Any religious government that rules without societal consent, or restricts this right, abrogates this conception of justice and sacrifices its legitimacy.

Democracy is both a value system and a method of governance. As a value system, it respects human rights, the public's right to elect their leaders and hold them accountable, and the defense of the public's notion of justice. As a method of governance, democracy includes the traditional notions of separation of powers, free elections, free and independent press, freedom of expression, freedom of political assembly, multiple political parties, and restrictions on executive power. Soroush argues that no government official may stand above criticism and that all must be accountable to the public. Accountability reduces the potential for corruption and allows the public to remove, or restrict the power of, incompetent officials. Democracy is, in effect, a method for "rationalizing" politics.[59]

The danger for a religious society is not the establishment of democratic government, as this would only preserve religion's role in government. It is instead that this society, for whatever reasons, loses its concern with religion, both at the individual and public level. No form of government is capable of forcibly making a people religious; this is something individuals choose for themselves.[60] In an increasingly secularized, irreligious society, a government that consistently applies the principles of fiqh would no more protect the role of religion than would a democratically elected, irreligious government. Such a society has lost the internal concern with religion necessary for maintaining a religious government. A religious government can only remain so if its citizens maintain their faith:

> [In] a religious society and a religious government, everything, including its government and law, rests on the believers' faith, and if this faith crumbles or changes, [the society's] government and religious law will be no different than in secular civil and legal systems. Islamic *fiqh* also may be implemented in a faithless and secular society with [some] profit. But both the practical success of Islamic *fiqh* and its existence and attractiveness are wound together in the faith and belief of the faithful.[61]

Soroush's conception of Islam and democracy has met with much criticism in Iran, both from members of the ulama (religious officials) and from lay religious intellectuals.[62] Some have argued that Soroush has a poor understanding of both Islam and democracy, for otherwise he would not attempt to reconcile the two. One critic, Hamid Payidar, maintains that democracy is inseparable from liberalism and secularism and hence fundamentally incompatible with Islam. He holds that as Islam distinguishes between the rights of Muslims and non-Muslims, any government that defends equal human rights is non-Islamic. In a democratic state, religion is no longer the basis of government and, he argues, this will lead to the disappearance of religion from public affairs. This in turn causes citizens in this democratic state to forget their religious heritage and treat religion as an obsolete relic. Finally, he laments that Soroush, by virtue of his large following among the country's youth, undermines the future generation's faith in Islam as a capable political force.[63]

Soroush's response to this criticism provides additional insight into his argument. He argues that the claim that Islam and democracy are totally incompatible confuses the interpretation of Islam with Islam itself. This position, according to Soroush, ignores the outside presuppositions that influence one's understanding of Islam. Inseparable from any religious understanding, these presuppositions ensure that the human interpretation of religion always differs from the religion itself. It is not Islam, then, but this critic's interpretation of Islam that is opposed to democracy—just as Soroush's interpretation supports democracy.

The question of equal rights for Muslims and non-Muslims in a Muslim society highlights this divergence between Soroush and his critic. Payidar argues that equality of rights among these two groups is forbidden in Islam (according to his interpretation). Soroush, in addition to his previous argument that human rights cannot be restricted to religiously derived rights alone, maintains that this approach to the question of Muslim and non-Muslim rights is flawed. He argues that in a democratic state, neither Muslims nor non-Muslims derive their human rights from their faith. For both, these rights are a product of their membership within the larger group of humanity. Since for Soroush faith is not the basis of rights, a non-Muslim is not required to renounce his or her faith in order to enjoy equal human rights in a Muslim society. Nor are Muslims required to renounce their faith in Islam as the one, true religion in order to accept equal rights for non-Muslims.[64]

At a different level, many critics have questioned Soroush's approach toward reconciling his understanding of Islam with democracy. They argue that Soroush overemphasizes the role of social consciousness[65] in determining political structures and pays too little attention to the institutional bases of a potential "religious democratic state." According to these critics, a publicly held understanding of Islam alone cannot provide the basis for a religious government. They argue that it must be founded on concrete religious institutions.[66]

The same critics also maintain that Soroush's position is neither theoretically sound nor historically accurate. It is theoretically weak because it does not present an institutional mechanism capable of translating public beliefs into political structures; rather it relies on the mere presence of these public beliefs alone. Moreover, it assumes both that this social consciousness is unified and that it will maintain its unity over time.[67] From a historical perspective, these critics argue that there are many religious societies in the contemporary world but no religious democratic states. The absence of democratic governments within Muslim societies suggests either that a social religious consciousness is an insufficient guarantor of democracy or that these societies are only superficially religious.[68]

These critics also reject Soroush's claim that modern conceptions of justice entail a notion of human rights with which religious understandings should and can conform. Instead they argue that today many religious societies—including Iran—do not espouse a general religious understanding that accepts these human rights.[69] In a modern religious society, then, publicly held religious values may prevent, rather than support, the establishment of a democratic state. These critics seek a response from Soroush that details, methodologically and institutionally, the way in which a religious democracy is established and maintained in a modern religious society.[70]

These criticisms challenge Soroush on a wide range of theoretical and historical issues. His critics point rightly to the absence within his framework of a developed institutional schema for a religious democracy. Given

Soroush's approach, this is a necessary absence. He argues that no under-standing of Islam can offer a detailed and effective blueprint for the foun-dation and administration of any form of religious government, democ-racy included.[71] It is wrong, he maintains, to judge the religious nature of a state based on the degree to which its institutions reflect some aspect of religion. The institutional role for religion in government is at best limited to the establishment of a legal code that incorporates, and is congruent with, fiqh.[72] Outside this restricted legal capacity of fiqh, according to Soroush, there is no way to institute religion in government. It is not insti-tutions but society that provides the religious foundation for the political system in Soroush's thought. A religious society's social consciousness will lend a "religious coloring" to all political affairs.

For Soroush's argument to be valid, it would have to explain the ab-sence of democratic regimes in modern religious societies. Many of his critics have argued that, on the basis of Soroush's argument, pre–revolu-tionary Iranian (pre-1979) society was an irreligious one, for it lived under a monarchical, rather than a religious, government.[73] Moreover, if this so-ciety was irreligious, then it would have been incapable of launching an Is-lamic revolution against the monarchy. Hence Soroush must either deny the religious character of prerevolutionary Iran—in the face of strong evi-dence to the contrary—or posit some arbitrary date at which the society passed from an irreligious to a religious phase.

Soroush's position on this can be read in either one of two ways. One reading can be taken from his frequent statements that "a religious society cannot have anything but a democratic government." This reading re-quires Soroush to label the majority of present-day religious societies that live under nondemocratic regimes as irreligious. The second reading re-quires attention to his qualifying statements, where he admits that non-democratic regimes may govern in a religious society, albeit through the use of force and without proper societal consent.[74]

Soroush also distinguishes between two types of religious societies.[75] The first is a society that is only superficially religious and does not possess a highly developed public religious consciousness. This society is superfi-cially religious in that its members only abide by their religious duties (i.e., prayer or fasting) without demonstrating a deep concern about the role of religion in their lives. Soroush does not deny the importance of religious duties but argues that, while anyone is capable of praying or fasting, these outward signs of faith do not reveal the depth of a person's inner faith. One may pray out of habit or obligation and not out of faith and love of God; so too with fasting.

In a truly religious society, according to Soroush, members observe these obligations with sincerity and are deeply concerned with maintain-ing the role of religion in their private and public lives.[76] On the basis of this distinction, Soroush argues that prerevolutionary Iran was, until a certain time, only superficially religious.[77] Iranians observed their religious obligations but lacked the deep faith that would provide the basis for a motivating, public religious consciousness. As the revolution demonstrated, this faith grew over time, marked by the emergence of both lay and clerical religious thinkers who prompted society to recognize its superficiality and rediscover its faith.[78]

The task for Soroush then is to describe precisely what constitutes a "religious society," beyond the rather vague statement that it reflects a powerful concern to maintain a public role for religion. One major feature of a religious society has already been mentioned—that it is a society in which no one understanding of religion prevails but multiple understandings coexist. A better understanding of Soroush's notion of a religious society and its religious consciousness, and the relationship of this notion to democracy, requires attention to his analysis of the clerical establishment This establishment undoubtedly plays a pivotal role in influencing the public's religious beliefs and hence in determining the role of religion in public affairs.

The Clerical Establishment

Soroush's concern that no religious interpretation claim final status led him to dismiss Islamic ideology, and any government founded on it. In discussing the problems of an ideological state, he referred to the negative impact of state-allied religious ideologues on the growth of religious knowledge. While this was a theoretical discussion of an ideological state in general, Soroush raises similar reservations about the role of the clerical establishment in contemporary Iran. He argues that the clergy and the centers of power are related in a way that prohibits the proper development of religious knowledge. In addition to this relationship, there are structural problems associated with the clerical establishment itself. Until these are recognized and reformed, neither religious knowledge nor public religious consciousness can evolve in the manner Soroush envisions.

Soroush argues that if religious knowledge is to evolve properly, the seminaries should meet certain conditions. Analysis of traditional religious texts based on the methods and findings of contemporary natural and philosophical sciences should be encouraged. Seminary students should be free to raise deep and wide-ranging questions about these texts. Above all, religion should not be confused with religious knowledge, and the respect and sanctity of the former should not be bestowed on the latter. The human nature of religious knowledge must be stressed, and students and teachers alike should set no boundaries in the study of this knowledge.[79]

Soroush acknowledges that this description reflects the ideal and that reality reveals another story. Indeed, the distinction between religion and religious knowledge is not stressed properly in the seminaries. Criticism of the classic Shii texts, produced by religious scholars over the ages, is interpreted as an attack on the fundamentals of religion itself. Seminary students hold back their questions regarding these texts for fear that they will be interpreted as lapses in faith. Soroush holds that while the boundary separating the core religious texts—the Quran, the hadith and the teachings of the imams—from questions of fallibility is maintained, it also unnecessarily extends to the teachings of select esteemed yet nevertheless fallible religious scholars. He identifies one reason for this gap between ideal and actual conditions as the failure among both seminary students and teachers to distinguish between religious knowledge and religion itself. This results in the elevation of certain esteemed scholarly religious texts to the same epistemological status as the core religious texts, entirely removing the former from the realm of criticism.[80]

These criticisms of the clerical establishment have earned Soroush a good deal of opposition, part of which can be attributed to the establishment's natural resistance to change. Reinforced by centuries of custom and tradition, the Iranian clerical establishment contains considerable organizational inertia. And when the call for change comes from the outside—for, regardless of Soroush's revolutionary or religious credentials, he is not a member of the ulama—organizational interests demand greater internal solidarity in response to the perceived external threat.

Yet the opposition to Soroush runs far deeper than mere organizational inertia. In fact, his criticisms of the seminary method of instruction carry profound political import. By arguing that religious knowledge is one branch of human knowledge and is not divine by virtue of its subject matter, Soroush denies any group the possibility of advancing one understanding of religion as the truth. And by calling for the use of a variety of methods in the study of religion, he undermines any one group's monopoly on religious studies. This dual criticism considerably weakens the power of both the seminary and the clerical establishment. The latter is no longer custodian of religious truth, and the former is no longer the sole method for arriving at this truth. The seminary becomes one among many centers for religious instruction, and the clerical establishment one among many groups of religious interpreters. The political consequence of this is that the clerical establishment, no longer the guardian of the truth, cannot justify a special role for itself in the political system. If religious knowledge is fluid and not the sole property of any one group, then it cannot function as a criterion for privileging one group over another in political affairs. Members of the clerical establishment then enter the political arena on a level playing field as lay members of society—and their political worth must be judged on their ability to carry out specific political tasks, not their possession of a qualitatively distinct form of religious knowledge.

Soroush's critiques also threaten the internal solidarity of the clerical establishment. In arguing that all religious theories should be questioned, he is concerned that no theory assume an extrahuman, divine status. A consequence of opening up all theories to criticism is the weakening of the socializing process within the seminaries. The seminaries follow a prescribed course of teaching, with prescribed texts, questions, and stages. These accepted methods, established over centuries of practice, constitute a key feature of the clerical identity. Any serious change in this course of teaching—either substantive or methodological—will result in a change in the socialization process of seminary students. A wider range of critical thinking, extending to fundamental reconsideration of pivotal texts or methods, would weaken internal clerical solidarity and cohesion. This would not only challenge the established notions of clerical identity but also weaken the establishment's ability to advance and defend certain common interests. If the clerical establishment is unable to maintain a dominant identity, it also will be unable to agree on where its group interests lie and how best to defend them against rival groups. Taken together, then, Soroush's criticisms so far provide a powerful challenge to the internal structure of the clerical establishment.

Beyond these internal criticisms lie deeper ones associated with the clerical establishment and seminary's role in Iranian society and government. The Islamic Republic is by definition a religious government, and "a necessity of a religious government is the empowerment of the clergy and the seminaries."[81] The clergy, who play a central role in government, are trained solely in the seminaries. The seminaries enjoy a special link to the government, one that, Soroush argues, restricts the range of academic inquiry in the seminary. Indeed, rather than provide a forum for the open criticism of religious knowledge and theories, the seminary reaffirms the ruling religious theories, according to Soroush. The need to encourage a rational intellectual climate is replaced with the need to teach in accordance with the ruling dogma. The seminary becomes the "ideologue and apologist for power," relinquishing its role as critic and teacher:

> [R]ather than guiding and criticizing the ruler, [the seminaries] will offer opinions and issue *fatwas* that meet [the rulers'] tastes, or they will close the door to debate concerning various theoretical issues. If in the seminaries, for example, the right to discuss the issue of *vilayat-i faqih* is not exercised, and opposing and supporting opinions are not freely exchanged, this is an indicator of a problem that must be removed.[82]

The seminary's social role also undermines its academic integrity and independence. In addition to its academic responsibilities, the seminary also trains students to provide moral education for the public. Soroush argues that in providing public guidance, preachers are often more concerned with maintaining popularity and expanding their audiences than in preserving their academic integrity. The result is that the integrity of religious knowledge is compromised by the need to popularize it. Any academic institution that assumes the task of public guidance faces this problem. The seminary must regulate its members and ensure that they do not vulgarize religion by introducing into sermons arguments that, while popular, are not based on a careful study of religious texts.[83]

The social role of preachers reveals a problem that is endemic to the clerical establishment itself. Soroush argues that the defining characteristic of this establishment is not the study of religion or the role of public moral guide or the attachment to political power. It is, rather, the derivation of income, or social or political status, from some form of religious activity—principally, academic teaching or preaching.[84] This relationship between religious activity—of any sort—and the means of one's livelihood is for Soroush the most pervasive problem facing the clerical establishment.

In accruing income (or status) through some form of religious activity, a person may compromise the integrity of religion in order to maximize his or her income.[85] The example of the preacher who popularizes religion in order to attain a wider audience, is applicable here as well, although it is not income that is sought but social status. This is not a problem encountered by the clerical establishment alone, according to Soroush. In any field, one may have the opportunity to advance one's livelihood through compromising the integrity of one's profession. Undoubtedly the establishment possesses methods for determining and maintaining a certain level of professional capability and integrity. For example, through required training and examinations the clerical establishment can set a professional standard for its members.[86]

Soroush maintains that while regulation limits the potential for corruption, it cannot remove it altogether. He particularly identifies those individuals who, having received their religious education, base their livelihood on the cultivation and defense of a particular notion of Islam as representing the greatest potential for corruption.[87] Their livelihood depends on the successful advancement of this religious interpretation, and to maximize the former they may compromise the latter. Soroush argues that even the existence of a reduced level of possible corruption should not be tolerated, for this corruption does not compromise only a professional ethic or standard; it also jeopardizes the integrity and sanctity of religion. To protect the purity of religion, the income incentive must be excised entirely from the clerical establishment. Religion must be removed wholly from the income/status equation: "religion must [exist] for religion's sake, not [for] financial income, political power, or social status/esteem."[88] This requires, in effect, the dissolution of the clerical establishment, for, in Soroush's view, only those individuals should pursue religious activity who do not aim to base their livelihood on this activity. The material needs of these individuals must be met from another source independent of religious activity before this activity is undertaken.[89]

By rejecting the existence of a class of individuals deriving income through religious activity and arguing instead for the replacement of this class with self-funded individuals, Soroush severely limits the potential size of the clerical establishment. In fact, as an establishment it will no longer exist: "In this way an academic society of religious scholars will come about but not a clerical guild."[90] According to Soroush, what is lost in size is made up for in quality: now those individuals engaged in religious activity are not motivated by personal gain but by a sincere desire to understand religion better and to cultivate this understanding among the public.[91] Soroush cites the prophet and the imams as examples of such sincere individuals. He recognizes that contemporary scholars and religious activists cannot duplicate the success and depth of understanding of the prophet and the imams but suggests that they should follow their example and seek religion only for its own sake and not for self-aggrandizement.[92] Soroush admits that this is a long-term goal, the first step of which is the realization of the problematic effects of the relationship between income and religious activity. This must be followed by gradual reforms toward the ultimate ends envisioned.

Soroush does not consider the clergy active agents in the problems outlined here. Instead, he sees these problems as an unintended but unavoidable consequence of the clerical establishment's structure: "In other words, the discussion is not about ill intention or ill behavior on behalf of the clergy. It is about a foundation that grew wrongly. . . . Freedom should not be sold at any price and the institutionalization [professionalization] of religious science, has as its first sacrifice the freedom of religious scholars."[93]

These structural criticisms constitute a serious challenge to the Iranian clerical establishment. By calling for a divorce of religious activity from any form of power—financial, political, or social—Soroush undermines the institutional linkages among the clerical establishment, the seminary, and the Iranian state. Yet, as Soroush's critics have asked, how can a government in a religious society be religious, in the absence of direct clerical involvement for the purpose of guarding and maintaining religious principles? Soroush's answer lies in part in the "society of religious scholars" that will replace the clerical guild and their relation to the public religious consciousness.

In his comments on the role of the Catholic Church in Europe, Soroush has provided an implicit example for the Iranian clerical establishment. The latter is well aware that one of the main features of modern Western society is the foundation of secular nation-states and the weakening of Church power within these states. Wishing neither to sacrifice their social and political influence nor to watch the religious bases of society give way to secularism, members of the Iranian clerical establishment recognize the need to avoid the Catholic Church's experience. Yet if one links Soroush's discussion of the Western experience with his criticisms of the clerical establishment in Iran, it appears that the latter may—unknowingly and definitely unwillingly—go the way of their Western counterparts.

Soroush argues that the Western reaction to the power of the Church and the public role of religion was not necessarily an attack on religion itself but, rather, a response to forces that used religion to prevent social, intellectual, and political change.[94] Had the Catholic Church not clung so steadfastly to a particularly notion of religion, and had it allowed for change, then the lay reaction against the Church and religion would not have been so strong.[95]

The implicit lesson for the Iranian clerical establishment is clear: rather than resist change at all costs (in order to maintain one vision of Islam), welcome and embrace change. The clerical establishment in Iran can avoid the fate of the Catholic Church in Europe only by allowing religious interpretations and theories to be reconciled with other branches of human knowledge. Likewise, the establishment must recognize that the best way to maintain a society's faith is not from above, through the imposition of a religiously derived notion of government, but from below, through the continuous process of religious reinterpretation. Soroush's "society of religious scholars" plays an essential role in this process.

In discussing the relationship between religion and democracy, Soroush has had to face the difficulty of relating his concept of social religious consciousness to practical political affairs. His critics have sought an explanation for how this social consciousness will guard against the secularization of society without religious institutions charged with precisely this task. Soroush's insistence that a government cannot guarantee the religious nature of society but rather that society determines the nature of government places a heavy burden on the role of social consciousness.

One method for strengthening this consciousness, he argues, is through allowing and promoting change in religious knowledge. This requires denying any one group a monopoly on religious knowledge and any theory a privileged status. Beyond these negative injunctions, there is also the need for positive growth in religious interpretations. The "society of religious scholars" plays a central role in stimulating this growth. According to Soroush, these individuals engage in religious activity solely out of a sincere motivation to understand religion and to spread this understanding. He identifies individuals such as Ali Shariati, Mehdi Bazargan, Ayatollah Khomeini, and Ayatollah Mutahhari as representative of this type of religious activist. These activists offer their notion of Islam not as a model to be copied but as an interpretation to be studied, debated, added to, and reformed. Soroush maintains that the free and lively interaction of these interpretations is an essential guarantor of a society's continued religious consciousness. This consciousness, so powerfully informed by these changing interpretations, will demand that politics remain congruent with religious values.

For Soroush, the establishment of a democratic government and the reform of the clerical establishment are necessary, but not sufficient, conditions for the promotion of an atmosphere conducive to the growth of religious knowledge. He also argues that crosscultural interaction plays an important and necessary role toward this end. In defending the need for this interaction, he calls for greater dialogue between Iranian and Western cultures.

Relations with the West

Perhaps no other issue provokes such polarized reactions, both in Iran and abroad, as that of Iranian–Western relations. Within the Western world there are those who predict a "clash of civilizations" with Islam and implicitly with Iran, which is seen as being at the forefront of the anti-Western battle. In Iran there is an equally heated concern over a Western "cultural invasion" (*tahajum-i farhangi*) that allegedly threatens to undermine the Iranian Islamic cultural identity. Between these two camps, those who call for a rational dialogue between the two sides run the risk of being labeled Islamic apologists or supporters of Western imperialism. Despite the increasingly polarized language of this debate, there is both the room and the necessity for constructive dialogue between Iranian and Western cultures. Soroush's position provides one way of conceptualizing this dialogue.

Soroush's argument that the religious sciences can grow only when engaged in an "intimate dialogue" with the nonreligious sciences provides the foundation for intercultural dialogue. The human sciences—understood in the most comprehensive way as including all the natural and social sciences—are not restricted by national boundaries.[96] Advancements made in one country must transcend their country of origin in order to influence the greater body of international scholarly thought; correspondingly, these advancements can only be made through an interaction with this wider scholarly community. The religious sciences in Iran, for example, can develop only when engaged in crosscultural scholarly interaction with other sciences.

Soroush defended this position during his time as a member of the Committee of the Cultural Revolution in Iran.[97] After the 1979 revolution in Iran there was a strong backlash against what was considered Western influences on the human sciences. Many argued that the Iranian higher educational system should be purged of these influences and that the subject matter and methodology of the system should be Islamicized. Soroush warned that this kind of thinking jeopardizes the growth of knowledge and aims at an impossible task. It is impossible, he argued, to replace the social sciences (which were at the forefront of the anti-Western attack) with Islamicized versions of them. The study of Islam is distinct from that of other fields, and the religious sciences are incapable of replacing the social sciences (the reverse is true as well).[98] Soroush argued that the emphasis should be not on the unification (*ittihad*) of the religious and nonreligious sciences (in order to Islamicize the latter) but rather on the interaction (*irtibat*) among these various fields.[99] By focusing on the links between religious and nonreligious knowledge, the universities can provide students with the necessary Islamic environment of learning.[100] Soroush argued finally that it is both possible and necessary to borrow se lectively from the West, without succumbing to a wholesale copying of Western culture.[101] This last point allowed him to extend his argument to larger issues of Iranian–Western interaction.

The catchword for anti-Western sentiments in Iran is *gharbzadagi*, "weststruckness."[102] Soroush's defense of intercultural relations comes partly in response to this concept. Soroush discerns two main themes in gharbzadagi arguments. The first regards any borrowing from the West as blind imitation and calls for a return to tradition.[103] Soroush rejects this position on the basis that it treats the West as an unified entity, such that the appropriation of anything Western is equated with the copying of the West as an entirety. For Soroush, the West is not a single entity but rather a compilation of diverse peoples, each with their own equally diverse cultures.[104] It is impossible to copy the West as a whole, because the "West" as a whole exists only as a fiction. Soroush promotes the selective acceptance of worthy Western achievements and the rejection of aspects of the West that do not merit borrowing.[105]

The second theme argues that Western dominance in all areas— cultural, political, and economic—is a constitutive feature of modernity. The West has arrived, and neither Iran nor any developing nation can resist its domination.[106] Gharbzadagi here is the recognition of and submission to this unfortunate historical reality. Soroush argues that this position suffers from a poor reading of history. It assumes the existence of an irresistible historical force that has placed the West in a dominant and Iran in a subservient position. It also suggests that, just as Western culture has fully arrived and proven its hegemony, so too has Iranian culture fully developed and proven its weakness. Soroush, on the other hand, maintains that no culture ever fully arrives but that all cultures change over time. To accept the principle of historical inevitability demands, in this case, the denial of the possibility of cultural change, and this possibility is a centerpiece of Soroush's argument.

In analyzing intercultural relations, Soroush calls for a move beyond labels such as gharbzadagi. He argues that selective borrowing from Western culture can benefit Iranian culture, provided that this borrowing is the result of free choice.[107] The only way for Iranian culture to grow is for it to open itself up to other cultures, to interact critically and freely with developments from outside of Iran. Selective, freely chosen interaction with the West does not amount to blind imitation of the West, which is the true meaning of gharbzadagi, according to Soroush.[108] Yet to emphasize Iran's pre-Islamic or Islamic identity and to exclude any Western influences, is just as dangerous as gharbzadagi.[109] Excessive nationalism or excessive religious puritanism threatens the rational climate necessary for cultural interaction and growth.[110]

Soroush's discussion of selective interaction applies also to the process of development. Modernity, like the West, should not be regarded as a unified phenomenon.[111] To recognize the diversity of experience within modernity is to allow for the potential to appropriate the lessons of some, but not all, of these experiences. Soroush dismisses the claim that there is only one path to development, which leads ultimately to a replication of a Westernized notion of modernity. He insists that aspects of modernity are compatible with a variety of cultures and that developing nations may appropriate these aspects and shape them to meet their own needs without falling victim to an inevitable process of Westernization.[112] Soroush neither denies the difficulty developing nations face in balancing cultural identity with development nor considers this difficulty insuperable. He suggests that among the first steps of overcoming this problem is for members of developing nations to avoid general, nondescriptive, dogmatic labels and to interact rationally, selectively, and consciously with foreign cultures and concepts.[113]

Conclusion: Soroush and New Trends in Critical Discourse

Soroush's arguments have earned him a substantial opposition, the most notable and active of which are the student group *Ansar-i hizbullah* (Supporters of the Party of God). According to this group, Soroush, among other crimes, undermines the religious faith of Iran's youth, promotes secularism, opposes vilayat-i faqih, is a liberal, questions several undisputed aspects of Islam, and is in league with the West. On numerous occasions in early 1996 the Ansar physically disrupted Soroush's university lectures in Iran with actions at times leading to attacks on both Soroush and his audience. These attacks, together with repeated threats on his life, led him to address a letter demanding guarantees of safety to then president Rafsanjani. No such guarantee was made, and violent disruptions of Soroush's public activities continued. After a particularly dramatic confrontation at Amir Kabir University in Tehran in May 1996,[114] Soroush left Iran for a period of eleven months, during which he engaged in a number of academic conferences in Europe and North America. Shortly after his return, his passport was confiscated and held for several months before he was allowed to resume travel. Since then he has continued to endure physical opposition from the Ansar, as well as constant criticism in their own and allied publications.

The new critical space inaugurated by President Khatami's election has allowed Soroush to respond forcefully and explicitly to his detractors. Soroush has emerged as a strong critic of social violence, lamenting publicly over the failure of the Islamic Republic's security forces to protect the country's cultural architects.[115] Soroush has also elaborated substantially on the relationship of his thought to the course of political reform in Iran. The public availability of terms such as *pluralism, democracy, civil society,* and *law,* have granted him the opportunity to articulate his thoughts within these terms. The best example of Soroush's position during this period are in a series of interviews published in the highly popular, yet now banned, daily paper *Jameah.*[116] In these interviews Soroush responds to his critics and spells out, in greater detail, the relationship between his own intellectual project and the direction of practical political change in Iran. The theme that emerges most strongly here is Soroush's recasting of his work as a multipronged defense of pluralism.[117]

At the heart of Soroush's project is the simple assertion that no religious interpretation is ever final. Recently he has defined this as a pluralist argument against unified, nonchanging forms of thought. He presents his intellectual project as a defense of pluralism understood as the acceptance, and coexistence, of multiple interpretations of religion, nature, and human experience. Soroush isolates several impediments to the growth of pluralism in Iran, some practical and some at the level of consciousness. He argues that Iran's long history of authoritarian rule has reinforced a belief that political and intellectual order must come from a single source: for example, a specific political leader or class or a specific intellectual doctrine. This political and intellectual dictatorship resists critique and prevents the emergence of the conditions necessary for plural interpretations of human experience. Such interpretations require both a free space for dialogue and the practical instruments of constructing dialogue: for example, a free press as the guarantor of "multiple sources of information."

Beginning from an endorsement of pluralism, Soroush has moved on to champion legal accountability, a strong civil society, human rights, political parties, increased freedom, and democracy as necessary for Iran's future. Establishment of these conditions will prevent any one theory of government, ideological doctrine, or political class from restricting social and political space. Soroush's defense of these reformist trends in Iran positions him in a particular relationship to "Islamic revivalism," understood as the reconciliation of Islam with the conditions of the modern Western world. Unlike his prerevolutionary predecessors, who sought Islamic methods of political rule, economic rationality, and social order, Soroush concentrates his efforts at the level of consciousness. Islamic revivalism, for Soroush, remains the continuous reinterpretation of the core religious texts, in harmony with advancements in the natural and social sciences. Soroush continues to offer no practical, organized structures for the manifestation of Islam in politics, economy, or society. He supports methods of governance, administration, and planning devoid of any religious content. He emphasizes, instead, the strengthening of individual and social consciousness through the expansion of Islamic studies and of the mystical components of religion.

Despite his recent adoption of a more secular language—the defense of democracy, freedom and civil society—Soroush remains committed to an expressive style heavily dependent on religious and poetic metaphor. Repeatedly he has admonished his fellow Iranian intellectuals to understand the deep religiosity of the Iranian people and to articulate their critiques through religion. In a religious society, according to Soroush, all reforms must operate through the language of religion. Hence even his recent articles in the monthly journal *Kiyan* display a parallel structure of religious and mystical metaphor and modern secular terminology. What remains unclear is to what extent this style will continue to reflect the "deep religiosity" Soroush sees in the Iranian public. The new political space created by the election of President Khatami has opened the doors not only to a range of new terms but also to a second, important trend: the return of a technocratic elite and a technocratic language. The early years of the Islamic Republic witnessed an intense debate between forces supporting revolutionary faith (*tahud*) and those promoting practical expertise (*takhasus*) in the administration of government. For many years the former group dominated, and major political, economic, educational, and social positions fell to the committed. In recent times technocrats (experts) have gained substantial ground as the terms of debate as well as the parcelling of office increasingly have turned to their favor. Iran's continuous social, economic, cultural, and political differentiation—a process Soroush supports—may tend, in the long run, toward the increasing fragmentation of reformist discourse. Whereas in the past, Iranian intellectuals have been drawn from diverse disciplinary backgrounds and have blended multiple languages in their critiques, critique may devolve more in the future on the technocratic critic with his or her specialized language. What role intellectuals like Soroush—who speak across specialized divides and in an idiosyncratic, mixed, metaphoric language—may play in this possible era of technical expertise remains to be seen. Although Soroush continues to generate active opposition among members of the clergy and the Ansar, and his considerable following remains, in the newly expanded critical Iranian landscape he certainly occupies a smaller percentage of the rhetorical space he once commanded.

This raises a final question, concerning the relevance of Soroush's expressive style and methodology to the establishment of a full range of critical discourse in Iran. Despite the greater independence and legitimacy that terms such as *civil society* and *democracy*—terms generally understood as Western and secular in Iran—have gained recently, Soroush continues to debate these terms' legitimacy in reference to religion.[118] Although these and like concepts undoubtedly cannot and should not remain uncontested, their continuous casting within the mold of religion by critics like Soroush may prevent the emergence of a full range of debate. As one voice among many, Soroush's position most certainly contributes to freer and open debate. Yet his repeated warnings to his secular contemporaries—to promote reform through religion, based on the undeniable religiosity of the Iranian people—demand that all political, social, and economic debate accommodate, in the final instance, religious categories of thought. This accommodation sounds to some like a reduction to, rather than a reconciliation of, secular and religious thought.[119] Whether the new terms of discourse can achieve anything greater than a legitimacy contingent on accommodation within religious categories remains to be seen, not only in Soroush's works but also in the audience to which he speaks. The outcome depends, no doubt, at least partially on the accuracy of Soroush's conclusion that in Iran, in the final analysis, all reform must move through religion.

8

ANWAR IBRAHIM

Activist Moderate

When Anwar Ibrahim organized a demonstration in Kuala Lumpur in 1980, he and his supporters were called "Malaysia's own Islamic zealots."[1] Other observers at the time identified the organization he led as one of the largest "fundamentalist" groups in the country.[2] Eighteen years later, when Anwar Ibrahim was tried in a highly visible court case on a variety of politically inspired charges, those charges did not include leading a religious opposition movement. He had been serving as deputy prime minister of Malaysia. Analysts spoke of him as "an unabashed globalist well suited to the modern world of markets and media,"[3] and many spoke of him as a "liberal."[4] Following his arrest, his supporters formed the Parti Keadilan Nasional (National Justice Party) under the leadership of his wife, Wan Azizah Ismail, in what many people recognized was the effort "to pick up the banner of Anwar's struggling *reformasi* (reform) movement aimed at . . . ushering in an era of democracy and political openness."[5] This transformation from a "charismatic" leader of an Islamic "fundamentalist" group into a globalist liberal advocating Southeast Asian reformasi appears dramatic. However, the change is more a measure of the transformation the religiopolitical context, both globally and in Malaysia, than a reflection of a dramatic change in the faith and views of Anwar Ibrahim himself.[6] As in many places, what was politically marginal in the 1970s became mainstream by the end of the twentieth century.

The mainstreams of Malaysian politics and society have been transformed in the decades since independence in the 1950s. One of the major themes in these transformations has been the gradual Islamization of perspectives. Intellectuals have been important in providing the ways to articulate these new perspectives, and Anwar Ibrahim has played a significant role in this process. In his own transformation from "charismatic fundamentalist" to "liberal reformer," he has reflected the changing mainstream of Malaysian politics and identities and has been, at the same time, a significant force in causing these changes. He has been, in these processes, an almost prototypical activist intellectual. One of his major concerns has been the articulation of new conceptualizations and paradigms, the classic role of the intellectual in times of great historic changes. However, as a leader of a significant student organization, a major Malaysian political figure, and now the symbol of reformasi in his country, Anwar Ibrahim has also been the classic political activist.

Anwar Ibrahim's self-description provides a good definition of "activist intellectual":

> I grew up in a time of great social transformation wherein the inter-play of ideas and events coincided with the rise of student activism, religious revivalism and political turmoil. Not content to be a mere bystander, I chose to be an active participant instead. I emerged from all this convinced that, while a life of contemplation and solitude can indeed be invigorating to the mind and the soul, a life of contemplation coupled with action and fraternity can be even more so.[7]

Basic Biography

Anwar Ibrahim was born in a northern town in Malaysia, Bukit Mertajam, in 1947, into a middle-class urban family. Both of his parents were active in the United Malays National Organization (UMNO), which had been formed in 1946 as an assertion of Malay political identity during the time when the British were reestablishing control following World War II. The town where he was born had a number of well-known religious schools, but his own education was secular, with religious education being provided in the afternoons. He received his secondary school education at the Malay College in Kuala Kangsar, a highly regarded school established by the British originally to provide an appropriate education for children of Malay ruling families. He attended this school from 1960 to 1966 and already exhibited his leadership abilities in a variety of activities, ranging from interscholastic debate to religious activities.

He was a student at the University of Malaya, where he concentrated in Malay studies and received his bachelor's degree in 1971. Early in his career as a university student, he became active in student affairs. Already in 1969, during his second year, he was president of two important student organizations, the University of Malaya Malay Language Society (PBMUM; Persatuan Bahasa Melayu Universiti Malaya) and the National Union of Malaysian Muslim Students (PKPIM; Persatuan Kebangsaan Pelajar-Pelajar Islam Malaysia). These groups tended to concentrate on issues of Malay identity, and Anwar's "early career as an activist centered far more upon issues of Malayness."[8] Anwar was, for example, responsible in these organizations for organizing the "Consciousness Raising Campaign," in which students went to live in rural areas on order the raise their consciousness of the problems of the Malay rural poor. "There was an *esprit de corps*, but a Malay one. The main aim was still to arouse the student spirit to struggle for the Malay race."[9] It was not until the early 1970s that there was a greater Islamic emphasis.

A major explosion of intercommunal violence in May 1969 became a turning point in the history of independent Malaysia. Malaysia is an ethnically pluralist society, with Malays representing only about half of the population and Chinese and Indians as major minorities. The Chinese controlled a significant proportion of the economy, and the 1969 riots involved attacks on what was seen as the privileged position of the Chinese. Following the 1969 riots, the government engaged in a major effort to improve the economic position of Malays in the country. Anwar Ibrahim and the groups he led played a significant role in advocating Malay rights. However, his Islamic commitment meant that he was an important factor in redefining Malay ethnic rights in more Islamic terms. Already his role as an activist intellectual, both articulating themes and working to implement them, was a key to his significance. A close associate from that early period recalled that it was he who began to "rationalize the theme of our struggle for socio-economic justice with the ideals of Islam."[10]

Soon this activism led to the establishment in 1971 of a more formal organization bringing together students and younger professionals who were concerned with issues of social and economic justice in Malaysia. Anwar recalled that at that time "we were impatient and angry about the plight of the Malays, their education, rural development, rural health. . . . We were very angry, disgusted and critical of the government. There seemed to be no moral foundation and no spiritual guidance. We turned to Islam to fill this vacuum and to look for solutions."[11] The new organization, Angkatan Belia Islam Malaysia (ABIM) reflected this dual focus of concern for Malay interests and the desire for Islamic renewal. It was Anwar who was the keystone for the new structure, both through his organizational leadership and his charismatic articulation of goals and aspirations.

In the early 1970s, Anwar's importance and visibility increased as student activism became an important part of the Malaysian political context. At first, many of the concerns were related to student-university issues or more internationally oriented protest demonstrations, like those in Kuala Lumpur during the 1973 Arab–Israeli war. However, a new militancy in off-campus demonstrations and a growing attention toward issues of governmental corruption and social and economic justice within Malaysia itself gave added significance to ABIM. In late 1974, developments reached a critical point. A series of open clashes between police and students demonstrating on a variety of issues[12] reached a climax in December. Peasants in Baling, in northern Malaysia, became upset by deteriorating economic conditions, and in November began a series of marches and demonstrations in protest. When the authorities forcibly stopped these protests, students on a number of campuses organized "demonstrations of sympathy and support for the undeniable social distress in Baling."[13] By early December, more than a thousand students had been arrested, and the government prepared to close university campuses in response to what became a major crisis.[14]

Anwar Ibrahim was among the students arrested, and he ultimately spent two years (1974–1976) in detention for his activities in the Baling crisis. Although government officials made the charge that the problems were the result of "communist" agitation and conspiracy, it was clear to most observers that ABIM under Anwar's leadership was the most important organizing force in the expanded protests. This represented a significant change in the nature of effective opposition to government in Malaysia. One informed observer at the time noted that the

> most formidable force in this new opposition to what is, in fact, a Malay Government, claims legitimacy from the principles of Islam. . . . Hitherto, the opposition was either nakedly communist or based on Chinese dissatisfactions. Whatever "red herrings" were drawn by the Government across the Baling upsurge, it was essentially and predominantly a confrontation between Malays and their Malay Government.[15]

Anwar, even in detention, remained in the forefront of the emergence of this new-style, Islamically oriented opposition, although in detention he had the time and opportunity for extensive reading in a wide range of subjects, including Western philosophy and Malayan history.[16]

Along with establishing ABIM, the emerging group created a private secondary school, Yayasan Anda, which became the base for a network of private schools. The new schools were created to provide an alternative to the government schools, presenting curricula that combined Islamic and secular modern education. In addition to his organizational activities, Anwar served as the headmaster for the school, and many others from the ABIM group worked as teachers in the school. By 1980 the school in Kuala Lumpur under his leadership had thirteen hundred students, with many living in a student hostel since they came from outside of the city, and was an important base for the broader efforts of Islamic renewal.[17]

During the 1970s, Anwar became more highly visible internationally and was influenced by and was a part of the developing global network of Muslim activist intellectuals. He served as a member of the United Nations Advisory Group on Youth (1973–1974) and was a representative for Southeast Asia in the World Assembly of Muslim Youth (1976–1982). He was among the first Muslim leaders to visit Iran after the Revolution in 1979. He and his group made special efforts to read and understand the major thinkers in the Islamic renewal movements of the twentieth century, notably reading the works of Sayyid Qutb, Hasan al-Banna,

KING ALFRED'S COLLEGE
LIBRARY

and Abu al-Ala al-Mawdudi. In addition, they had direct personal contacts with major contemporary activist intellectuals, who played an important role in articulating the Islamist positions of the day. In Malaysia itself, the young Islamists had close relationships with Syed Naguib al-Attas, who was dean of the arts faculty at the National University. One theme that emerged from these discussions was an "understanding of the comprehensiveness of Islam as *ad-deen* (way of life),"[18] a concept that is at the heart of the Islamist understanding of Islam. Internationally, Anwar had a variety of connections. He had come to know the prominent Islamist scholar Ismail al-Faruqi in the early 1970s when Faruqi taught for a time in Malaysia. Faruqi's ideas played an important role in shaping Anwar's ideas.[19] Islamic scholars from Indonesia were also important in helping to shape ABIM's Islamist mode. These included Deliar Noer, an Indonesian academic teaching in Australia, and, in the early 1970s, Imaduddin Abdul Rahim. However, Imaduddin's approach was relatively militant and hardline, while the ABIM leadership did not "agree with such a black and white interpretation of the struggle for Islam."[20] This reflected the developing approach of Anwar, which was to be strong in advocacy but to avoid extreme positions that could lead to militancy.

Although Anwar Ibrahim was very careful to remain within the bounds of legal opposition, he came to be viewed as one of the major figures in the alternatives to the political establishment of UMNO and its allies that had dominated Malaysian politics since independence (and before). ABIM, and Anwar himself, had worked with the more explicitly Islamic party, Partai Islam se-Malaysia (PAS). It had been thought that if or when Anwar became a direct participant in Malaysian politics, it would somehow be in the framework of PAS. As a result, it came as a great surprise to many when he joined UMNO and won a parliamentary seat in the general elections of 1982. "It was a move that shocked the country and distressed his followers in ABIM. His followers in PAS were stunned as they had considered him a potential leader of the party."[21]

Anwar had become convinced that he could accomplish more for the Islamization of Malaysia by becoming a key member of the leadership than by remaining in the opposition. UMNO itself had recently, in 1981, come under the new leadership of Mahathir Mohamad, who was well known to Anwar. Mahathir had been an early member of UMNO but had come into conflict with the party leadership in 1969. Anwar worked with him during his time in opposition in the early 1970s and came to know him quite well.[22] Mahathir later was in the cabinet in a variety of positions, and Anwar was convinced that Mahathir's commitment to the Islamization process was significant. Many of Anwar's old associates felt betrayed, while many others joined with him in the effort to establish a greater Islamic orientation within the political establishment itself.[23] In this way, 1982 marks the transformation of Anwar from the most visible leader of the

Islamically-oriented opposition to one of the major figures in the ruling political establishment.

In UMNO, Anwar gradually moved through the ranks of the leadership with great skill. Almost from the very beginning, he held cabinet positions. In 1983 he became the minister of sport, youth, and culture, and from 1984–1986 he served as minister of agriculture. From 1986 until 1991 he was minister of education, where he played an important role in giving a more formal place to Islam in curricula at all levels and especially in higher education. He worked closely with the International Islamic University (IIU) in Kuala Lumpur, which had been established in 1983, to create the Faculty of Islamic Revealed Knowledge and Human Sciences and basic departments in most of the social sciences and humanities. In 1991 he became minister of finance and emerged as a leading advocate of the globalist "liberal" approach to economic policy. In 1993 he was named Deputy prime minister, and most observers expected that he would be the eventual successor to Mahathir.

The Asian economic crises of 1997-1998 put great pressure on the relationship between Mahathir and Anwar, his minister of finance and deputy prime minister. Mahathir reacted strongly to the crisis with a rhetoric that alarmed the world financial leaders, and Anwar emerged as "the moderate, rational voice reassuring the international business community."[24] Tension apparently built up between the two leaders and came to a head in September 1998, when Anwar was relieved of all of his posts after refusing to resign. He then began a series of appearances that gained growing popular support for general political reform. At the end of the month, he was arrested and charged with a variety of crimes, including corruption and sexual misconduct. During his trial, his physical appearance indicated that he had been beaten, but he remained resolute in the affirmation of his innocence. In a series of trials that many called political show trials, he was convicted of corruption in April 1999 and sexual misconduct in August 2000 and sentenced to extended prison terms.

A new era in the career of Anwar, and the history of the Islamic revival in Malaysia, began with his removal from office in 1998. In the brief period before his arrest, he laid the foundation for a new reform movement and party through a series of addresses and demonstrations that attracted thousands of supporters. Public leadership of this movement was assumed by his wife, Wan Azizah Ismail; she is an ophthalmologist trained in the Royal College of Surgeons in Dublin. She and Anwar were married in 1980, and she was not a highly visible figure until the events of September 1998. With Anwar in prison, she moved quickly to create the Parti Keadilan Nasional (National Justice Party) to provide an institutional base for the reform movement. The basic positions of the party and movement emphasize the importance of democracy and the recognition of the fundamental pluralism of Malaysian society. When it was formed, it had the potential for providing a bridge between the different major opposition groups, the primarily Chinese Democratic Action Party (DAP) and the explicitly Islamic PAS. In this it continued the intermediate position that Anwar had maintained within Malaysian politics between Muslim and non-Muslim and also between militantly Islamic and more secular Malay groupings. A basic question following Anwar's conviction was the degree to which he would remain in control. Supporters of Mahathir see Wan Azizah as "only a proxy leader, or a trustee for her husband,"[25] while she realistically said, "People do ask whether Anwar is behind this. . . . He is, in a way, but he's also behind bars. So I have to sink or swim."[26] The future of Anwar Ibrahim as an activist intellectual was unclear at the end of the 1990s.

Defining a Moderate Islamic Activism

Anwar Ibrahim is an action-oriented intellectual. He has played a significant role in conceptualizing and articulating the Islamic revival in Malaysia, but this has been done primarily through speeches and articles and organizational activities rather than through the writing and publication of major scholarly monographs and studies. His contributions to the reconceptualization of Islamic life have been the products of actions in the political and social arenas, in contrast to the more self-conscious rearticulations of the Islamic heritage found in the many books of an intellectual like Hasan Hanafi. An important part of Anwar's evolution as an activist intellectual has been the shift from the role of the "charismatic leader of opposition," whose intellectual positions were presented through specific activities like the Baling demonstrations, to that of the political leader who gave special attention to defining broad policy principles while a member of the cabinet.

The basic positions taken by Anwar in these two different stages of his career are fundamentally the same. The core of his intellectual activism has been and continues to be a conscious commitment to social justice and equality whose foundation is the faith and teachings of Islam. The changes are in the ways of implementing that commitment and also in the modes of interpreting and understanding the fundamental principles of Islam. It is in this regard that observers have been correct in identifying him as a "fundamentalist." Local custom and historical habit and tradition, in this perspective, have less importance than careful thought and action based on the believer's understanding of the fundamentals of Islam.

While Anwar has been committed to activist involvement, his positions were moderate rather than extremist. On virtually every significant issue, his positions and actions represented a medial position between extremes. However, his moderate intellectual positions were strongly advocated through direct involvement in affairs. His mode of operation was not passive, nor did he advocate disengagement from issues and events. In general terms, his views represented positions between those of advocates of violent confrontation, like some radical communists or militant jihadists, and of those who, like the Dar al-Arqam movement, advocated pious withdrawal from society. He also stood between the extremes of the secularist Westernizers in Malaysian society and the old-fashioned conservatives who wanted no changes in their "traditional" society.

The Era of Opposition Activism

From the time that Anwar Ibrahim emerged as a student leader in the late 1960s until he joined UMNO and Mahathir's cabinet in 1982–1983, Anwar was a highly visible activist whose positions tended to be defined through his activities. Three activities provide a key to the new Islamic intellectual that he represented: the early work in supporting Malay consciousness, the Baling affair, and the schools that were established under his leadership by ABIM.

Ethnic consciousness. Anwar's earliest activism came in student groups dedicated to raising the ethnic and cultural consciousness of Malays in Malaysia. In the 1960s, the issue of a national language was of great importance. Before independence, "the education system was extremely fragmented along ethnic lines," and following independence in 1957 there "was a shift in education policy . . . which reflected the urgency of creating national unity that a newly independent plural society faced."[27] Steps were taken to establish Malay as the national language in a period when there was great concern about the survival of Malay culture and growing awareness of the problem of the Malay poor, especially in the rural areas. Although the National Language Act establishing Malay as the national language was passed in April 1967, it involved compromises that preserved a special position for English. Students and others demonstrated actively against the compromise, with some schools being closed for a time as a result.[28]

It was in this turmoil that Anwar Ibrahim began his career as activist intellectual, taking up the issue of supporting Malay language and preserving Malay culture. However, his concern was not the abstract intellectual concern of cultural preservation alone; it also involved a sense of the need for social and economic justice. As a leader of the Malay Language Society at the University of Malaysia, he helped to organize the "Consciousness Raising Campaign" in 1968, which brought students together with rural Malay villagers. The goals included providing the students with a better understanding of the foundations of Malay culture and the villagers with help in overcoming their poverty.[29] At the same time, during 1968–1969, a series of violent intercommunal confrontations between Malays and Chinese took place, reaching a climax in the major riots of

May 1969. Students from the Malay Language Society and other Malay groups were actively involved in these developments as well.

In general terms, both the positive and negative dimensions of this activism were primarily ethnic in the goals that were defined. However, the close relationship between the Malay identity and Islam led people like Anwar to give more consideration to the Islamic dimension. In a later discussion of "the Asian renaissance," he provided the underlying reasons for the transition from ethnic activism to Islamic advocacy:

> To seek cultural empowerment is to bring ourselves up to a level of parity with other more self-confident cultures. It involves rediscovery of what has been forgotten through ages of weakness and decay; it involves renewal and reflowering. . . . Genuine renaissance would not be possible without a rediscovery, reaffirmation and renewed commitment with the universals within our culture, that is, the idea of human dignity founded upon spiritual substance, moral well-being and noble sensibility.[30]

Anwar's early activism reflected his concern for social justice and equality but expressed in terms that were more tied to ethnic identity than Islam. However, by the early 1970s there had been a significant shift in emphasis, and the establishment of ABIM in 1971 reflected the new approach.

The Baling crisis. By the time of the Baling incidents in 1974, Anwar was clearly identified with the cause of advocacy of Islamic renewal, and the support given to the rural Malay poor was defined in terms of the Islamic call for equality and social justice. By the end of the Baling crisis, it could be said that "the potent force in Malaysia, where 80 percent of the people are from impoverished rural communities and the burgeoning intelligentsia is of rural origin and still holds fast to Islam, is ABIM."[31] The activism reflected the complex mixture of the call for economic justice and affirmation of Malay identity concerns.

> The active involvement of Anwar and his supporters in the Baling demonstrations, which clearly cut across ethnic lines, in the urban connection, implicitly raised class-like issues of exploitation of workers and peasants alike. This suggests a commitment to more universalistic reforms. Yet detractors argue that, for all its surface class-like character, Baling was essentially in defence of the Malay peasant, who was both its source and symbol.[32]

ABIM defined its call for social and economic justice in terms of the universal principles expressed in Islam, and by 1980 it could be reported that Anwar "has found a wide echo for his movement's charges of widespread corruption and exploitation of the poor of all ethnic groups."[33]

ABIM's schools. The content of Anwar's message can be seen in the cur-

ricula of the school he headed. It is often said that Islamic movements proclaim that "Islam is the solution" but do not provide content for what that
solution means. By the end of the 1970s, it would have been difficult to
make that charge against ABIM unless one ignored the record of policies
advocated during and after the Baling crisis and, more particularly, the
content of what was taught in the ABIM schools. The schools represented
a significant synthesis and coming-together of educational traditions.
"The goal of these schools . . . is to combine religious and secular education patterns in such a way that pupils can both sit for the national pro-
motional examinations which open the doors of occupational opportunity
to government and private sector and receive a solid religious and moral
foundation for life as good Muslims."[34] Students studied both religious
subjects and modern scientific subjects, recognizing that ABIM did not see
"modern science" as being fundamentally in conflict with Islam.

This approach was grounded in the project that was developing at this
time of "the Islamization of knowledge." A global network of Muslim
scholars, led by Ismail al-Faruqi, was active in this effort, which was institutionalized with the establishment of the International Institute of Islamic
Thought (IIIT) in Virginia. Anwar Ibrahim was a cofounder of the Institute
and an active supporter of the broader project. In this perspective, "the reform of education is the Islamization of modern knowledge itself. . . .
As disciplines, the humanities, the social sciences, and the natural sciences
must be reconceived and rebuilt, given a new Islamic base, and assigned
new purposes consistent with Islam."[35] It is possible to consider the ABIM
schools of the 1970s as pioneers in this type of reform. It did not represent
a rejection of modern science but the development of a perspective that
put modern science into a conceptual framework that was different from
the usual Western materialist and secular perspective. The so-called fundamentalism of Anwar and ABIM was neither intellectually obscurantist nor
Luddite in its attitude toward modern science and technology. It simply
gave priority to moral values and social justice in the effort to understand
the implications of modern science and technology for contemporary
human life.

Political and Social Positions

The message that is presented in Anwar Ibrahim's activities of the 1970s
and early 1980s is quite clear, and it has implications for issues that were of
importance in the broader debates of the late-twentieth-century Islamic
resurgence. The issues of an "Islamic state," pluralism, and the "role of
women" have been frequently debated, and they were not ignored by
Anwar and ABIM. However, the distinctive positions of activist moderation
taken by Anwar had a very important impact on the development of the
debates about political Islam in Malaysia. In contrast to many other coun-

tries, where the most visible participants in debates and conflicts are at the extremes, Anwar's "charismatic" and activist advocacy of moderation had a strong influence of the evolution of Islamist politics in Malaysia.

An Islamic state. PAS and many of the Islamists in Malaysia advocated the establishment of an "Islamic state" and the formal implementation of the Shariah in Malaysia. This followed a common pattern for Islamist movements in the 1970s. However, Anwar did not follow this pattern. His vision was of the gradual Islamization of society through the efforts of dedicated individuals and groups like ABIM working to transform society "from the bottom up" rather than imposing an Islamization "from the top down." In this approach, calling people to adherence to an authentic understanding of Islam was the major obligation of the Muslim dedicated to Islamic renewal. The term for this "call" was *dakwah*, which became a major identification for the programs of Islamic revival in Malaysia. The concept of dakwah emerged gradually in the 1970s as the mission of the various Islamic groups and movements, and it took many different forms. As ABIM emerged under Anwar's leadership as the largest and most visible Islamist movement, it played an important role in defining dakwah in the Malaysian context.

Anwar's definition of dakwah was distinctive in a number of ways. In contrast to similar movements elsewhere in the Muslim world, and other groups in Malaysia like PAS, the emphasis was on broader principles. "It did not see Islam in the black and white manner that the later *dakwah* adherents did. . . . It believed in Islamizing the *ummah* first along a gradual, moderate, and progressive path."[36] In contrast to other movements, this means that ABIM identifies many of the specific demands of other movements as giving too much emphasis to "the ritualistic aspects of Islam," which are, in ABIM's view, secondary to the main mission of creating a just and equitable society.[37]

One consequence of this perspective is that Anwar did not actively call for the establishment of an Islamic State or the immediate enforcement of specific rules of Islamic law. In his view, dakwah would transform society on the long run, and only then would it be possible formally to proclaim an Islamic state and the full implementation of Islamic law. His views were clearly presented in an interview in 1980:

> Questions about the creation of an Islamic state were put off by Mr. Anwar, who stresses that much education is necessary before the matter can arise. "We should first have a truly just economic society," he said. "Then we can apply Islamic law. I don't see it in the very near future." If such a just society could be created, he added, "I would not rule out chopping off of hands"—the Koranic penalty for theft.[38]

However, the full implementation of Islamic law would require the prior establishment of a just society.

Anwar provided an important intellectual alternative in the debates arising out of the growing "Islamic resurgence" in Malaysia, as well as the broader Muslim world. A movement of more typical Islamic resurgence had also been developing in Malaysia. PAS had been in existence since the 1950s and represented a revivalist tradition similar to that of the Muslim Brotherhood in Egypt at that time. Its demands were more typical, and by the late 1970s, PAS "called not just for a vague Islamic state, but for alterations in the federal constitution to bring it more in line with Islamic law and administration."[39] Without the activities of Anwar and ABIM, it is probable that the debates and tensions involved in the Islamic revival of the 1970s and 1980s would have taken a more typical form of clashes between "secular" modernizing establishments and generically defined "Islamists," divided between those calling for jihad and the less militant. Anwar's intellectual formulations shaped the form and content of the debates of the Islamic revival in a distinctive way.

A pluralist society. One of the most important dimensions of Anwar's vision of dakwah and the long-term Islamization of society is his acceptance of the reality of the ethnic and religious diversity in Malaysia. He believes that this is a distinguishing characteristic of Malaysia in the Muslim world and that Malaysia can be an example for other Muslim societies.[40] Although he began his career as an activist in the movement for affirming Malay rights and identity, the creation of ABIM signaled his acceptance of a more universalistic Islamic mission. Increasingly, he came to oppose ethnic nationalism and "racism" as being contrary to Islam. Initially, this was expressed more in terms of defining the Muslim community, but Anwar developed a more broadly inclusive conceptualization of pluralism in an Islamic perspective.

The theme of the annual congress of ABIM in 1979 was "Islam is the solution for the problems of a plural society," and Anwar's major address to this meeting emphasized Islam's opposition to discrimination and racism.[41] The framework of the position is Islamic, and it argues that Islam provides a foundation for society in which all people have real freedom. However, in contrast to more typical or conservative Islamist presentations, there is an emphasis of the authentic pluralism of Islamic faith and tradition, when rightly understood. Anwar, for example, uses Umar, who was the second successor to the Prophet Muhammad as leader of the Muslim community, as a good example, noting that "Omar's rule was . . . instructive for the administration of a multi-ethnic society, for his realm comprised many non-Muslims (*dhimmi*), and his policy was to allow complete freedom of worship, guaranteeing their protection in return for obedience."[42] In a speech in 1994, he reiterated this theme by pointing to the example of Spain under Muslim rule and expressing the hope for a "global convivancia" in that tradition.[43]

In this area, Anwar has also had an impact on the ways that political debates and policies have been formulated in Malaysia. Again, although

Malaysia politics were dominated by the issue of Malay rights and ethnic tensions following the riots of 1969, there was a move away from extreme positions of ethnic support during the 1970s. The middle position presented by Anwar and ABIM played an important role in this transition.

Women. Anwar is a strong advocate of equality for women and sees this as an important dimension of the broader call for social and economic justice. However, this is presented within an Islamic framework that emphasizes the importance of the contribution of women to family life, child-rearing, and societal morality. Modest, Islamically appropriate dress is expected, and gender separation in public is encouraged. In this as in most other aspects, the ABIM position as it was articulated by Anwar represented a moderate position between the extremes of the more fundamentalist groups like PAS and Dar al-Arqam on the one hand and urban secular lifestyles on the other.

In a report of a series of interviews with women in the early 1980s, the type of woman who was described as most likely to be associated with ABIM presents this picture of committed moderation:

> Unlike the Islamic Republic *dakwah* students, she does not believe that music is sinful, that concerts, sports, and cultural events are bad for mind and soul. . . . She does not believe that Islam is the straightjacket religion that the *surau* people have made it out to be. . . . She is *dakwah*, but her increased religiosity only applies to her personal life. She doesn't tell others to dress or behave like her.[44]

Education for women has been a high priority in Anwar's approach and ABIM's programs from the very beginning. Young women were an important part of the student body of the schools established by ABIM in the 1970s and have played a significant role in the contributions of ABIM to the Islamic revival in Malaysia. The first graduates of Anwar's school in 1974 were among the very first women at the University of Malaysia to wear the distinctive modern Islamist covering on campus.

The expectation of modest dress did not reflect an expectation that women would be in seclusion. Instead, women were expected to take an active role in the development of society. The expectations of people like Anwar were clearly expressed by Khalijah Mohammed Salleh, a professor of physics at Universiti Kebangsaan Malaysia:

> Traditionally *Muslim* women were visibly seen as wives and mothers. Currently more and more of them are gaining access to higher education and hence into the labour market. . . . To enable the women to participate in nation building there are several strategies that can be considered. First is . . . education, training and opportunities. . . . Other strategy is the paradigm shift by man with regards to [the] man–woman relationship. Rather than looking upon

women as being subordinates to men, it would benefit both parties to regard each other as partners that complement each other. [This] [p]aradigm shift would also mean that men would have to consider household chores as responsibilities to be shared with their wives."[45]

One excellent example of this concept of partnership at work is the role of Anwar's wife, Wan Azizah Ismail. Following their marriage in 1980, she established an active medical practice and primarily treated women. Following his arrest in September 1998, she immediately emerged as the leading figure in the reform movement, speaking as actively as her husband had done before his imprisonment. Although conservatives in groups like PAS expressed reservations about having a woman lead a political party (and thus potentially the country as well), activist moderates in the "tradition" of Anwar had no problem with the emerging role of Wan Azizah Ismail. This provides another illustration of the character of the Islamic revivalism of activist moderation that had been conceptualized and established by Anwar Ibrahim in the 1970s.

Activism within the Establishment

When Anwar Ibrahim joined UMNO in 1982, he transformed his position from most visible spokesperson in the opposition to rapidly rising star in the Malaysian political establishment. He argued that he was convinced that Mahathir, the new prime minister, was serious in his commitment to effective Islamization and had already begun a program that promised to reduce corruption and increase government efficiency significantly. The conclusion Anwar drew was that he could more effectively work to achieve his goals by working from within rather than against the government. He had already had a positive experience working with Mahathir in the early 1970s and had been encouraged in taking this step in 1882 by the internationally known Islamist scholar Ismail al-Faruqi.

In his new position, Anwar did not change his broad overall goals or perspectives. However, as both a policy-maker and one responsible for implementing policy, he began to articulate his positions more carefully in terms of a broader conceptual framework. Many intellectuals, when they take administrative and executive posts, tend to stop the effort of conceptual definition and articulation. Anwar, in contrast, took the opportunity to present a number of broad conceptual frameworks for policy as he assumed different cabinet positions. As minister of education and then of finance, he had the opportunity to rearticulate his ideas about culture and economics in the context of actual policy planning. He did not write comprehensive monographs or broader systematic analyses, but in his speeches and shorter writings, important themes emerge. He fulfilled his role as an intellectual while being directly involved in the affairs of government.

Anwar presented important conceptualizations of major issues, both domestic and global, from the perspective of the Islamic revival in which he had been engaged since the early 1970s. The major themes that emerge in his presentations are the need for a broad new paradigm for sociopolitical and economic development and the definition of that paradigm in ways that recognized broader religious and moral values; a new understanding of the nature of pluralism in multireligious societies and the world as a whole; and, in particular, an emphasis on the importance of intercivilizational dialogue as the only possible alternative to a deadly clash of civilizations. In these discussions, Anwar generally presented his ideas at two different but complementary levels. At one level, his thinking was directly concerned with the specific issues faced by Muslims and the particular challenges of defining an adequate Islamic response. At the second level, he presented his ideas in more global and inclusive terms. In this second area, Anwar was going beyond and redefining (but not contradicting) his earlier conceptualizations.

The new paradigm. Anwar was convinced that the older Western understanding of the processes of development represented an outmoded paradigm that even in the West was being amended or rejected. In the mid-1980s, he argued: "a new paradigm in development studies has slowly emerged."[46] This was seen as being in the context of the failure of both Marxist and secular materialist paradigms in terms of their applicability for the developing world. Following the collapse of communism in Eastern Europe, he developed this argument further, noting that "Marxism failed precisely because of its flawed vision of man. It severs man from his moorings in faith, viewing him as nothing more than a cypher, a cog in a brutal machine called the state. There was no place for ethics, morality or spirituality."[47] Older Western modernization theory had a similar gap in its emphasis on the secular development of economics. "Much of the definition of development originating from the West has rejected any reference to moral and ethical considerations. Cultural preservation is regarded as retrogressive in the march for development."[48] Western paradigms did not recognize that the "final aim of economic pursuit is the development of man, not the Promethean man of secular humanism who relentlessly seeks to conquer, but rather man as envisaged by the great traditions of East and West."[49]

The solution was to define a new paradigm that would be properly rooted in local traditions and not simply be a blind borrowing from the West. Anwar approached the definition of this new paradigm at two levels, a specifically Islamic one and a more broadly Asian one.

Anwar's Islamic paradigm was different from many of the programs and approaches advocated by more typical Islamist groups in that it did not start with advocating the implementation of the specifics of Islamic law as they had come to be defined in medieval Muslim society. In Islamic history, two contrasting approaches to tradition had developed. One said that it was important to follow as closely as possible precedents that had been set by previous generations. This is the approach of taqlid, or imitation. The second approach utilizes informed independent analysis, or ijtihad, in determining what actions should be taken. In Anwar's view, Islam "is essentially a pragmatic religion with a keen sense of historical direction. Muslim thinkers ruled out the acquisition of knowledge simply by imitation (taqlid)."[50] Although many Muslims in the past, and still in the present, in Anwar's view, had exercised taqlid, the real strength and dynamism of Islam was built on the continuing revitalization provided by ijtihad.[51]

Within this framework, Anwar presented two historically established Islamic concepts as vital to the exercise of independent judgment in defining and implementing the new paradigm. Anwar noted efforts by some modern Muslim scholars to relate classical formulations to current conditions in order to bridge the gap between old theory and contemporary practice. In particular, he cited the importance of giving emphasis to the classical principle of maslahah, which was the concept of public welfare or the common good, as a basis for determining policy. This procedure had been advocated and utilized by some important modernist Islamic scholars, like the late Mahmud Shaltut, Shaykh al-Azhar (1958–1963).[52] In describing the Islamic approach to economic policy and the market economy, Anwar noted a second traditional Islamic concept that illustrates how Islam encourages an active free market but sees the need for just regulation. Despite a "favourable disposition towards the market, Muslim societies in the past saw the need to introduce the institution called hisba to oversee fairness in market dealings, to check against monopoly and manipulation."[53]

Maslahah and hisba in the context of the presentation of the new paradigm also illustrate the mode of approach envisioned by Anwar. As was true in the 1970s, he was not interested in enforcing "ritualistic" details; his mode of operation was to work within a broader framework or principles like the common good and fair regulation. The new paradigm did have an important economic component, but it was within the broader framework of Islamic religious and moral values. This approach opened the way for efforts to encourage the establishment institutions like the Islamic Bank. However, the broader goal was the creation of a just and equitable economic system. As a result, Anwar's work as finance minister is not associated with the more typical Islamist campaigns to implement specific aspects of the traditionally understood economic teachings of Islam. Instead, Anwar

spearheaded the government's programme to identify and assist the hardcore poor. Eradicating absolute poverty through budgetary allocations and direct aid was central to his mission as finance minister. His commitment to low-cost housing and his relentless drive to coax the private sector to join hands with the government in providing shelter to the homeless has won him accolades from the general public.[54]

Anwar presents his priorities clearly:

The proponents of the imposition of Muslim laws or the establishment of an Islamic state are confined to the periphery. Southeast Asian Muslims prefer to concentrate on the task of ensuring economic growth and eradicating poverty instead of amputating the limbs of thieves. They would rather strive to improve the welfare of the women and children in their midst than spend their days elaborately defining the nature and institutions of the ideal Islamic state. They do not believe it makes one less a Muslim to promote economic growth, to master the information revolution and to demand justice for women.[55]

The new paradigm as conceived by Anwar is not, however, to be an exclusively Islamic one. He also conceives it in the broader terms of "Asian values." The starting point for this perspective is a recognition of the failure of Western development paradigms as they were applied in Asia and the difficulties created by the experience of past European imperial control. However, Anwar emphasizes that he does "not follow a policy of discarding the West. We are not anti-West. We have strong views against some Western attitudes and policies. We believe in engagement between the East and the West."[56] A crucial part of the new paradigm is the establishment of a new consciousness of "Asian values" so that "Asia could take the lead in engaging the West in continuous dialogue."[57]

Anwar is relatively specific in identifying the components of this paradigm involving Asian values.

What we envisage for Asia as a whole in the next century is that it should become a greater contributor to the advancement of human civilization. The Asian intellectual community must henceforth expend a significant part of its resources to[ward] nurturing and promoting the Asian heritage, especially those elements in the culture and traditions which not only characterize Asian identity but also contribute to the enrichment of a universal humane society. Among the elements, the most fundamental relate to the harmony of society through good governance, the sanctity of the family, tolerance towards diversity, and compassion for the weak and the unfortunate.[58]

Special attention has been given to the interactions between Islam and Confucianism in the development of this common Asian front. In an address opening an international seminar, "Islam and Confucianism," in Kuala Lumpur in 1995, Anwar said: "It is our conviction that a civilizational dialogue between Islam and Confucianism would greatly contribute towards global peace and understanding. Here are two great traditions of the world whose adherents have generally been living, if not in perfect harmony with each other, certainly not in antagonism and discord, for the better part of the last one thousand years."[59] Among the "striking similarities" he mentioned was the refusal of both Islam and Confucianism "to detach religion, ethics, and morality from the public sphere. . . . A Muslim would have no difficulty identifying with the Confucian project to restore trust in government and to transform society into a moral community."[60]

Anwar made a special effort to recognize "Asian" perspectives and approaches in the concrete world of policy and government planning. For example, in discussions involved in the plans in the major Ecomedia City 2020 project, he advised that special attention be given to the recommendations made by Kisho Kurokawa regarding "ecotechnology and its relationship to architectural and urban plannning." These recommendations were based on "the philosophy of symbiosis, a concept which underlies most Asian philosophies."[61]

The keystone of this new paradigm becomes a cultural renaissance that provides the foundation for giving a more meaningful role to traditional concepts and values in the society of the future. Anwar recognizes that this involves a dangerous balancing of affirmation of separate identities and a sense of the universal human community. He notes that there must be a constant effort to avoid falling into the traps of religious fanaticism and ethnocentrism in the process of reviving of the grand civilizational traditions of Asia along with trying to defend the local cultures against homogenization in the experience of globalization. To explain this he developed a special conceptualization of pluralism to understand how to balance the global and local elements of contemporary affairs.

Pluralism. Anwar's conceptualization of pluralism starts from the recognition of the reality of diversity in human society. Within this framework, the experience of Malaysia has special relevance because its internal diversity is so central to its experience as a society and country. From the Malaysian experience it is possible to see the positive dimensions of diversity:

> Nations can actually grow and prosper by accepting the fact of cultural diversity, strengthening themselves by learning about their differences as well as by reinforcing the values they share in common. Malaysia is a case in point. It can justifiably claim to be Asia in microcosm – a country with a truly diverse population in terms of ethnicity, culture and faith. Admittedly this has not come about by choice. One might even say that we were forced by circumstances and history to become a nation, not by dissolving our respective identities and loyalties, but by transcending them.[62]

This experience provides a basis for developing the conceptualization further. Toleration of differences is, in Anwar's view, an important starting point but only a beginning. Already in the 1970s, he and his colleagues in ABIM attacked "cultural jingoism" and "tribalism" as threats to Malaysian survival. Anwar began to argue that the diversity was not simply a challenge but represented a major positive resource for Malaysian in particular, and Asians in general. People needed to "transcend" their differences but not eliminate them. The Southeast Asian context provides an important lesson in Anwar's conceptualization:

> Southeast Asians will not forget that since time immemorial, their region has been the theater in which the great civilizations have crossed paths. But they are honest enough to know that the region is not a great melting pot. The collective memory of each community is as strong as ever, and each holds dearly to its identity. Yet Southeast Asia is moving toward greater cohesiveness. . . . The people of various faiths in Southeast Asia are proceeding beyond mere tolerance.[63]

"Transcending tolerance" becomes a crucial part of the new paradigm developed by Anwar as the basis for a strong society. Going beyond mere tolerance is not just virtuous but is, on the long run, a necessity for human survival. The strength of democracy rests on the existence of diversity. Authoritarian regimes, according to Anwar, forget "that dissent is also a true barometer of the democracy we uphold. A case can be easily made, not for mere tolerance, but rather for the active nurturing of alternative views."[64] In this context, pluralism becomes an essential foundation for a strong democracy and, even more, a necessary part of a healthy and dynamic society. Within this perspective, lack of diversity becomes a weakness.

Anwar believes that this acceptance of pluralism that transcends tolerance is a clearly Islamic position. In a speech on civilizational dialogue, he cited the verse in the Quran: "Oh mankind! Verily we have created you all from a male and a female, and have made you into nations and tribes that you may come to know one another."[65] Constructively recognizing the implications of this divine revelation involves affirmation of both distinctiveness and global humanity.

> We believe that a revitalization of tradition, with all its cultural and intellectual richness, is the most effective countervailing force against religious fanaticism and ethnocentrism. In the context of Islam, this process of revitalization comprehends the reassertion of the values of justice (al-adl), tolerance (al-tasamuh) and compassion (al-rahmah). These values have enabled Muslims, throughout history, to accept diversity not merely as a fact but as an essential fea-

ture of human civilization to be celebrated. Because of diversity, man becomes richer through the impetus of the quest to know and understand one another."[66]

This creates, in Anwar's view, a context of constructive living together by diverse groups of people, both in individual societies and in the broader emerging global community. He describes this condition with a term that was developed to describe the religiously pluralistic society in the Iberian Peninsula under Muslim rule: *convivencia*. In its historic sense, and as Anwar uses it, the term "is loosely defined as 'coexistence,' but carries connotations of mutual interpenetration and creative influence. . . . [In Spain] it is the coexistence of the three groups [Muslims, Christians, and Jews], but only as registered collectively and consciously in the culture of any one of them."[67]

In Anwar's paradigm, convivencia is seen as the Islamic form of pluralism, but this is a vision that is quite different from the typical Islamist programs of making a place for non-Muslims in a traditionally conceived Islamic society. Primacy is given to the values of social and economic justice and equality, which are recognized as being fundamental to other great traditions of religious faith as well as Islam. This represents a special balancing of the particular and the universal. Anwar defines this in his call for the "Asian Renaissance":

[I]ts societies must be prepared to transform themselves and discard the harmful residue from the past—tribalism, narrow-mindedness and fanaticism. It is not the case that Asia must lose its identity, but it must renew its commitment to core values such as justice, virtue and compassion, that are in themselves universal. Creativity, imagination and courage is [sic] needed to translate these values into reality.[68]

This pluralist vision becomes the key to Anwar's understanding of the future global role for Islam and for Asia. It is the foundation for his call for civilizational dialogue.

Civilzational dialogue. People have long discussed the relationships among the civilizations of the world and have noted both the conflicts and the constructive interactions. However, in 1993, Samuel Huntington wrote an article that popularized the terminology of "the clash of civilizations" and set the terms of much discussion and debate concerning world affairs during the 1990s.[69] Although Huntington's analysis was global in its coverage, it concentrated attention on the relations between Islam and the West and did so in a way that emphasized stark contrasts:

The underlying problem for the West is not Islamic fundamentalism. It is Islam, a different civilization whose people are convinced of the superiority of their culture and are obsessed with the inferiority of their power. The problem for Islam is not the CIA or the U.S. Department of Defense. It is the West, a different civilization whose people are convinced of the universality of their culture and believe that their superior, if declining, power imposes on them the obligation to extend that culture. These are the basic ingredients that fuel conflict between Islam and the West.[70]

Anwar, like many Muslim intellectuals, as well as analysts in the West, was aware of the "clash of civilizations" paradigm and rejected it for a variety of reasons. In an informal interview, Anwar argued that

the psyches are different, the cultures are different. Many things about America I like to emulate. But I don't need to be an American. . . . We should be modern; we should be democratic. We should not condone corruption or oppression in any form, or deny basic rights. . . . But don't tell me that democracy and freedom can only be preached by some countries and political leaders in the West.[71]

The response of many people to Huntington's perspective was to call for a dialogue of civilizations, not a clash. Both as an intellectual and as a political leader, Anwar joined in this effort. In this, he again defined an important position of activist moderation. He identified common positions of advocacy that had emerged in the encounter between the West and "the civilizations of the East." He noted that the intelligentsia from the East faced the choice of

whether to remain loyal to one's traditions or to depart for a way of life perceived as superior. They generally fall into two categories. There are those who foreswore everything from the West because of their passionate and tenacious hold on everything from their own traditions. And then there were those who, overwhelmed by the dazzling light of Western civilization, became renegades to condemn their own.[72]

Both of these types of intellectuals had essentially accepted Huntington's fundamental premise of profound and unbridgeable differences between civilizations.

Anwar rejected the concept of almost absolute otherness. "We are already in fundamental agreement, in that we subscribe to the universal quest for truth and the pursuit of justice and virtue. . . . In our disjointed world, therefore, with so much ugliness, violence and injustice, there cannot be a nobler aim and vocation than the realization of values which unify humanity, despite the great diversity of climes and cultures."[73] The universals become an essential part of the cultural rebirth. The rediscovery of tradition in cultural rebirth "must inevitably involve a synthesis with other cultures, including those from the West. Genuine renaissance would not be possible without our rediscovery, reaffirmation and renewed commitment with the universals within our culture."[74]

Civilizational dialogue becomes the necessary policy framework for Anwar's conceptualization of pluralism. "For us, the divine imperative as expressed in the Qur'an is unambiguous. Humanity has been created to form tribes, races and nations, whose differences in physical characteristics, languages and modes of thought are but the means for the purpose of lita'arafu—'getting to know one another.'"[75] In a world of dangerous confrontations, civilizational dialogue is a necessity for human survival and progress. However, this dialogue "must be an encounter among equals, between cherished ideals and values that will serve to challenge our pride and end our prejudices."[76] In this dialogue, continuations of both the old imperialist attitudes of the "civilizing mission" and fundamentalist rejections of the West as an enemy are not appropriate and only threaten human survival. But civilizational dialogue is a means to a goal, not the goal itself, in Anwar's view. This "dialogue has become an imperative at a time when the world has shrunk into a global village. For it is a precondition for the establishment of a convivencia, a harmonious and enriching experience of living together among people of diverse religions and cultures."[77] This means that the "primary motif of civilizational dialogue must be a global *convivencia*."[78]

Conclusion

Anwar's new paradigm has both explicitly Islamic and more generally defined conceptual foundations. It provides the basis for an activist Islamic "moderatism" that is in contrast to the more typical Islamic "fundamentalisms" and the common reformist secularisms that are found in many parts of the world. Anwar's moderate position is not a position of compromise; it is an affirmation of the conviction that moderation is an Islamic imperative and that Islam is fundamentally a "middle path." This conviction then provides the basis for a new conceptualization of pluralism as an active good and of civilizational dialogue as a necessary part of Islamic faith and practice.

Anwar's evolution from a charismatic student leader to an activist moderate provided the basis for his articulation of a significant Islamic activism. Over the years he played a vital role in the developing discourse of Islam in Southeast Asia and the broader Muslim world. Even as a political prisoner, his mode of activism continues to provide a well-known and influential model for intellectuals and movements. By combining activism and involvement in public affairs with a continuing intellectual effort to conceptualize what he was doing and what was happening in the world around him, he is a highly visible example of a Muslim activist intellectual in the final decades of the twentieth century.

9
ABDURRAHMAN WAHID
Scholar-President

In October 1999, Abdurrahman Wahid, a prominent Islamic leader, became the first elected president in Indonesia's history. As leader of the Nahdatul Ulama, (the renaissance of religious scholars), Abdurrahman Wahid heads the biggest Islamic organization in the world's largest Muslim country, Indonesia, where 87 percent of the population of 220 million are Muslim. The Nahdatul Ulama (NU) is a predominantly conservative, rural-based, sociocultural organization with some thirty-five million members (approximately 20 percent of Indonesia's population), headed by a man best described as a modern, urban liberal Muslim intellectual. Abdurrahman Wahid, popularly known as Gus Dur, is an intellectual/activist who attracts and repels modernists and traditionalists alike. While some have charged that he is too close to government, government officials have feared his influence and "interference." The head of Indonesia's largest Islamic organization, he nevertheless warns against those Islamic reformers who would reassert Islam's role in politics.

Abdurrahman Wahid was born into a prominent Javenese Muslim family in 1941 in Jombang, East Java, a district in Indonesia known as a center for Islamic learning. Both his grandparents were prominent religious leaders, founders of important "pesantrens" that educated thousands of students. *Pesantren* ("the place of the *santri*," those learned in sacred scripture) in the Indonesian-Muslim tradition refers to Islamic residential educational institutions or schools. Pesantrens educate the students who board there in religious sciences; the master, or *kiai*, a combination of religious scholar and Sufi (mystic) guide, also offers religious instruction and guidance to the outside community. Wahid's paternal grandfather, Hasyim Asyari (Hashim Ashari), studied in Mecca and, shortly after his return, founded a pesantren at the turn of the century (1898). Abdurrahman's grandfather came to be recognized as a great Islamic scholar, writing in both Javanese and Arabic. He founded the

Nahdatul Ulama but is also remembered as a preeminent Sufi leader (Naqshbandi shaykh). Abdurrahman's maternal grandfather also studied at Mecca and established his own pesantren. Both grandfathers became prominent Islamic leaders, were acknowledged leaders of the ulama, and were active in the Indonesian nationalist movement.

Abdurrahman's father, Wahid Hashim, was educated in the pesantren system and later became vice-chairman of his father's pesantren; he also was a national political leader. Active in the anti-Dutch nationalist movement, he was one of the founders of the Masjumi party and of the postindependence modern Indonesian state. After independence, the family moved to Jakarta in 1950, where Abdurrahman's father became minister of religious affairs, a position he held until his tragic death in an auto accident at the age of thirty-eight. Wahid Hashim was one of the formulators of the Jakarta Charter, the preamble to Indonesia's Constitution, and of the Pancasila, a set of five basic principles, which forms the basis for Indonesia's national ideology. Abdurrahman's experience as a teenager of witnessing the constitutional debates (1956–1959) had a formative influence on his belief regarding the relationship of Islam to the state. In particular, the religious compromise that produced the formula or doctrine of Pancasila, the principle of belief in one God or supreme principle, which was formulated to include all of Indonesia's faiths, convinced him of the certain"failure of formalizing Islam in the life of a state like Indonesia."[1]

The first of six children, Abdurrahman's educational formation combined modern and traditional religious education. Despite the fact that his family was so closely associated with the pesantran system and that he was literally born in a pesantran, he was enrolled in the government or public school in 1946 at the age of six. (Although he was actually born in 1941, his birth date was changed to 1940 in order to enroll him early.) He attended government primary and high schools and subsequently (1957–1964) spent almost six and a half years studying in four pesantren, among them Pesantren Tegalrejo at Magelang and Pesantren Krapyak in Yogyakarta. Here he studied Arabic, Islamic law, and hadith (Prophetic traditions). It was a time of austerity and long hours spent memorizing and studying texts. During this time he also taught (1959–1963) at a pesantren in Jambong. His formal education was supplemented by exposure to different currents of thought and culture. His family introduced him to a diverse group of people. Family friends with whom he socialized, and at times lived with, included ulama of the modernist Muhammadiya, as well as a diverse group of prominent NU ulama and Europeans (the beginning of his love of European classical music).

After completing his studies in the pesantran system, Abdurrahman traveled to the Arab world (Egypt and Iraq) and Europe for higher studies. He studied at al-Azhar University in Cairo (1964–1966) and at the Arts Faculty of the University of Baghdad (1966–1970) and served as chairman of the Association of Indonesian Students in the Middle East from 1964 to

1970. Because al-Azhar, the oldest center of Islamic learning in the Muslim world, has long been a training ground for Indonesian religious families, the Islamic modernist movement of Egypt's Muhammad Abduh (d. 1905) had spread to Southeast Asia in the early twentieth century, where it had a significant impact. However, Abdurrahman was disappointed with the level of instruction at al-Azhar and spent much of his time in libraries reading and in the coffee shops of Cairo listening and participating in intellectual discussions and debates on culture and politics, in particular the merits of nationalism and socialism. This was the period of the ascendancy of Arab nationalism and socialism; among the more prominent forms were Nasserism and Baathism in Syria and Iraq.

Dissatisfied with al-Azhar, Abdurrahman went to Baghdad, where he enrolled at the university during the early years of the Baath party's rule. In contrast to al-Azhar, he now encountered a more secular, Western-style approach to education. The faculty of Islamic law had been absorbed into the faculty of letters and transformed into a department of religion, and he was shocked to find several Communist professors on its faculty. [2] He studied Arabic literature and culture as well as European philosophy and social thought. During this period, he became convinced that Islam had to be reinterpreted, and that change in Islamic teachings was necessary to bring them into conformity with modern science and knowledge. Although he completed his coursework and exams for a master's degree, the death of his mentor delayed his ability to write his thesis, so he went to Europe to pursue doctoral studies. However, frustrated by European language requirements for advanced study, he spent the better part of mid-1970 to 1971 traveling in Europe. He would later teach himself French, English, and German.

Returning to Indonesia, Abdurrahman married, began to have a family, and moved back to his grandfather's pesantren. Abdurrahman now devoted his time to teaching students and training teachers. He occupied a variety of positions in the pesantren network, including that of dean at Hasyim Asyari (Hasan al-Ashari) University (1972–1974) and secretary general of the Pesantren Tebuireng in Jombang (1974–1980). In 1974 he joined with others in creating the Committee for the Development of Pesantrens in order to revitalize the pesantren system by expanding its economic base and impact. They networked with other pesantrens and persuaded government agencies to fund development projects, from clean water and energy to mathematics and technology.

As in his youth, Abdurrahman Wahid continued to be involved with and influenced by diverse currents of thought, national and international. After moving to Jakarta in 1977, he became active in intellectual and religious circles, participating in forums with prominent progressive Muslim thinkers like Nurcholish Madjid, as well as with non-Muslims. It was then that he emerged as a public intellectual and national commentator on current events, visible in public meetings, the media, and the press, in particular in the prominent weekly magazine *Tempo*. He also expanded his contacts with social movements in the Third World, traveling extensively. In particular, he visited Latin America, where he became quite familiar with Catholic social movements and liberation theology. He met with Archbishop Oscar Camara in Brazil and other leaders and became familiar with the thought of liberation theologians such as Leonardo Boff. Moreover, he observed the development of Christian base communities and bank-credit unions that had been established to help the poor. These experiences have influenced his later life and work.

Modern Reformer but Not Islamic Modernist

Abdurrahman Wahid is truly an enigma. He is neither a conservative traditionalist nor an Islamic modernist. A liberal thinker, he is leader of the largest traditionally based Islamic organization. An innovative intellectual with the air of a lay professional or intellectual, he presides over an organization of ulama, religious scholars, whose organization, the Nahdatul Ulama (Revival of Religious Scholars), was founded in 1926 to defend the interests of traditional Islam and counter the threat of modernism. The NU has functioned as both a socioreligious movement and a political party. Yet in 1984 at its Twenty-Seventh Congress at Situbondo, Abdurrahman Wahid was elected to lead NU with a new team of younger leadership, marking a turning point in its history. His impeccable family credentials and connections to NU, as well as his own personal, intellectual, and political talents, enabled him then and throughout the years to retain his leadership, though not uncontested. The twenty-seventh Congress redefined NU's relationship to the government, accepted Pancasila as the sole foundation of the state, broke with the Muslim political party, United Development Party (PPP), and set a new agenda with a heavy emphasis on social activism.

Abdurrahman sought to strengthen the NU leadership and to revitalize its membership through fostering a younger leadership at the grassroots level, and Indonesia's oldest and largest traditionalist organization emerged with a reformist leadership. In many ways, it reflected Abdurrahman himself, a progressive thinker and activist with an abiding appreciation of the strengths of traditionalist Islam. He is a man who bridges the worlds of traditional Islamic scholarship and "modern" thought, espousing a reformist intellectual synthesis and social agenda that distinguishes between unchanging religious doctrines or laws and legitimate accomodation and social change. This ideal was reflected in his comments on an independent-minded pesantren religious leader (kiai) who could be inflexible on some religious issues but accommodating in many other social situations: "The answer lies with the ability of Kiai Ali to discern between issues which are of essential importance to religion and those which are not; the ability to arrive at an accommodation with the demands of the day without forfeiting the original persona that is the source of the profoundest religious values."[3] In contrast to many modernizers, secular and Islamic, in the Muslim world who excoriate the ulama for the backwardness and failures of Muslim societies, Abdurrahman Wahid emphasizes the importance of the ulama in Islamic reform: "It is only in this way that dynamic leadership of the pesantren will be able to prevent a protraction of the crisis in the pesantren, and develop the pesantren to become an educational and social institution that is truly capable of facing the challenges of time."[4] Abdurrahman was not blind to the failings of many of the traditionalist ulama and their institutions. He sought to revitalize the ulama and the pesantren system, integrating the best of Islamic traditional thought and culture with the best of modern Western thought. His goal was to link intellectual and social reform in order to revitalize NU and the Muslims of Indonesia. For this he placed a heavy emphasis on revitalization through the expanded presence and role of a younger leadership in the pesantren, who would be "able to bring together the practical requirements for progress (especially the material ones) with the religious traditions which they have inherited from earlier generations."[5]

NU's new direction reflected the transition occurring in Indonesian society. Throughout the 1970s and the 1980s, Indonesia's Suharto had controlled and coopted Islam. The government used a carrot-and-stick approach, funding religious leaders and projects and stifling its Islamic opposition. At the same time, the government moved swiftly against any and all opposition. Students criticizing the government or passing out pamphlets were imprisoned as easily as those who waged armed insurrection in Sumatra. Muslim opposition was often branded deviant or fundamentalist (as Khomeneism or radical Islam) and charged with being fueled by support from Libya and Iran. The effectiveness of the government in controlling political Islam tended to foster a shift in activist energy to the social and cultural spheres.

At the same time, broader indigenous factors encouraged the growth of Islamic revivalism or influence. Among the more important were: a dissatisfaction with Western secular solutions to social and political problems; a rejection of what were seen to be undesirable aspects of modern Western value systems; a greater sense of pride and identity among Muslims, fostered by the Islamic world's greater prominence in global economic and political affairs; and the expansion of efforts by foreign Muslim governments and groups to spread the faith.[6]

Like many other parts of the Muslim world, mosques proved fertile centers for recruitment and organization of disaffected students. This was all the more so since the government had banned student organizations in the universities, making the Islamic groups and Islamic discourse the major vehicle for dissent. A prominent Indonesian Muslim scholar observed:

"The mosque has become a sanctuary for the expression of political dissatisfaction and frustration."[7] Students were critical of the failures of development, corruption, the growing disparity between rich and poor, and conspicuous consumption in a society with limited opportunities for the younger generation. This trend dovetailed with the emergence of a modern Islamically oriented generation of Muslim intellectuals educated in Europe and America. The closure of the political door led to a greater focus on the relevance of Islam to social and economic development. Abdurrahman Wahid and many of those attracted to him are among that generation of Islamic neomodernists, who include others like Nurcholish Madjid, Jalalludin Rakmat, Dewan Rahardjo, and Amien Rais. All advocate a progressive Islam, one that is democratic, pluralistic, and tolerant. However, their visions differ. In contrast to Nurcholish Madjid and others such as Amien Rais, former leader of the Muhammadiya, who have advocated the Islamization or re-Islamization of Indonesian society, Abdurrahman emphasizes the Indonesianization, the indigenization or contextualization (*pribumisasi*) of Islam. By this he means the blending of Islamic belief and values with local culture: "The source of Islam is revelation which bears its own norms. Due to its normative character, it tends to be permanent. Culture, on the other hand, is a creation of human beings and therefore develops in accordance with social changes. This, however, does not prevent the manifestation of religious life in the form of culture."[8]

Suharto had insisted that all organizations accept Pancasila as their sole ideology. The 1985 Law of Mass Organizations forced all organizations to do so. Thus Pancasila became not only the sole political but also the sole social ideology. While many had expected NU to resist the government, the new direction it adopted at its congress in 1984 signaled the decision to avoid direct involvement in the political system. At the same time, NU withdrew its longstanding and majority membership in the PPP, the major grouping of Muslim parties — a decision that displeased many of the older NU leaders. For the new leadership, NU was at a critical transitional stage. Like many other organizations, NU did not simply cower to the government but rather chose to remove itself from a potentially confrontational path in order to be free or to be left alone to focus on concentrating on the social (rather than overtly political) transformation of society. Withdrawal from politics enabled NU, under Abdurrahman's leadership, to focus more on socioeconomic and cultural development. However, this was to be a transitional strategy: "We must be careful to denote our non-political nature. . . . Perhaps by the mid-1990s we shall be able to impose our political views."[9] Indeed, despite its withdrawal from formal politics, NU enjoyed significant indirect political influence, proving effective as a major political pressure group. Wahid remained active in politics, forming shifting alliances over the years. In the period leading up to the fall of Suharto, he was a critic of the excesses of the government and a supporter of Megawati Sukarnoputra, the daughter of Indonesia's first president, Sukarno, who called for the replacement of Suharto through open and democratic elections. In the post-Suharto era, Wahid formed his own political party, the National Awakening Party, which garnered 13 percent of the popular vote.

In many ways, Abdurrahman Wahid might be called an Islamic modernist or neomodernist, except that in Indonesia, Islamic modernism is often associated with those who ultimately wish to implement Islam in public life. The Islamic modernist movement of Egypt's Muhammad Abduh and Jamal al-Din al-Afghani was brought to Indonesia by Southeast Asian Muslims who had returned from study at Egypt's al-Azhar University. Islamic modernism rejected a blind adherence to medieval Muslim doctrines and, responding to the challenge of modernity, called for a bold reinterpretation (ijtihad) of Islam. Modernists asserted the compatibility of Islam and modern science and technology. They claimed the right to bypass past interpretations and go directly to Islam's two material sources, the Quran and Prophetic Traditions, to formulate new responses to modern questions and issues. The modernist agenda included religious, educational, legal, and social reform. The disciples of Islamic modernism in Southeast Asia came to be known as the Kaum Muda ("new faction"), propagating their message and implementing their agenda through schools, journals, and associations.[10] Groups like the Muhammadiya—Indonesia's other major Muslim organization, founded in 1912 in Yogyakarta, which, in contrast to NU's rural base, is urban-based—proved very effective in creating a widespread network of modern Islamic schools and providing social services. The Muhammadiya, like the majority of Islamic modernists, advocates greater implementation of Islam in society.

However, Abdurrahman represents a form of Islamic modernism that encountered stiff opposition and was often suppressed. He may be seen as following the school of thought, sometimes referred to as Islamic liberalism, espoused by the Egyptian Ali Abd al-Raziq, a young Egyptian religious scholar. Abd al-Raziq maintained that religion and politics were separate and distinct spheres in Islam from the time of the Prophet Muhammad to the present. In his book *Islam and the Sources of Political Authority*, he argued that neither the caliphate nor any specific Islamic system of government ever existed or is required by Islam,[11] thus advocating the separation of religion and the state. These views cost him his job at al-Azhar University after his position was condemned by a council of senior ulama. A similar position was espoused by another religious scholar, Khalid Muhammad Khalid, in his *From Here We Start*, only to retracted in 1981 in a subsequent book in which he declared that Islam is both religion and state (*din wa dawla*).[12]

Despite the traditionalist roots of the NU, Abdurrahman Wahid has followed an accomodationist path that goes beyond that of his more traditional predecessors and of modernist organizations like the Muhammadiya. In particular, he advocates the separation of religion and the state, for which he is criticized by Islamic modernists and political activists. At the same time, his stature as a religious scholar and political leader and his use of Islamic discourse have at times also been a worry to secular Muslims, including government leaders.

Three pillars of Abdurrahman's thought are: (1) the conviction that Islam must be creatively and at times substantively reinterpreted or reformulated in order to be responsive to the demands of modern life; (2) his belief that, in the Indonesian context, Islam should not be the state religion; and that (3) Islam should be an inclusive, democratic, pluralistic force rather than an exclusive state ideology.

Abdurrahman Wahid believes that contemporary Muslims have two choices or paths: a more traditional legal-formalistic Islam or a more universal, cosmopolitan, pluralistic, Islamically informed worldview. The universalism of Islam is reflected in its monotheism (tawhid), law (fiqh), and ethics (akhlaq). These result in Islam's deep concern for human dignity: "The principles of being equal before the law, of protection of society from despotic powers, of the maintenance of the rights of the weak and of the limitation of the authority of political power, are reflections of Islamic concern with human dignity."[13]

Islamic legalism is the product of the past, a distorted historical reality; the latter is the agenda for contemporary Islamic reform. Historical Islam reveals the movement or transition from dynamism to legal formalism, as Islam became institutionalized primarily through law. Abdurrahman believes that Islam began as a dynamic reformism that exalts the status of mankind as God's viceregent (khalifah) on earth, responsible for witnessing, propagating, and implementing God's righteous way of life. However, the early tendency to formalize and institutionalize Islam's message produced instead a rigid, oppressive reality: "we are presented now with an Islam that oppresively puts human life within the narrow confinements of a rigid viewpoint: the demand for the so-called 'sharia state,' the equivalent of what is known in Western thought as theocracy."[14]

The extent to which law became the means whereby Islam was institutionalized meant that the legal framework became the mechanism by which jurists controlled and assured a more uniform interpretation, subjecting every aspect of life in Islam to "legal imprimatur." This process, Abdurrahman believes, produced a hegemony of law and legal scholars, one that was able to limit alternative theological and legal interpretations and check the "excesses" of philosophy, mysticism, and the humanities in general. The effects were intellectually devastating: "the humanities, liberal arts, and sciences suffer greatly to the extent that they entirely ceased to develop in Islam during the last six centuries."[15] While diversity continued to exist, it was always in tension with the legal-formalism of orthodox or, more accurately, orthoprax Islam, whose religious experts, ulama, saw themselves as the guardians of Islam whose task it was to legitimate the ideas and activities of all Muslims.

This legal-formalistic Islam is grounded, then, in a more rigid literalist approach to scripture, a monolithic vision of Islam that demands "a monocultural environment for its religious expression, with rigorous conformity to the prescribed life pattern and no room for any deviation."[16] It seeks to formalize Islam in the life of the state. Idealizing Islam as a social system, it seeks to impose and implement past Islamic law, albeit superficially, on the present, with little concern for change and cultural pluralism, generating a fortress mentality that proves socially disruptive.[17] Its comprehensive reassertion of Islam as a total way of life, which increasingly has taken the form of an "Islamic fundamentalism," runs the risk of degenerating into a religious sectarianism that alienates other national groups and becomes a separatist movement.[18]

Abdurrahman Wahid rejects the reduction of Islam to a stifling legal-formalism as both an aberration and a major obstacle to Islam's response to global change: "the whole situation has to be changed if Islam is asked to contribute to the formulation of a new world civilization in the future."[19] The concept of the Muslim as simply a subject of the law must be broadened. Recognition of "the need for a concept of man in Islam," that is, of the multifaceted Muslim and a dynamic Islamic tradition, requires a transformation based on fundamental values such as free will and the right of all Muslims, both laity and religious scholars (ulama) to "perpetual reinterpretation" (ijtihad) of the Quran and Traditions of the Prophet in light of "everchanging human situations."[20] This process, Abdurrahman believes, will produce a dynamic (rather than static legalistic) cosmopolitan Islam more suited to and capable of responding to the diverse realities of modern life.

Not blindly bound to past interpretations and institutions, cosmopolitan Islam seeks to reinterpret and reformulate Islam's attitude toward life. Abdurrahman believes that the challenge that Muslims face today is to render change with some kind of continuity with the past. He advocates a creative process that rediscovers and extracts the essence of religion from the totality of Islam, "the positive legacy of the past." This essence of Islam should function as an inspirational rather than (as in the past) a legal basis for national life. Thus, cosmopolitan Islam is more concerned with political culture than political institutions; cosmopolitan Islam exists in the informal structures rather than the formal political and legal institutions of the state. It is expressed in the individual lives and morality of people, informing the social ethics of the community and its sense of a transnational or universal identity (membership in the worldwide Islamic community, ummah).

In contrast to many Islamists today, Abdurrahman rejects the notion that Islam should form the basis for the nation-state's political or legal system: "there is no need for a nation-state with Islamic law."[21] He regards the enshrining of Islamic principles in law as a Middle Eastern tradition alien to Indonesia.[22] Instead he believes that Indonesian Muslims should apply a moderate, tolerant brand of Islam to their daily lives in a society where "a Muslim and a non-Muslim are the same" in a state in which religion and politics are separate.[23]

The cornerstone of Abdurrahman's worldview is pluralism, for it is the plurality of peoples and ideas that form the essential context of modern life. The new global outlook of cosmopolitan Islam is one that recognizes the need for a substantial reformulation of "existing civilizations,' institutional as well as spiritual frameworks of moral and human behaviour." This outlook will respond to universal basic rights, recognize and respect other faiths, ideologies, and cultures, and absorb the best that modern science and technology have to offer.[24] Cosmopolitan Islam produces a more flexible formulation of Islam whose pluralism and tolerance are more appropriate to the modern realities of Indonesia. Abdurrahman was the first official figure to publicly denounce the riots of 1996, in which most of the participants were NU members. In addition to advocating tolerance toward Christians, he called for official recognition of Confucianism as a religion in Indonesia.[25] However, his political pluralism seemed to test the limits of many Muslims when in mid-1994 he visited Israel and called for the establishment of relations with Israel. He further aggravated traditionalist Muslims and the ulama (many members of NU) when he criticized, as meddling in politics, the Indonesian Council of Ulamas for their call for Muslims to vote for parties with Muslim candidates. Moreover, he insisted that the Indonesian government should be a secular coalition rather than a coalition of Islamic parties.[26]

An accomodationist, pluralistic approach of cosmopolitan Islam is not without its dangers. Accomodation and acculturation can over time produce an identity whose Islamic character is dissipated or that simply comes to be perceived as non-Islamic. To safeguard its Islamic character, the product of the reinterpretation of Islam Abdurrahman believes that cosmopolitan Islam is dependent on a continuity with its Islamic past or heritage that draws its inspirational and moral base from the sources of Islam (the Quran and Prophetic Traditions). To enhance its promotion in the broader populace, indigenous Islamic institutions outside the modern sector, such as the traditional pesantren system, must be identified and utilized in regenerating the Indonesian Muslim community. The challenge for contemporary Muslims is to articulate and preserve an authentic identity informed by their Islamic heritage but open to the cosmopolitan realities of a global environment: "to find an identity that will develop a sense of belonging to Islam, but at the same time still retain a sense of belonging to a larger and wider association with groups motivated by world ideologies, other faiths and global concerns."[27]

Islam and Development

The diversity of the Muslim world is reflected by (witnessed in) the enormous diversity of the Indonesian archipelago itself. Abdurrahman Wahid sees Indonesian Muslims as sharing many of the common problems of

Muslims throughout much of the Muslim world but facing them in their quite distinctively diverse and pluralistic context. Indonesia, with its three thousand islands stretched out along a 3,200 mile arc, is a vast collection of religious and cultural groups. It has been significantly influenced by its pre-Islamic, Hindu-Buddhist legacy as well as the diverse Islamic interpretations and orientations of its peoples—the militant conservatism of the Muslims of Acheh, the more nominal, syncretistic approach of Java embodied in Suharto's government and many of its citizens, the militant brands of contemporary Islamic activism. Abdurrahman has championed the belief that Indonesia can and must provide an example that counters the stereotypes of Islam and Muslim states as radical, antimodern, antidemocratic, and intolerant:

> All that the West sees in Islam is radicalism and its incompatibility with modern, open, democratic politics. Indonesia, however, has the opportunity to show that politics based on confession—as it is in Algeria and Iran—is not the only way. Not only can modernity and open politics exist in a Muslim-majority society, as it can here in Indonesia, but it can be nurtured so that democracy can flourish well in Islam.[28]

Islam, Nationalism, and Democratization

The relationship of Islam to the nation-state is a major issue for modern Muslims. Historically and religiously, Muslims have had multiple identities as members of tribes, clans, families, and villages, yet they also have possessed an underlying unity or overriding identity based in a common sense of religious identity and solidarity. This belief is articulated in Islam's concept of the ummah, the Islamic community. Thus Muhammad's unification of disparate tribes in Arabia was based on the assertion of a common religious bond that was to transcend tribal and ethnic identities. The ummah took on more transnational and global dimensions as Islam spread and was transformed into a central empire, or caliphate, and subsequently into a network of sultanates that stretched from Timbuktu to Sumatra. Despite their diversity, they shared a common sense of universal identity and shared Islamically legitimated institutions and values. However, the impact of European colonial rule and the subsequent emergence of modern Muslim states presented a new challenge to Islam and Muslims.

Southeast Asian Islam, like other parts of the worldwide Islamic community, or ummah, shared the struggle for independence. In the first part of the twentieth century, a double pattern prevailed: resistance to both the political and the cultural penetration of the West. Islam and Muslims across the globe were concerned with throwing off the yoke of European colonialism and gaining independence. At the same time, many charged that there was a fundamental contradiction between Western and Islamic values. Some questioned and others rejected the excessive materialism/consumerism and individualism of the West and even its technology. Others called for the need to balance Western individualism and materialism with Islam's emphasis on community and spirituality.

In the several decades since national independence, a cross-section of Muslim countries have struggled with issues of political legitimacy, national identity/unity, and the relationship of religion to national development in a world in which the presuppositions of development and modernization theory presumed a Western, secular path. Abdurrahman identifies many issues and realities in nation-building. The difficulties nation-states face include the need to create national integration in the face of communalism, establish the rule of law, and develop viable economic frameworks for the equitable distribution of wealth. At the same time, he maintains that many rely on sociopolitical engineering, authoritarianism, political suppression, and violence to impose their vision. Governments that rely on social control rather than consultation increasingly employ violence and repression and create a climate that contributes to radicalization and violence against the state. Islamic movements are faced with "the choice of following either a radical approach or a gradual response in their struggle for social justice, equal treatment before the law and freedom of expression."[29]

Abdurrahman Wahid believes that in the postindependence period, the Southeast Asian experience contrasts with much of the Muslim world. Many Muslims initially opposed modern nationalism and continue to debate the compatibility of Islam and the nationalism. However, in Southeast Asia what clearly emerged from the independence movement was an acceptance of the nation-state—recognition by the majority in Indonesia and Malaysia of the bond between Islam and nationalism. Over the years political parties and organizations continued to play an "informal" role in society while social organizations flourished in Indonesia and Malaysia. In contrast to many parts of the Muslim world where the resurgence of Islam has been primarily political, Abdurrahman argues that the movement for greater Islamization of society in Southeast Asia has been occurring for some time and that it has been primarily cultural rather than political. In Indonesia, organizations like the Muhammadiya developed a network of more than fifteen thousand schools, as well as hospitals and clinics, and NU, in addition to supporting its pesantren system—some seven thousand pesantrens spread across Indonesia—turned to development projects. In Malaysia the Islamic Youth Movement of Malaysia (ABIM) and PAS (Parti Islam Sa-Malaysia), the more conservative Islamic party, both in their members and sociopolitical activities, are religioculturally inspired or motivated. (Many would argue that PAS has played a more aggressive political role and sought to establish an Islamic state.) The Malaysian government's ruling party (United Malay National Organization; UMNO) has included many former members of Islamic movements, in particular ABIM, whose former founder and charismatic leader Anwar Ibrahim became Malaysia's finance minister and deputy prime minister.

A Theology of Liberation

Central to Abdurrahman Wahid's cosmopolitan Islamic worldview and work is his bottom-up strategy and thus significant involvement in development projects. His ideology is the product of diverse religious and cultural currents. It is based not only on his Indonesian Islamic background and experience but also on the work of Muslim thinkers and activists in the broader Muslim world such as Egypt's Hasan Hanafi and Iran's Ali Shariati, as well as Christian liberation theologians. His direct experience with liberation theology in Latin America in particular had a significant impact on his view of Islam and its role in the world as well as of religion and Third World development in general.

In addressing the problems of development, Abdurrahman casts Islam as itself the basis for a theology of liberation. Like the Iranian Ali Shariati and many other contemporary Muslim ideologues and activists, Abdurrahman identifies Islam as a liberating religion whose very origins were concerned both with religious and social reform. Thus religion is concerned not only with the individual but also with the community; not only with the next life but also with this life. Like modern Islamic leaders in many parts of the Muslim world, Abdurrahman recognized the need to relate Islam to the socioeconomic crises in many Muslim societies. An Islamically informed approach to development (moral and social) is embodied in Muhammad's and the Quran's protest against social injustice, the establishment of the first Islamically guided community at Medina, and the expansion and propagation of Islam, which led to the creation of a vast cosmopolitan empire and civilization.

Ali Shariati legitimated his reformist Islam by claiming to appropriate Alid Shiism, the original sociopolitically revolutionary spirit of islam and Ali, its first imam or leader, as distinguished from that of Safavid Shiism, the quiescent, establishment religion of a clergy coopted by imperial rulers. Abdurrahman Wahid also preaches an Islam of social activism. Influenced by liberation theology's notion of "conscientization," he speaks of the need for Muslims to develop a "new conscience," one that responds to the dire social realities of the majority. Thus, his cosmopolitan Islam, which attempts to adapt Islam to the diverse and changing realities of Muslim life, includes a pronounced emphasis on the relationship of religion to development, in particular poverty and other social ills that afflict the majority of society: "Social justice should be made a religious as well as a political paradigm."[30] The sociocultural activities of indigenous institutions such as the pesantren system should become a vehicle for the socioeconomic transformation of society and thus contribute to the "real task of development, i.e. to liberate mankind from all constraints, whether structural, cultural, or political, still obstructing the full development of man's potentialities."[31]

The Escapism of Fundamentalism

For Abdurrahman, religion is a significant variable in the development process. However, it constitutes a major obstacle for governments, often resulting in an adversarial relationship between the state, which is responsible for the formulation and implementation of national ideology and political life, and the leadership of religious movements. The causes of Islamic revivalism in Southeast Asia reflect issues of faith/identity and dissatisfaction with the political, economic, and social failures of society. The impact and dislocation caused by the clash of values that accompanies the cultural penetration of the West causes many to perceive and react to the "danger" and "threat" of Westernization and modernization. The experience of alienation and marginalization, stemming from the inability of many to integrate themselves (their lives and family values), educational institutions, and economic enterprises into the new modern mainstream, creates a climate in which "[f]undamentalism becomes an attractive 'escape way' to regain in an inner way what they lose in the outer one."[32]

While he uses the term *fundamentalism*, Abdurrahman acknowledges the problems with its popular usage. Fundamentalism is a Christian term misapplied to Muslims. Moreover, given its common and popular denotations of extremism and radicalism, its equation with an exclusivist and narrow-minded attitude, the term is often a source of confusion rather than clarification. In a sense, he notes, fundamentalism is an appropriate description of a Muslim who simply wishes to observe or be faithful to the basic "fundamentals," that is, fundamental sources of his or her religion. Abdurrahman distinguishes between Islamic militants and fanatics or fundamentalists. Islamic movements draw their strength from the extent to which religion informs and transforms their ideology and activities. Political ideals are drawn from religious beliefs, mundane or profane convictions are sacralized, and failure and persecution are regarded as part of an eternal struggle (jihad and martyrdom) against oppression and injustice. Militants are those who are concerned with fundamental issues of self-identity but accept and work within the social and political system. Many combine modern educations with a conscious reappropriation and reformulation of a religiously informed modern Islamic identity. This is reflected in personal morality and dress, new forms of socioeconomic activity such as interest-free banking and finance, schools, and social welfare. They demonstrate the ability of Islam to inspire and motivate Muslims to find solutions to the failures and problems of the modern nation-state: "As long as those efforts constitute attempts to reiterate Islamic values, without totally abandoning the process of modernization in the whole region, it is impossible to apply the label Fundamentalism to them."[33] In contrast, fundamentalists are a minority of extremists or fanatics who reject the social and political framework. They oppose not just a specific government but the very idea of the nation-state itself. They are small and sporadic movements, often confused with the majority of Islamically oriented but more mainstream youth. They withdraw from mainstream society physically and ideologically. Some live in communes; all reject the political and religious establishment, prefer or profess there own narrow "far out view of Islam," and condemn the majority of Muslims who participate in national political life. Though their violent outbursts challenge and disrupt the system from time to time, Abdurrahman believes that they continue to have only local significance and have proven incapable of developing nationally or regionally.[34] Because the state often regards religious movements as a threat to national unity and development, it tends to restrict or coopt religion. Governments attempt to weaken or control religious movements through harassment or the creation of heavily funded rival movements or simply to coopt movements through the use of funds. Because Islamic movements provide a cohesive and well-organized alternative (comparable) to the state, confrontation with government is often inevitable. Abdurrahman bases his assessment on the examples of Islamic movements in the Muslim world, Catholic movements in Latin America, and Catholic priests who defend the rights of Muslim minorities in the southern Philippines.

Abdurrahman Wahid believes that most governments close their eyes to a fundamental issue in the development of their societies when they ignore issues of faith and identity and reduce national problems solely to political, socioeconomic, and technical factors. The failure of governments to address deep-seated issues of identity and the relationship of faith to national identity/ideology and institution-building runs the long-term risk of contributing to greater instability, "risking the dangers of massive social explosions."[35] Marriages of convenience are short-lived; long-lasting creative solutions are needed to determine the relationship of religion and the state.

As throughout the history of the Indonesian state, the politics of religion in the 1990s proved a challenge that often put Abdurrahman Wahid at odds with the government, the military, and fellow Muslim intellectuals and politicians alike. President Suharto attempted in the 1990s to broaden his base of support among observant (versus nominal) Muslims. His "turn" more to Islam included making the pilgrimage to Mecca (hajj), introducing new legislation and programs on religious education and religious courts, and approving the creation of ICMI (Association for Indonesian Muslim Intellectuals), an organization of intellectuals and government officials. Among the ICMI leadership were Nurcholish Madjid, a prominent intellectual and leader of Paramedina, a reformist organization; Amien Rais, a U.S.-trained political scientist and head of the Muhammadiyah; Ado Sasono, a social activist; and Islamic activists, like Imad ad Deen, who had previously been among the staunchest critics of Suharto's New Order. Conspicuously absent was Abdurrahman Wahid, who maintained that ICMI leaders compromised their independence and adopted a tactic to infiltrate and Islamize the government and society. He charged that ICMI's agenda, to create an Indonesian society infused with Islamic values in a 90 percent Muslim-majority country would reconfessionalize Indonesian politics, undermine national unity and religious and political pluralism, threaten non-Muslims and nominal Muslims alike, and contribute to sectarian strife. Abdurrahman regarded the creation of an Islamic society in Indonesia as "treason against the constitution because it will make non-Muslims second class citizens."[36]

To counter ICMI, Abdurrahman joined forty-five intellectuals to create the Forum for Democracy. In contrast to ICMI's linkage of Islam and democratization and the desire of its Muslim intellectuals and activists to Islamize Indonesian society, the Forum provided a platform to promote Abdurrahman's secular democratic vision. It was based on Pancasila, with its equal recognition of all religions and separation of religion and the state, as the sole national ideology. Because religious tolerance is a prerequisite for democratization, he argued that only nonpolitical, pluralistic Indonesianized Islam recognizes the equality of all citizens necessary for the promotion of true democracy in a Muslim-majority society like Indonesia. Abdurrahman remained critical of both ICMI and the government, maintaining that the ICMI's Islamization of Indonesian society would mean inequality and second-class citizenship for minorities and lead to sectarian strife and religious fanaticism. While Suharto's New Order was secular, it was not democratic. It was dependent on a military-derived vision of an "integralistic secularism," which emphasized the totality of the state and lacked separation of powers, a system of checks and balances, and the independence of civil society from state control.[37] The impact of the Forum was greatly hampered by its broad and diverse opposition: the Suharto government, the Muslim intellectuals of ICMI and some Muslim religious leaders and organizations, and the military, who were as opposed to Abdurrahman's and the Forum's democratic and liberal ideas as to ICMI's talk of Islamization.

If contemporary Islam has too often been seen as monolithic, inflexible, and extremist, Abdurrahman Wahid and Indonesian Islam have offered a counterimage of the diversity, creativity, and dynamism of contemporary Muslim societies. Like many Islamic activist intellectuals, he is the product of a traditional and a modern education. A progressive thinker and reformer, he remains intimately linked to his traditionalist heritage. Though a Muslim modernist, he is the leader of the world's largest ulama organization. While he shares much in common with other reform-minded Indonesian activist intellectuals, he nevertheless has parted company with many over his vision of Islam and its relationship to state and society. While some call for an Islamization of Indonesian society to reflect the demographic realities of the world's largest Muslim country and its Muslim majority population, Abdurrahman and, under his leadership, NU, have insisted on the promotion of Islam in individual life and within the Muslim community but its separation from government. His liberalism has often strained relations with older, more conservative members of NU (in 1994 he narrowly defeated his government-favored opponent by 174 to 142 votes to win a third term as NU chairman) as well as the government and military.

At the same time, his progressive thinking, championing of democracy, religious tolerance and advocacy of human rights have won praise from younger, reform-minded NU activists, liberal intellectuals, non-governmental organizations, and Christian and Chinese minority leaders and businessman.

The example of Abdurrahman Wahid also highlights the problems that can arise when religious leaders and organizations mix religion and politics. His intellectual flexibility, independence, and pragmatic politics have often led some to charge opportunism. Others have seen him as a master politician, a consensus builder, Indonesian style. Balancing his role as an Islamic leader/scholar and Chairman of NU, an organization of ulama, with that of a progressive reformer and secular political leader has required him to compromise and to shift alliances, seeming at times to move from one marriage of convenience to another. At times a strong critic of Suharto's military-backed government, he was also willing to make substantial compromises. A critic of the Indonesian Armed Forces, he accepted and cultivated its support, particularly in the early 1990s when Suharto turned to Islam or the Islamization of politics to counterbalance the influence of the military. Nowhere was political pragmatism more pronounced than in the late 1990s, when he willingly worked closely with both Megawati, former president Sukarno's daughter, who opposed Suharto, and Tutu, Suharto's daughter, who was a potential vice-presidential nominee. In the aftermath of national elections, while calling for national reconciliation, he continued to move easily among contending political leaders and forces: state officials, the military, and the opposition—at one point calling for a trio to lead the country (Megawati, who had garnered the most votes, Amien Rais, and himself), at others distancing himself from Megawati. In the end, after Amien Rais was elected Speaker of Parliament, Abdurrahman, a compromise candidate between B. J. Habibie and Megawati, was elected president of Indonesia by the parliament, and Megawati was appointed vice-president, in October 1999.

For much of Indonesia's modern history, both Sukarno and Suharto sought to keep a tight control on Islamic leaders and organizations. Indonesia, the largest Muslim country in the world, was often characterized as a state in which the majority of the population were nominal Muslims and in which both the ruler and the military marginalized and at times suppressed the role of religion in Muslim politics. In the late Suharto years, Islam became a more visible political presence and political force. In the post-Suharto period, as Indonesia attempts to move away from a legacy of authoritarian government on a path of democratization, defining the nature of Indonesian Islam and its relationship to public life in a pluralistic society, the debate between Abdurrahman Wahid's vision of an Indonesianized Islam and the visions of those who advocate a more Islamized society, will prove critical.

NOTES

Introduction

1. Edward Shils, "Intellectuals," in *International Encyclopedia of the Social Sciences*, ed. David L. Sills (New York: Macmillan, 1968), 7:399.

2. Roberto Michels, "Intellectuals," in *Encyclopaedia of the Social Sciences*, ed. Edwin R. A. Seligman (New York: Macmillan, 1932), 8:118.

3. Clyde W. Barrow, "Styles of Intellectualism in Weber's Historical Sociology," *Sociological Inquiry* 60, 1 (February 1990): 47.

4. Julien Benda, *The Treason of the Intellectuals*, trans. Richard Aldington (New York: Norton, 1969; New York: Morrow, 1928), pp. 43–44.

5. Ibid., p. 139.

6. J. P. Nettl, "Ideas, Intellectuals, and Structures of Dissent," in *On Intellectuals: Theoretical Studies, Case Studies*, ed. Philip Rieff (Garden City, NY: Doubleday, 1969), p. 93; see also the discussion of "qualitative dissent," pp. 64–70.

7. Edward W. Said, *Representations of the Intellectual* (New York: Random House, 1994), p. 11.

8. Nettl, "Ideas," p. 69.

9. Shils, "Intellectuals," p. 399.

10. Said, *Representations*, p. 11.

11. Benda, *Treason*, pp. 45–46, 51.

12. Tibor Huszar, "Changes in the Concept of Intellectuals," in *The Intelligentsia and the Intellectuals: Theory, Method and Case Study*, ed. Aleksander Gella (London: Sage, 1976), pp. 79–83.

13. Paul Johnson, *Intellectuals* (New York: Harper and Row, 1988), p. 1.

14. Ibid., pp. 1–2.

15. See, for example, the analysis in Raymond Aron, *The Opium of the Intellectuals*, trans. Terence Kilmartin (New York: Norton, 1962), chap. 9.

16. Said, *Representations*, p. 120.

17. Nettl, "Ideas," p. 117.

18. Max Weber, *Essays in Sociology*, ed. and trans. H. H. Gerth and C. Wright Mills (New York: Oxford University Press, 1958), p. 176.

19. Seymour M. Lipset and Asoke Basu, "The Roles of the Intellectual and Political Roles," in *The Intelligentsia and the Intellectuals: Theory, Method and Case Study*, ed. Aleksander Gella (London: Sage, 1976), p. 121.

20. Ibid., p. 121.

21. Ibid., pp. 121–22.

22. Edward Shils, "The Intellectuals and the Powers," in Rieff, *On Intellectuals*, p. 41. See also his discussion in Shils, "Intellectuals," 7:406.

23. Max Weber, *The Sociology of Religion*, trans. Ephraim Fischoff (Boston: Beacon Press, 1963), p. 120.

24. *Ulama* is the plural, in Arabic, for *alim*, or "one who possesses knowledge" (ilm). Ulama are, literally, the "people of knowledge."

25. Shils, "Intellectuals and Powers," p. 41.

26. Marshall G. S. Hodgson, *The Venture of Islam* (Chicago: University of Chicago Press, 1974), 1:238.

27. Ibid., 1:238.

28. This is a modified version of the translation in Ibn Khaldun, *The Muqaddimah: An Introduction to History*, trans. Franz Rosenthal (New York: Pantheon, 1958), 1:460.

29. Roy P. Mottahedeh, *Loyalty and Leadership in an Early Islamic Society* (Princeton: Princeton University Press, 1980), p. 138.

30. A helpful introduction to this scholar and his school is George Makdisi, "Hanabilah," in *The Encyclopedia of Religion*, ed. Mircea Eliade (New York: Macmillan, 1987), 6:178–88.

31. Quoted in Akbar S. Ahmed, *Discovering Islam: Making Sense of Muslim History and Society* (London: Routledge, 1988), p. 51.

32. H. A. R. Gibb, "Constitutional Organization," in *Law in the Middle East*, ed. Majid Khadduri and Herbert J. Liebesny (Washington, DC: Middle East Institute, 1955), p. 27.

33. Hamid Enayat, *Modern Islamic Political Thought* (Austin: University of Texas Press, 1982), p. 11.

34. E. I. J. Rosenthal, *Political Thought in Medieval Islam* (Cambridge, England: Cambridge University Press, 1962), p. 45.

35. Ibid., p. 44.

36. Victor E. Makari, *Ibn Taymiyyah's Ethics: The Social Factor* (Chico, CA: Scholars Press, 1983); see, especially, chap. 8.

37. George Makdisi, "Ibn Taymiyah," in Eliade, *Encyclopedia of Religion*, 6:570.

38. Rosenthal, *Political Thought*, pp. 52–53.

39. John O. Voll, "Renewal and Reform in Islamic History: Tajdid and Islah," in *Voices of Resurgent Islam*, ed. John L. Esposito (New York: Oxford University Press, 1983), pp. 32–47.

40. See, for example, the discussions in Abd al-Muta'al al-Sa'idi, *al-mujaddidun fi al-Islam min al-qarn al-'awwal ila al-rabi' 'ashar* [Renewers in Islam from the first century to the fourteenth] (Cairo: Maktabah al-Adab, n.d.), and Abu al-Ala Mawdudi, *A Short History of the Revivalist Movement in Islam*, trans. al-Ashari (Lahore: Islamic Publications, 1976).

41. Shils, "Intellectuals and Powers," p. 43.

42. Lipset and Basu, *Roles*, pp. 130–31.

43. Ibid., pp. 135–43.

44. Albert Hourani, *A History of the Arab Peoples* (London: Faber and Faber, 1991), p. 302.

45. Hisham Sharabi, *Arab Intellectuals and the West: The Formative Years, 1875–1914* (Baltimore: Johns Hopkins Press, 1970), p. 3.

46. Alvin W. Gouldner, *The Future of Intellectuals and the Rise of the New Class* (New York: Continuum, 1979), p. 1.

47. Sharabi, *Arab Intellectuals*, pp. 132–33

48. S. M. H.Mashoor, *Muslim Heroes of the Twentieth Century* (Lahore: Sh. Muhammad Ashraf, 1978), pp. 51–58.

49. Anwar el-Sadat, *In Search of Identity: An Autobiography* (New York: Harper and Row, 1977), pp. 12, 13, 17.

50. James A. Bill and Carl Leiden, *The Middle East, Politics and Power* (Boston: Allyn and Bacon, 1974), pp. 39, 45. Emphasis added.

51. James A. Bill and Robert Springborg, *Politics in the Middle East*, 3rd ed. (Glenview, IL: Scott, Foresman, 1990), p. 78

52. Khaldun, *The Muqaddimah*, 1:459, 461.

53. H. A. R.Gibb and Harold Bowen, *Islamic Society and the West*, vol. 2, *Islamic Society in the Eighteenth Century*, pt. 2 (London: Oxford University Press, 1957), p. 107.

54. Ibid., pp. 112–13.

55. F. H. el Masri, introduction, to *Bayan wujub al-hijra ala 'l-'ibad*, by Uthman Ibn Fudi (Khartoum: Khartoum University Press, 1978), p. 9.

56. Muhammad b. Ali al-Shawkani, *al-qawl al-mufid fi adalah al-ijtihad wa al-taqlid* (n.p.:n.n., 1929/1347), p. 3.

57. John L. Esposito, *Islam and Politics*, 3rd ed. (Syracuse, NY: Syracuse University Press, 1991), p. 129.

58. Menahem Milson, "Medieval and Modern Intellectual Traditions in the Arab World," *Daedalus* (Summer 1972): 24.

59. Ibid.

60. *Memoirs of Hasan al Banna Shaheed*, trans. M. N. Shaikh (Karachi: International Islamic Publishers, 1981), pp. 112–13.

61. Ibrahim M. Abu-Rabi', *Intellectual Origins of Islamic Resurgence in the Modern Arab World* (Albany: State University of New York Press, 1996), pp. 37–38

62. Albert Hourani, *Arabic Thought in the Liberal Age, 1798–1939* (London: Oxford University Press, 1962), p. 75.

63. Nikki R. Keddie, "Intellectuals in the Modern Middle East: A Brief Historical Consideration," *Daedalus* (Summer 1972): 44.

64. The most thorough discussion of this person and his impact is R. S. O'Fahey, *Enigmatic Saint: Ahmad Ibn Idris and the Idrisi Tradition* (London: Hurst, 1990).

65. Nikki R. Keddie, "Afghani, Jamal al-Din al-," in *The Oxford Encyclopedia of the Modern Islamic World*, ed. John L. Esposito (New York: Oxford University Press, 1995), 1:27.

66. Sharabi, *Arab Intellectuals*, p. 51, citing Shakib Arslan, *Limadha ta'akhkhar al-muslimun*.

67. Mustafa Mahmud, *Rihlati min al-shakk ila al-'iman* (Cairo: Maktabah al-Jadid, 1989).

Chapter 1. Ismail Ragi al-Faruqi

1. Ismail Ragi al-Al-Faruqi, *On Arabism: Urubah and Religion* (Amsterdam: Djambatan, 1962), pp. 2–3.

2. Ibid., p. 5.

3. Ibid., p. 207.

4. Ibid., p. 211.

5. Ibid., p. 209.

6. Ibid.

7. Ismail R. al-Al-Faruqi, *Islam and Culture* (Kuala Lumpur: ABIM, 1980), p. 7.

8. Ibid.

9. As quoted in M. Tariq Quraishi, *Ismail al-Al-Faruqi: An Enduring Legacy* (Plainfield, IN: Muslim Student Association, 1987), p. 9.

10. Ismail Raji al-Al-Faruqi, *Tawhid: Its Implications for Thought And Life* (Kuala Lumpur: International Institute of Islamic Thought, 1982), p. ii.

11. In later life, al-Faruqi translated and edited ibn Abd al-Wahhab's writings on tawhid: *Sources of Islamic Thought: Three Epistles on Tawhid by Muhammad ibn Abd al-Wahhab* (Indianapolis: American Trust Publications, 1980) and *Sources of Islamic Thought: Kitab al-Tawhid* (London: I.I.F.S.O., 1980).

12. Ibid., p. 7.

13. Ibid., p.7.

14. Ibid., p. 73.

15. Ibid., p. 16.

16. Ibid.

17. John L. Esposito, ed., *Islam and Development: Religion and Sociopolitical Change* (Syracuse, NY: Syracuse University Press, 1980); Ismail R. al-Al-Faruqi, ed., *Essays in Islamic and Comparative Studies, Islamic Thought and Culture, Trialogue of the Abrahamic Faiths* (Herndon, VA: International Institute of Islamic Thought, 1982).

18. Ismail al-Al-Faruqi, *Islamization of Knowledge* (Herndon, VA: International Institute of Islamic Thought, 1982) and "Islamizing the Social Sciences," *Studies in Islam* (April 1979): 108–21.

19. For a presentation of IIIT's vision, see I. R. al-Faruqi and A. H. AbuSulayman, *Islamization of Knowledge: General Principles and Workplan* (Herndon, VA: International Institute of Islamic Thought, IIIT, 1981).

20. In addition to *Christian Ethics*, see, for example, "Islam and Christianity: Diatribe or Dialogue," *Journal of Ecumenical Studies* 5, 1 (1968): 45–77; "Islam and Christianity: Problems and Perspectives," in *The Word in the Third World*, ed. James P. Cotter (Washington, DC: Corpus Books, 1968), pp. 159–81; "The Role of Islam in Global Interreligious Dependence," in *Towards a Global Congress of the World's Religions*, ed. Warren Lewis (Barrytown, NY: Unification Theological Seminary, 1980), pp. 19–38; and "Islam and Other Faiths," and *Historical Atlas of the Religions of the World* (New York: Macmillan, 1975).

21. Al-Faruqi, *Historical Atlas*, p. 21.

22. Ibid., p.10.

23. Ibid., p. 11.

24. Ibid., p. 21.

25. Ibid., p. 32.

26. Ibid., p. 32.

27. Ibid, p. 33.

28. Ibid., p. 33.

29. Ibid, p. 54.

30. Ibid.

31. Stanley Brice Frost, Foreword to al-Faruqi, *Christian Ethics*, p. v.

Chapter 2. Khurshid Ahmad

1. Khurshid Ahmad, notes from interview with the authors at Islamic Foundation, Leicester, England, June 1988, p. 2.

2. Ibid.

3. Abul Ala Mawdudi, *The Islamic Law and Constitution*, 6th ed. (Lahore: Islamic Publications, 1977), p. 130.

4. Ahmad, interview, June 1988.

5. Khurshid Ahmad, *The Religion of Islam* (Lahore: Islamic Publications, 1967), pp. 6–7.

6. Ibid., p. 18.

7. Syed Abul Ala Mawdudi, foreword to *Islam and the West*, by Khurshid Ahmad (Lahore: Islamic Publications, 1967), p. v.

8. Ahmad, *Islam*, p. 61.

9. Ahmad, interview, June 1988.

10. Khurshid Ahmad, introduction to *Islamic Economics: Annotated Sources in English and Urdu*, compiled by Muhammad Akram Khan (Leicester, England: Islamic Foundation, 1983/1403), p. 7.

11. Introduction to *Contemporary Aspects of Economic Thinking in Islam*, ed. (American Trust Publications, 1973), p. xv.

12. See, for example, the important study done in a relatively traditional mode, Abdul-Hamid Ahmad Abu-Sulayman, "The Theory of the Economic of Islam," in *Contemporary Aspects*, pp. 9–54.

13. Khurshid Ahmad, "Economic Development in an Islamic Framework," in *Islamic Perspectives*, ed. Khurshid Ahmad and Zafar Ishaq Ansari (Leicester, England: Islamic Foundation, 1979/1399), p. 226.

14. Syed Abul Ala Maududi, *Economic System of Islam*, ed. Khurshid Ahmad (Lahore: Islamic Publications, 1984), p. 9.

15. Ibid., p. 13.

16. Ahmad, *Religion of Islam*, p. 16.

17. Ahmad, "Economic Development," p. 232.

18. Ibid., p. 230.

19. Ahmad, *Religion of Islam*, p. 8.

20. "Movement That Intendes to Shape Its Own Future," interview with Khurshid Ahmad, *Arabia: The Islamic World Review* 6 (February 1982/Rabi al-Thani 1402): 54.

21. Mawdudi, *Economic System*, p. 91.

22. Ibid., pp. 165–66.

23. See, for example, *Christian Science Monitor*, February 8, 1988.

24. Ahmad, "Economic Development," p. 226.

25. Ibid.

Chapter 3. Maryam Jameelah

1. Maryam Jameelah, "This Stranger, My Child," in *Memoirs of Childhood (1945–1962): The Story of One Western Convert's Quest for the Truth* (Lahore: Muhammad Yusuf Khan, 1982), p. 7.

2. Ibid., p. 5.

3. Ibid., p. 40.

4. Ibid., p. 87.

5. Ibid., p. 91.

6. Ibid., p. 108.

7. Maryam Jameelah, *Islam in Theory and Practice* (Lahore: Muhammad Yusuf Khan, 1976), p. 11.

8. Ibid., p. 193.

9. Maryam Jameelah, *At Home in Pakistan (1962–89)* (Lahore: Muhammad Yusuf Khan 1990), preface.

10. Maryam Jameelah, *Islam and Western Society* (New Delhi: Adam Publishers, 1982), p. 2.

11. *Memoirs*, p. 215.

12. Ibid., p. 24.

13. Maryam Jameelah, *Islam and Modernism* (Lahore: Muhammad Yusuf Khan, 1971), p. 59.

14. Ibid., p. 69.

15. *Islam and Western Society*, pp. 21–22. See also *Islam and Modernism*.

16. *Islam and Modernism*, p. 153.

17. *Islam and Western Society*, p. xi.

18. Jameelah, *Islam in Theory and Practice*, pp. 13, 15.

19. *Islam and Western Society*, p. 289.

20. Ibid., pp. 252, 271, 301.

21. Albert Hourani, as quoted in Jameelah, *Islam and Western Society*, pp. 267, 269.

22. *Islam and Western Society*, p. 13.

23. Ibid., pp. 12–13.

24. Ibid., p. 46.

25. Ibid., p. 47.

26. *Memoirs of Childhood*, p. 215.

27. *Islam and Western Society*, p. 17–19.

28. Ibid., p. 19.

29. Ibid., pp. 23–24.

30. Maryam Jameelah, *Westernization versus Muslims* (Lahore: Mohammad Yusuf Khan, 1978), p. 5.

31. William Hunter, *Our Indian Musalmans: Are They Bound in Conscience to Rebel against the Queen?* as quoted in Jameelah, *Westernization versus Muslims*, p. 7.

32. Lord Cromer, *Modern Egypt*, as quoted in *Westernization versus Muslims*, p. 9.

33. *Islam and Western Society*, p. xii.

34. Ibid., pp. 43–44, 46.

35. Maryam Jameelah, *Islam versus Ahl al-Kitab Past and Present*, 3rd ed. (Lahore: Muhammad Yusuf Khan, 1983). *Islam in Theory and Practice*, p. 36.

36. *Islam and Western Society*, p. 301. *Islam in Theory and Practice*, p. 67.

37. *Islam in Theory and Practice*, pp. 113–14.

38. Ibid., p. 392.

39. Maryam Jameelah, *Islam and Modern Man* (Lahore: Muhammd Yusuf Khan, 1976), pp. 13–14.

40. Ibid., p. 16.

41. Maryam Jameelah, *Islam and the Muslim Woman Today* (Lahore: Muhammad Yusuk Khan, 1976), p. 6.

42. Ibid., p. 6.

43. Ibid., p. 9.

44. Ibid., p. 9.

45. Ibid., pp. 21, 27.

Chapter 4. Hasan Hanafi

1. Much of the biographical information in this chapter comes from an an autobiographical account that Hasan Hanafi included in one of his major works, *al-din wa al-thawrah fi Masr, 1952–1981*, vol. 6, *al-usuliyyah al-islamiyyah* (Cairo: Maktabah Madbuli, 1989), pp. 207–91. Because of the importance of nuances in parts of this work, Hanafi provided the authors with a personally prepared rough translation. We have done supplementary translation work for purposes of clarification of our understanding and also to provide specific quotations for this text. The reference to Hanafi's arrival to France is 6:226.

2. These phrases are drawn from titles of books and addresses by Hanafi as well as his own self-descriptions in conversations about his goals.

3. *Al-din*, 6:208.

4. The most complete discussion by Hanafi of the Islamic Left appears in a journal he originated, only publishing one issue, which is widely known and cited. In it he worked to present the definition and positions of this mission: "Madha ya'ni al-yasar al-islami," *al-yasar al-islami* 1 (1981): 5–48.

5. "Madha," p. 5.

6. An interesting account of this is provided by one of the participants in Zaynab al-Ghazali, *Ayyam min hayyati* (Cairo: Daral-Sharuq, 1980/1400).

7. *Al-din*, 6:212.

8. Ibid., 6:212.

9. Ibid., 6:217.

10. Ibid., 6:219.

11. Ibid., 6:219.

12. Ibid., 6:221.

13. For the discussion of these activities, see ibid., 6:218–20.

14. Ibid., 6:223–24.

15. Ibid., 6:226.

16. Ibid., 6:226.

17. Ibid., 6:238.

18. Ibid., 6:241.

19. Ibid., 6:229.

20. Ibid., 6:235.

21. Ibid., 6:236–37.

22. Hasan Hanafi, *Les Methodes d'Exegese, Essai sur la Science des Fondement de la Comprehension 'Ilm Usual al-Fiqh* (Cairo: Imprimeries Nationale, 1965).

23. *Al-din*, 6:231. "The processes of linguistic pseudo-morphology" is Hanafi's translation of the phrase "amaliyyat al-tashakkil al-lughawi."

24. Ibid., 6:232.

25. Hasan Hanafi, *L'Exegese de la Phenomenologie, l'Etat actuel de la Methode Phenomenologique et son application au phenomene religieux* (Cairo: Dar al-Fikr al-Arabi, 1977).

26. Hasan Hanafi, *La Phenomenologie de l'Exegese, Essai d'une Hermeneutique Existentielle a partir du Nouveau Testamnent* (Cairo: Dar al-Fikr al-Arabi, 1977).

27. *Al-din*, 6:250.

28. Ibid., 6:250.

29. Ibid., 6:252.

30. Ibid., 6:252.

31. Ibid., 6:255.

32. Ibid., 6:255.

33. Ibid., 6:256–57.

34. Hasan Hanafi, "Kamilo Turiz, al-qadis al-thai'r," in *Qadaya mu'asirah*, vol. 1, *Fi fikrna al-mu'asir* (Beirut: Dar al-Tanwir, 1983), pp. 297–334.

35. *Al-din*, 6:258.

36. Ibid.

37. These papers from the 1970s were published in Hassan Hanafi, *Religious Dialogue and Revolution: Essays on Judaism, Christianity and Islam* (Cairo: Anglo-Egyptian Bookshop, 1977).

38. *Al-din*, 6:258. For his full argument, see *Religious Dialogue*, pp. 182–97.

39. Hanafi published a series of essays that are collected in *al-din wa al-thawrah fi masr, 1952–1981*, vol. 6, *al-usuliyyah al-islamiyyah* (Cairo: Maktabah Madbuli, 1989), pp. 94–188.

40. *Al-din*, 6:261.

41. Hasan Hanafi, *Muqaddimah fi 'ilm al-istighrab* (Cairo: Daral-Fanniyyah, 1991).

42. See, for example, the discussion of this incident in *aljadid* 3, 18 (May 1997): 3.

43. See, for example, the discussion in Wa'il al-Ibrashi, "Khittah Dhabh Hasan Hanafi," *Ruz al-yusuf*, 22 December 1997, pp. 22–25.

44. A good short summary of this "lifetime project" can be found in Issa J. Boullata, "Hanafi, Hasan," in *The Oxford Encyclopedia of the Modern Islamic World* (New York: Oxford University Press, 1995), 2:97–99.

45. One clear presentation of his analysis appears in some short essays Hanafi wrote in the late 1960s. See, for example, "al-isalah wa al-mu'asirah," in *Qadaya*, 1:49–53.

46. Ibid., 1:49.

47. Ibid., 1:49–50.

48. See, for example, Elie Chalala, "A New Book Debunks Muhammad Abed Al Jabberi's Theory, Sources, and Interpretations," *aljadid* 3, 17 (April 1997): 16.

49. Robert D. Lee, *Overcoming Tradition and Modernity: The Search for Islamic Authenticity* (Boulder, CO: Westview Press, 1997), p. 6.

50. Hassan [*sic*] Hanafi, "Hermenutics [*sic*] as Axiomatics," in *Religious Dialogue*, p. 1.

51. Ibid., p. 2.

52. *Al-din*, 6:228.

53. This discussion is primarily drawn from Hasan Hanafi, "Method of Thematic Interpretation of the Quran," in *Islam in the Modern World*, vol. 1, *Religion, Ideology and Development* (Cairo: Anglo-Egyptian Bookshop, 1995), 407–28.

54. Ibid., 1:408.

55. Ibid., 1:418. There are a number of spelling errors in the published text, which have been corrected in this quotation for purposes of clarity and ease of reading.

56. This paragraph is a summary of the description of method in ibid.,

1:418–21. Again there are corrections of spelling in quotations as they are presented in the text.

57. Hasan Hanafi, "The Relevance of the Islamic Alternative in Egypt," in *Islam in the Modern World*, vol. 2, *Tradition, Revolution, and Culture* (Cairo: Anglo-Egyptian Bookshop, 1995), p. 54.

58. Ibid., 2:54–55.

59. Ibid., 2:53.

60. "Mahda," pp. 31–32.

61. Ibid., p. 35.

62. Hasan Hanafi, "From Dogma to Revolution," in *Islam*, 2:105–7.

63. Ibid., 2:107–8.

64. Ibid., 2:110–11.

65. Ibid., 2:131.

66. See, for example, Muhammad Abduh, *The Theology of Unity*, trans. Ishaq Musaad and Kenneth Cragg (London: Allen and Unwin, 1966), especially pp. 66–75, 107–8.

67. "From Dogma," 2:132.

68. This discussion is a summary of the views presented in ibid., 2:140–44.

69. Ibid., 2:141. Emphasis added.

70. Ibid., 2:140–41.

71. Ibid., 2:145.

72. Ibid., 2:145.

73. Ibid., 2:146. There are a few editing changes in this quotation.

74. Ibid., 2:146.

75. Ibid., 2:146. The text has been edited slightly.

76. Ibid., 2:147.

77. Ibid., 2:110.

78. *Al-din*, 6:245.

79. The most thorough presentation of this is Hasan Hanafi, *Muqaddimah fi 'ilm al-istighrab* (Cairo: Madbuli, 1991), although he has written many essays on this subject and this larger volume is, in part, a compilation of those ideas in a more systematic form.

80. Hasan Hanafi, "From Orientalism to Occidentalism," in *Islam*, 2:355.

81. Ibid., 2:354.

82. Ibid., 2:357.

83. Ibid., 2:358. The text has been slightly edited for clarity.

84. Ibid., 2:364.

85. Ibid., 2:365.

86. This can be seen, for example, in a paper he presented at a conference in Venezuala in 1990, published as "New Social Science," in *Islam*, 2:447–71.

87. Ibid., 2:458.

88. Ibid., 2:458–59.

89. Ibid., 2:469. The text has been edited slightly for clarity.

Chapter 5. Rashid Ghannoushi

1. The epigraph is from Linda Jones, "Portrait of Rachid Ghannoushi," *Middle East Report* (July–August 1988): 19.

2. Interview with Rachid Ghannoushi, Wayland, Mass., Dec. 1989, p. 12.

3. Ibid.

4. Ibid.

5. Ibid.

6. "Nobody's Man—But a Man of Islam," in *The Movement of Islamic Tendency: The Facts* (London, 1987), p. 82.

7. Ibid., p. 80; similar comments appear in Abdelwahhab El-Effendi, "The Long March Forward," *Inquiry* (October 1987): 50.

8. Ibid., p. 84.

9. Ali, p. 30.

10. Ali Laridh, p. 32.

11. Dirk Vanderwalle, "From New State to the New Era: Toward a Second Republic in Tunisia," *Middle East Journal* (Autumn 1988): 603.

12. Ben Ali Discusses Opposition Parties, Democracy," *FBIS-NES*, 29 December 1989.

13. Halliday, p. 26.

14. "The Autocrat Computes," *Economist*, 18 May 1991, pp. 47–48.

15. *Middle East* (September 1991): 18.

16. "Useful Plot," *Economist*, 1 June 1991, p. 38.

17. Rachid Ghannoushi, interview with the authors, Wayland, MA, December 1989.

18. Ibid.

19. Emad Shahin, *Political Ascent: Contemporary Islamic Movements in North Africa* (Boulder, CO: Westview Press, 1997), p. 229.

20. Ibid., p. 235.

21. Rachid Ghannoushi, "What We Need Is a Realistic Fundamentalism," *Arabia* (October 1986): 13.

22. Ibid., p. 14.

23. Ibid., p. 13.

24. Ibid.

25. Ghannoushi, interview, December 1989.

26. Ibid.

27. Ibid.

28. Ibid.

29. Rachid Ghannoushi, "Deficiences in the Islamic Movement," *Middle East Report* (July–August 1988): 23.

30. Ibid., p. 23.

31. Ibid., p. 24.

32. Ibid.

33. Rachid Ghannoushi, "The Battle against Islam," *Middle East Affairs Journal* 1, 2 (Winter 1992/1413): 7.

34. Rachid Ghanniushi, "Again . . . We and the West," *Maqallat* (n.d.): 56.

35. *London Observer*, 19 January 1992.

36. Rachid Ghannoushi, interview with the authors, London, 5 February 1993.

37. Ibid.

38. Ibid.

39. Ibid.

40. Ibid.

41. Ghannoushi, "Battle against Islam," p. 3.

42. Rachid Ghannoushi, "Secularism in the Arab Maghreb," in *Islam and Secularism in the Middle East* (New York: New York University Press, 1999), p. 101.

43. Ibid., p. 111.

Chapter 6. Hasan al-Turabi

1. A biography of this ancestor appears in the traditional collection of biographies of Sudanese religious teachers, Muhammad al-Nur Ibn Dayf Allah, *Kitab al-Tabaqat fi Khusus al-Awliya wa' al-Salihin wa al-ulama wa al-Shu'ara fi al-Sudan*, ed. Yusuf Fadl Hasan (Khartoum: Khartoum University Press, 1971), pp. 160–73.

2. See, for example, the analysis in P. M. Holt, "Holy Families and Islam in the Sudan," in *Studies in the History of the Near East* (London: Frank Cass, 1973), pp. 121–34.

3. This is the *Mukhtasar* (summary of Maliki law) by Khalil ibn Ishaq.

4. Interviews with the authors, March 1992 at a discussion at the University of Bergen, Norway, in 1993, Muhammad Abu Salim and R. S. O'Fahey agreed with the assertion that Wad al-Turab was probably the first Sudanese mahdi.

5. Hasan al-Turabi, interviews with the authors, March 1992.

6. Ibid.

7. Abdelwahab El-Affendi, *Turabi's Revolution: Islam and Power in Sudan* (London: Grey Seal, 1991), p. 63.

8. Many accounts of the origins of the Islamic movement in Sudan, including Turabi's own, note the importance of the Communist "threat" in leading to the creation of the Sudanese Islamist groups in the late 1940s and early 1950s. See, for example, Hasan al-Turabi, *al-Harakah al-Islamiyyah fi al-Sudan* (Cairo: al-Qari' al-Arabi, 1991), pp. 22–24.

9. El-Affendi, *Turabi's Revolution*, p. 63

10. Ibid., p. 170.

11. Hasan al-Turabi, *Tajdid al-fikr al-Islami* (Jiddah: al-Dar al-Sa'udiyyah, 1987/1407), p. 191.

12. Ibid., p. 191.

13. Ibid., p. 191.

14. Ibid., pp. 35–36.

15. Ibid., p. 198.

16. S. Abul A'la Maududi, *A Short History of the Revivalist Movement in Islam*, trans. al-Ash'ari (Lahore: Islamic Publications, 1976), p. 38.

17. El-Affendi, *Turabi's Revolution*, p. 171.

18. Sayyid Qutb, *Ma'alim fi al-tariq* (Cairo: Dar al-Sharuq, n.d.), p. 14.

19. El-Affendi, *Turabi's Revolution*, p. 172.

20. Hassan Turabi, "The Islamic State," in *Voices of Resurgent Islam*, ed. John L. Esposito (New York: Oxford University Press, 1983), p. 245.

21. Hasan al-Turabi, *Adwa' ala al-mushkilah al-dustiriyyah* (Khartoum: al-Matba'ah al-Hukumiyyah, 1967), p. 3.

22. Turabi, *Adwa'*, p. 37.

23. Hasan al-Turabi, *Tajdid 'usul al-fiqh al-islami* (Khartoum: Maktabah Dar al-Fikr, 1980/1400), p. 6.

24. Ibid., p. 7.

25. Ibid., p. 8.

26. M. Bernand, "Kiyas," in *The Encyclopaedia of Islam*, (Leiden: Brill, 1980), 5:239.

27. See the sections on "limited qiyas" (p. 23) and "broad qiyas (pp. 24–25) in Turabi, *Tajdid usul*.

28. Ibid., pp. 29–30.

29. Abdel Salam Sidahmed, *Politics and Islam in Contemporary Sudan* (New York: St. Martin's Press, 1996), p. 106.

30. This draft constitution was supported by a parliamentary majority but was never approved because the government coalition dissolved the parliament for other reasons before approval was given.

31. Sidahmed, *Politics and Islam*, pp. 102–3.

32. *al-Mithaq al-Islami*, 15 December 1967, quoted in El-Affendi, *Turabi's Revolution*, p. 79.

33. Ja'far Numayri, *al-Nahj al-Islami Limadha?* (Cairo: al-Maktab al-Masri al-Hadith, 1980).

34. Gabriel R. Warburg, "The Sharia in Sudan: Implementation and Repercussions," in *Sudan, State and Society in Crisis*, ed. John O. Voll (Bloomington: Indiana University Press, 1991), p. 94.

35. Nayal Abu Qurun and Awad al-Jid Ahmad, interviews with the authors, Khartoum, August 1984. For a report based on these and interviews with Turabi and other Brotherhood leaders at that time, see John O. Voll, "The Political Impact of Islam in Sudan: Numayri's Islamization Program," research study prepared for the U.S. Department of State, INR/LAR, order no. 1722-420140, September 1984 (Washington, DC).

36. Turabi, *al-Harakah*, p. 244.

37. Ibid.

38. El-Affendi, *Turabi's Revolution*, p. 163.

39. Turabi, *al-Harakah*, p. 244. Emphasis added.

40. Quoted in Warburg, "The Sharia," p. 98.

41. Turabi, *al-Harakah*, pp. 137–38.

42. Ibid., p. 140.

43. Hasan al-Turabi, *al-mar'ah bayn ta'alim al-din wa taqalid al-mujtama'* (Jiddah: al-dar al-sa'udiyyah, 1984/1404). A translation of this has been published as Hasan Turabi, *Women in Islam and Muslim Society*, trans. (London: Milestones, 1991).

44. Abdelwahab El-Affendi, introduction to Turabi, *Women*, p. 2

45. Turabi, *Women*, p. 5.

46. Ibid., p. 11.

47. Ibid., p. 21.

48. In Arthur L. Lowrie, ed., *Islam, Democracy, the State and the West: A Roundtable with Dr. Hasan Turabi* (Tampa, FL: World and Islam Studies Enterprise, 1993), p. 28.

49. Turabi, *Women*, pp. 38–39.

50. Ibid., p. 41.

51. Ibid., p. 46.

52. Ibid., p. 44.

53. Ibid., p. 47.

54. Sondra Hale, *Gender Politics in Sudan* (Boulder, CO: Westview Press, 1996), p. 193.

55. Hale, *Gender Politics*, p. 217.

56. In Lowrie, *Islam, Democracy*, p. 47.

57. Hasan Turabi, "Principles of Governance, Freedom, and Responsibility in Islam," *American Journal of Islamic Social Sciences* 4, 1 (1987): 1.

58. The National Committee for the Islamic Constitution, *Mudhdhakirah 'an al-dustur al-Islami al-kamil li-jumhuriyyah al-Sudan* (Memorandum concerning

the fully Islamic constitution for the republic of the Sudan) (Khartoum: n. p., 1967).

59. Ibid., p. 6.

60. Ibid., p. 5.

61. Ibid., p. 11.

62. Ibid., p. 5.

63. Ibid., p. 10.

64. The text used here is *The Democratic Republic of the Sudan Gazette (Attorney Generals Chambers), Authentic English Translation of the Permanent Constitution of the Sudan* (issued 8 May 1973).

65. Nayal Abu Qurun and Awad al-Jid Ahmad, interviews, August 1984.

66. *Dustur al-jibhah al-Islamiyyah al-qawmiyyah* (n.p., n.d.), pp. 6–7.

67. Official English translation of *Draft Constitution of the Republic of the Sudan* (April 1998), p. 1. This is the text distributed following the Constitution's ratification by the Assembly and the popular referendum.

68. National Islamic Front, *Sudan Charter: National Unity and Diversity*, pt. 2, b-3 (January 1987). (English text distributed by NIF.)

69. El-Affendi, *Turabi's Revolution*, p. 148.

70. Turabi, *al-Harakah*, p. 155.

71. El-Affendi, *Turabi's Revolution*, p. 149.

72. Turabi, *al-Harakah*, p. 155.

73. John Garang, *John Garang Speaks* (London: KPI, 1987), p. 23.

74. Garang, speech, 10 August 1989, quoted in Ann Mosely Lesch, *Sudan: Contested National Identities* (Bloomington: Indiana University Press, 1998), p. 169.

75. Lesch, *Sudan*, p. 177.

76. Quoted in Lesch, *Sudan*, p. 157.

77. *Sudan Focus* 4, 4/5 (April/May 1997). The full text of the agreement was published in this issue.

78. Turabi, *al-Harakah*, p. 157.

79. *Washington Post*, 22 February 1999.

Chapter 7. Abdolkarim Soroush

1. This essay is a revised version of an earlier essay, *Debating Religion and Politics in Iran: The Political Thought of Abdolkarim Soroush* (New York: Council on Foreign Relations, 1996).

2. A number of Soroush's student followers in England have established a website devoted to coverage of Soroush, including biographical information, news updates, press reports, translated articles, and commentaries. See www.seraj.org.

3. For coverage of opposition to Soroush, see, among others, Robin Wright, "Iran's Greatest Political Challenge," *World Policy Journal* 14, 2 (1997): 67–74; and the coverage on the Seraj website.

4. Soroush's tenure in this Council is a point of much controversy. During the Cultural Revolution in Iran the universities were closed and a number of professors and syllabi purged. Many of Soroush's critics contend that Soroush actively participated in this process and hence his current defense of free dialogue is hypocritical at best. Soroush has responded that his tenure began after the closure of the universities and that he consistently worked toward the

rapid reopening of the universities. Soroush eventually parted with the Council, after a period of four years, due to differences which have yet to receive adequate articulation. For more on this topic, see Afshin Matin-asgari, "Abdolkarim Soroush and the Secularization of Islamic Thought in Iran," *Iranian Studies* 30, 1–2 (1997): 97, and the coverage of Soroush's biography in Mahmaoud Sadri and Ahmad Sadri, *Reason, Freedom, and Democracy in Islam* (New York: Oxford University Press, 2000). Matin-asgari also provides particularly good and concise coverage of Soroush's intellectual development, from a different angle than the one offered here.

5. The presentation here draws on materials readily available at www.seraj.org, especially the interview reproduced from Sadri and Sadri's forthcoming study of Soroush.

6. See especially Matin-Asgari, "Abdolkarim Soroush," on Soroush's on this period.

7. Abdolkarim Soroush, "*Qabz va bast* dar mizan-i naqd va bahs" (*Qabz va Bast* at the level of critique and discussion), *Kiyan* 1, 2 (1991): 5. A full elaboration of Soroush's theory of religion can be found in Abdolkarim Soroush, *Qabz va bast-i tiorik-i shariat* (The theoretical contraction and expansion of the Sharia) (Tehran: Muassassah-yi farhangi-yi sirat, 1990); this work originally appeared as four separate articles in the monthly journal *Kayhan-i Farhangi* from 1988 to 1990. The publication of the articles sparked a controversial debate within Iranian intellectual circles, reflected within the pages of *Kayhan-i Farhangi*. For a summary of this debate, see Mehrzad Boroujerdi, "The Encounter of Post-Revolutionary Thought in Iran with Hegel, Heidegger, and Popper," in *Cultural Transitions in the Middle East*, ed. Serif Mardin (New York: Brill, 1994), pp. 248–55.

8. *Qabz va bast-i tiorik-i shariat*, p. 99.

9. "*Qabz va bast* dar mizan-i naqd va bahs," p. 9.

10. *Qabz va bast-i tiorik-i shariat*, p. 158.

11. Ibid., 156.

12. Ibid., pp. 147, 162. See also Abdolkarim Soroush, *Ilm chiist? Falsafah chiist?* (What is science? What is philosophy?), 10th ed. (Tehran: Muassassah-yi farhangi-yi sirat, 1987), pp. 23, 108. Soroush admits his own worldview is based on the philosophical school of realism, in which there is a difference between an object (i.e., religion) and the perception of an object (i.e., religious understanding). For a criticism of this realist position, see Ahmad Naraqi, "Fahm-i amiqtar?" (A deeper understanding?), *Kiyan* 3, 11 (1993): 16–20.

13. He identifies cosmology, anthropology, linguistics and epistemology as the non-religious sciences that most influence the study of religion. See Abdolkarim Soroush, "Pasukh bih naqd-namah-yi 'Sabat va taghir dar andishah-yi dini'" (Reply to the critical essay 'Constancy and change in religious thought'), *Kiyan* 2, 7 (1992): 17.

14. Ibid., and "*Qabz va bast* dar mizan-i naqd va bahs," p. 10.

15. *Qabz va bast-i tiorik-i shari'at*, p. 262.

16. "*Qabz va bast* dar mizan-i naqd va bahs," p. 11; also *Qabz va bast-i tiorik-i shariat*, p. 118.

17. *Qabz va bast-i tiorik-i shariat*, p. 25.

18. Ibid., p. 24, and *Ilm chiist? Falsafah chiist?* pp. 211, 221.

19. *Qabz va bast-i tiorik-i shariat*, pp. 44, 120, and "Pasukh bih naqd-namah-yi 'Sabat va taghir dar andishah-yi dini,'" p. 16.

20. *Qabz va bast-i tiorik-i shariat*, p. 185.

21. Ibid., p. 104.

22. See Abdolkarim Soroush, "Farbih-tar az idioloji" (More comprehensive than ideology), *Kiyan* 3, 13 (1993): 2–20. For a criticism of this article, see Jahangir Salihpur, "Naqdi bar nazariyah-yi 'Farbih-tar az idioloji'" (A critique of 'More comprehensive than ideology'), *Kiyan* 3, 15 (1993): 47–49, and by the same author, "Din-i asri dar asr-i idioloji" (Modern religion in the age of ideology), *Kiyan* 4, 18 (1994): 36–41. "Farbih tar az idioloji," together with many of Soroush's other *Kiyan* articles, was later collected and printed in a book by the same name; see Abdolkarim Soroush, *Farbih-tar az idioloji* (More comprehensive than ideology) (Tehran: Muassassah-yi farhangi-yi sirat, 1993). As many of Soroush's books are collections of articles or speeches originally published or delivered elsewhere, the titles of the books often do not reveal the content of the individual chapters. Hence most chapters are referred to here by their individual titles.

23. "Farbih-tar az idioloji," p. 4.

24. Ibid.

25. For Soroush's views on Shariati, see, among others, "Shariati va jamaah-shinasi-yi din" (Shariati and the sociology of religion), *Kiyan* 3, 13 (1993): 2–12, and "Duktur shariati va baz-sazi-yi fikr-i dini" (Dr. Shariati and the reconstruction of religious thought), in Abdolkarim Soroush, *Qissah-yi arbab-i marifat* (The tale of the masters of knowledge) (Tehran: Muassassah-yi farhangi-yi sirat, 1994), pp. 381–440. For an overview of the ideological background of the Iranian Revolution, see Hamid Dabashi, *Theology of Discontent: the Ideological Foundations of the Islamic Revolution in Iran* (New York: New York University Press, 1993).

26. "Din, idioloji, va tabir-i idiolojik az din" (Religion, ideology, and the ideological interpretation of religion), *Farhang-i touseh* 1, 5 (1993): 11–12. This is a roundtable discussion on ideology in which Soroush participated.

27. Ibid., pp. 10–12.

28. "Farbih-tar az idioloji," p. 13.

29. Soroush raises this argument in the context of Shariati's thought. Shariati promoted the introduction of ideology in society yet opposed the existence of an official class of religious interpreters. Soroush identifies this tension and argues that, had Shariati realized the essential connection between an ideological society and state-allied ideologues, he would not have supported an ideological society. For Shariati's discussion of this, see Ali Shariati, *Tashayyu-i alavi va tashayyu-i safavi* (Alavi Shiism and Safavi Shiism), vol. 9 in *Collected Works* (Tehran: Intisharat-i tashayyu, 1980). For Soroush on Shariati, see "Farbih-tar az idioloji," pp. 7, 14.

30. "Farbih-tar az idioloji," p. 13. See also Abdolkarim Soroush, "Aql va azadi" (Reason and freedom), *Kiyan* 1, 5 (1992): 13–25.

31. "Farbih-tar az idioloji," p. 13.

32. Ibid., p. 19.

33. Ibid., p. 8.

34. Ibid.

35. Abdolkarim Soroush, "Idioloji-yi dini va din-i idiolojik" (Religious ideology and ideological religion), *Kiyan* 3, 16 (1993–94): 25.

36. Abdolkarim Soroush, "Jamaah-yi payambar pasand" (A society admired by the Prophet), *Kiyan* 3, 17 (1994): 21.

37. "Bavar-i dini, davar-i dini" (Religious belief, religious arbiter), in *Farbih-tar az idioloji*, p. 49.

38. Ibid., p. 49.

39. Ibid., p. 50.

40. Ibid., p. 52. For a discussion of the task government faces in distributing justice, see Abdolkarim Soroush, "Danish va dadgari" (Knowledge and the administration of justice), *Kiyan* 4, 22 (1994–95): 10–15.

41. "Bavar-i dini, davar-i dini," p. 52.

42. Ibid., p. 50.

43. Ibid., p. 52.

44. Ibid., p. 57.

45. Abdolkarim Soroush, "Khadamat va hasanat-i din" (The functions and benefits of religion), *Kiyan* 5, 27 (1994): 12, 13. Soroush argues here that God did not give religion to humanity as a blueprint for the ordering of external life but rather as a guide to teach the inner order necessary to prepare for the afterlife. For a related discussion, see "Din-i dunyavi" (Worldly religion), *Iran-i farda* 4, 23 (1995–96): 50–53.

46. Abdolkarim Soroush, "Saqf-i maishat bar sutun-i shariat" (The ceiling of livelihood upon the pillar of the Sharia), *Kiyan* 5, 26 (1995): 28. See also Abdolkarim Soroush, "Mana va mabna-yi sikularizm" (The meaning and basis of secularism), *Kiyan* 5, 26 (August–September 1995): 4–13; "Khadamat va hasanat-i din," 13; and Abdolkarim Soroush, "Idioloji va din-i dunyavi" (Ideology and this-worldly religion), *Kiyan* 6, 31 (1996): 2–11.

47. "Saqf-i maishat bar sutun-i shariat," p. 28.

48. "Farbih-tar az idioloji," p. 11.

49. Abdolkarim Soroush, "Tahlil-i mafhum-i hukumat-i dini" (Analysis of the concept of religious government), *Kiyan* 6, 32 (1996): 2.

50. See "Arkan-i farhangi-yi dimukrasi" (The cultural pillars of democracy), in *Farbih-tar az idioloji*, 269–72; and "Mabani tiorik-i libiralizm" (The theoretical bases of liberalism), in *Razdani va roshanfikri va dindari* (Augury and intellectualism and pietism), 2nd ed. (Tehran: Muassassah-yi farhangi-yi sirat, 1993), pp. 153–54. For an early discussion on democracy in the context of the Islamic Republic, see "Musahabah-yi duktur surush ba ustad-i shahid piramun-i jumhuri islami" (Dr. Soroush's interview with the martyred professor on the Islamic Republic), in Murtaza Mutahhari, *Piramun-i inqilab-i islami* (On the Islamic revolution) (Tehran: Intisharat-i sadra, 1995), pp. 125–41.

51. Abdolkarim Soroush, "Hukumat-i dimukratik-i dini?" (A religious democratic government?), *Kiyan* 3, 11 (1993): 12.

52. "Hukumat-i dimukratik-i dini?" p. 12. For a related discussion, see Abdolkarim Soroush, "Akhlaq-i khudayan: akhlaq-i bar-tar vujud nadarad" (The morality of the gods: There is no higher morality), *Kiyan* 4, 18 (1994): 22–32, and "Az tarikh biamuzim" (Let us learn from history), in *Taffaruj-i sun: guftarhay-yi dar maqulat-i akhlaq va sanat va ilm-i insani* (Essays on the human sciences, ethics, and art) (Tehran: Intisharat-i surush, 1987), p. 265.

53. "Hukumat-i dimukratik-i dini?" p. 15.

54. Ibid.

55. "Bavar-i dini, davar-i dini," p. 56; and "Hukumat-i dimukratik-i dini," pp. 14–15.

56. "Bavar-i dini, davar-i dini," p. 56.

57. Abdolkarim Soroush, "Mudara va mudiriyat-i muminan, sukhani dar nisbat-i din va dimukrasi" (The tolerance and administration of the faithful: A talk on the relationship between religion and democracy), *Kiyan* 4, 21 (1994): 11. This issue of *Kiyan* is devoted entirely to discussions of religion and de-

mocracy and includes three articles in response to Soroush's "Hukumat-i dimukratik-i dini?"

58. "Bavar-i dini, davar-i dini," p. 51.

59. "Mudara va mudiriyat-i muminan, sukhani dar nisbat-i din va dimukrasi," p. 4.

60. Ibid., p. 8.

61. Ibid.

62. For articles critical of Soroush's position on democracy, see Aliriza Alavi, "Hakimiyat-i mardum dar jamaah-yi dindaran" (The rule of the people in the society of the religious), *Kiyan* 4, 22 (1994–95): 26–30; Hasan Yusifi Ashkuri, "Paraduks-i islam va dimukrasi?" (The paradox of Islam and democracy?), *Kiyan* 4, 21 (1994): 24–29; Maqsud Farastkhah, "Rabitah-yi din va siyasat dar jamaah-yi dini" (The relationship between religion and politics in a religious society), *Kiyan* 4, 18 (1994): 33–35; Bijan Hikmat, "Mardum-salari va din-salari" (Leadership of the people and leadership of religion), *Kiyan* 4, 21 (1994): 16–23; Muhammad Javad Ghulamriza Kashi, "Chand pursish va yik nazar piramun-i nazariyah-yi 'Hukumat-i dimukratik-i dini'" (A few questions and a position on 'A religious democratic government'), *Kiyan* 3, 14 (1993): 26–31; Majid Muhammadi, "Ghusl-i tamid-i sikularizm ya nijat-i din" (The ceremonial baptism of secularism or the rescue of religion), *Kiyan* 4, 21 (1994): 30–34; Hamid Payidar, "Paraduks-i islam va dimukrasi" (The paradox of Islam and democracy), *Kiyan* 4, 19 (1994): 20–27; Jahangir Salihpur, "Din-i dimukratik-i hukumati" (A ruling democratic religion), *Kiyan* 4, 20 (1994): 6–11; and Murad Saqafi, "Mardum va farhang-i mardum dar andishah-yi siyasi-yi shariati va surush" (People and the culture of people in the political thought of Shari'ati and Soroush), *Goftogu* 1, 2 (1993–94): 25–39. See also the 7 November 1995 issue of *Subh*, entitled "Vijah-yi barrasi-yi ara va aqaid-i duktur surush" (A special analysis of the opinions and ideas of Dr. Soroush), which contains thirteen critical articles by various Iranian thinkers.

63. Payidar, "Paraduks-i," pp. 22–27.

64. "Mudara va mudiriyat-i muminan, sukhani dar nisbat-i din va dimukrasi," pp. 6, 14.

65. Although Soroush does not use the term "social consciousness" in his argument, it is my opinion that this is the best English equivalent of Soroush's position.

66. Farastkhah, "Rabitah-yi," pp. 33–34; Hikmat, "Mardum-salari?" p. 21.

67. Farastkhah, "Rabitah-yi," pp. 33–35; Muhammadi, "Ghusl-i," p. 33.

68. Farastkhah, "Rabitah-yi," p. 34; Hikmat, "Mardum-salari?" p. 23; Muhammadi, "Ghusl-i," p. 33.

69. Muhammadi, "Ghusl-i," p. 33.

70. Ibid.

71. "Khadamat va hasanat-i din," p. 12.

72. Ibid., p. 14.

73. Hikmat, "Mardum-salari?" p. 22; Muhammadi, "Ghusl-i," p. 32.

74. "Mudara va mudiriyat-i muminan, sukhani dar nisbat-i din va dimukrasi," p. 9.

75. "Musalmani va abadi, kafiri va kam-rushdi" (Muslimness and development, unbelief and underdevelopment), in *Farbih-tar az idioloji*, pp. 315–17.

76. Ibid., pp. 315–17.

77. Ibid., p. 312.

78. Soroush raises this point in discussing the role of Ayatullah Khomeini

as a religious revivalist. See Abdolkarim Soroush, "Aftab-i diruz va kimyayi-yi imruz" (Yesterday's light and today's guide), *Kayhan-i farhangi* 6, 3 (1988): 4–7. For a related discussion, see Abdolkarim Soroush, "Dark-i azizanah-yi din" (The sincere perception of religion), *Kiyan* 4, 19 (1994): 2–9.

79. Abdolkarim Soroush, "Intizarat-i danishgah az hauzah" (The university's expectations of the seminary), *Salam*, 5 January 1993, pp. 5, 8. See also Abdolkarim Soroush, "Taqlid va tahqiq dar suluk-i danish-juyi" (Imitation and investigation in university student behavior), *Kiyan* 1, 1 (1991): 12–17.

80. "Intizarat-i danishgah az hauzah," p. 5. For a highly critical response to "Intizarat-i danishgah az hauzah," see Ayatullah Nasir Makarim-Shirazi, "Bih aqidah-yi man majmuah-yi in sukhanrani avvamzadagi-yi ajibi ast" (In my opinion the whole of this talk reflects extreme vulgarism), *Salam*, 5 January 1993, p. 8.

81. Ibid.

82. Ibid.

83. Ibid.

84. Abdolkarim Soroush, "Hurriyat va rauhaniyat" (Freedom and the clerical establishment), *Kiyan* 4, 24 (1995): 4. This article led to a heated debate in Iran, in which the leader of the Islamic Republic, Ayatollah Seyyed Ali Khamenei, commented indirectly yet unmistakably to Soroush's criticisms. See *Ittilaat* (Tehran ed.), 10 September 1995, p. 7, and "Saqf-i maishat bar sutun-i shariat," p. 31. In order to prevent the further politicization of the discussion, the editors of *Kiyan* decided in their October–November 1995 issue to cease publishing any articles related to "Hurriyat va rauhaniyat." See *Kiyan* 5, 27 (1995): 2. For an extremely critical response to Soroush's position, see "Harf-ha-yi kuhnah va malal-avar dar zar-varaq-i andishah va taffakur" (Old and tiresome words under the cover of thought and reflection), *Subh*, 2 January 1996, pp. 7, 14.

85. "Hurriyat va rauhaniyat," p. 4. This is an issue with which Ayatullah Mutahhari was also concerned, although Soroush's position is considerably more far-reaching than Mutahhari's. For an article that questions Soroush's reading of Mutahhari and challenges his description of the clerical establishment, see Ali Mutahhari, "Ustad mutahhari va hall-i mushkil-i sazman-i rauhaniyat" (Professor Mutahhari and the solution of the problem of the clerical establishment), *Kiyan* 5, 25 (1995): 12–15.

86. Ibid., p. 5.

87. "Saqf-i maishat bar sutun-i shariat," p. 30.

88. "Hurriyat va rauhaniyat," p. 6.

89. Ibid., p. 8.

90. Ibid., p. 8.

91. Ibid., pp. 8–9.

92. Ibid., p. 8. For an example of the type of religious activist Soroush envisions, see his article on Mehdi Bazargan, "An kih bih nam bazargan bud nah bih sifat" (He who was a merchant in name, not in character), *Kiyan* 4, 23 (1995): 12–20. The article's title is a play on words that reveals the essence of Soroush's point. *Bazargan* in Persian means "merchant," and Soroush argues that Mehdi Bazargan was a merchant in name alone and not in character, as he would not compromise or sell his belief in religion. Although written before his criticisms of the clerical establishment, this provides an excellent illustration of Soroush's ideal religious activist.

93. "Hurriyat va rauhaniyat," p. 10.

94. See "Sih farhang" (Three cultures), in *Razdani va roshanfikri va dindari*, p. 146.

95. Ibid.

96. Abdolkarim Soroush, "Ma'rifat, muallifah-yi mumtaz-i mudernizm" (Knowledge, the distinguished products of modernism), *Kiyan* 4, 20 (1994): 5; "Ulum-i insani dar nizam-i danishgahi" (The human sciences in the university system), in *Taffaruj-i sun*, pp. 198, 199; and Boroujerdi, "Encounter," p. 242.

97. For Soroush's position on the relationship between the religious and nonreligious sciences, within the context of the Cultural Revolution, see "Ulum-i insani dar nizam-i danishgahi," pp. 190–202, and "Huvviyat-i tarikhi-i va ijtimayi-yi ilm" (The historical and social identity of knowledge), in *Taffaruj-i sun*, pp. 203–27.

98. "'Ulum-i insani dar nizam-i danishgahi," p. 195.

99. Ibid., p. 195.

100. Ibid., pp. 200–202.

101. Abdolkarim Soroush, "Gharbiyan va husn va qubh va shuun va atvar-i anan" (The Westerners and their goodness, baseness, honors and manners), *Kayhan-i farhangi* 1, 2 (1984): 17, and "Sih farhang," p. 117.

102. For the classic articulation of *gharbzadagi*, see Jalal Al-i Ahmad, *Gharbzadagi* (Weststruckness) (Tehran: Intisharat-i ravaq, 1962). For an English translation, see Ahmad Alizadeh and John Green, trans., *Weststruckness*, (Lexington, KY: Mazda, 1982).

103. "Sih farhang," pp. 111–12, and "Vujud va mahiyat-i gharb" (The existence and essence of the West), in *Taffaruj-i sun'*, pp. 240–42.

104. "Gharbiyan va husn va qubh va shuun va atvar-i anan," p. 15; "Sih farhang," p. 111; and "Vujud va mahiyat-i gharb," p. 244.

105. "Sih farhang," p. 112, and "Vujud va mahiyat-i gharb," p. 250. For Soroush's position in relation to his critics, see Boroujerdi, "Encounter," pp. 242–44.

106. "Vujud va mahiyat-i gharb," pp. 242–44.

107. "Gharbiyan va husn va qubh va shuun va atvar-i anan," p. 18, and "Sih farhang," pp. 119–21.

108. "Sih farhang," p. 128.

109. Ibid.

110. On the potential dangers of a religious society in which the excessive intensity of religious faith threatens the rational climate Soroush envisions, see Abdolkarim Soroush, "Dindari va khardvarzi" (Pietism and rationalism), *Kiyan* 3, 12 (1993): 8–14.

111. See "Marifat, muallifah-yi mumtaz-i mudernizm."

112. Abdolkarim Soroush, "Maishat va fazilat" (Livelihood and virtue), *Kiyan* 5, 25 (1995): 9.

113. "Musalmani va abadi, kafiri va kam-rushdi," p. 334. In one of his early postrevolutionary works, Soroush lamented the increasingly dogmatic, polarized language of intellectual debate in Iran. See Abdolkarim Soroush, *Idioloji-yi shaitani: dugmatizm-i niqabdar* (Satanic ideology: Masked dogmatism), 4th ed. (Tehran: Intisharat-i baran, 1982).

114. For coverage of this event, see issue number 229 of the weekly Tehran paper *Mobin*.

115. In addition to the interviews in *Jameah* cited hereafter, on the problem of violence see the March 1999 interview with Soroush in *Kiyan*, 45.

116. See Jameah, issues of 16, 17, 18, 20, 28, 29, and 30 June 1998.

117. For more on pluralism, see Abdolkarim Soroush, *Kiyan*, 36.

118. For a particularly clear example of this, see his discussion of civil society in Adbolkarim Soroush, "Din va jamaah-yi madani" (Religion and civil society), in *Jamaah-yi madani va iran-i imruz* (Civil society and contemporary Iran) (Tehran: Intisharat-i naqsh va nigar, 1998), pp. 106–40. For a criticism of Soroush's approach that corresponds closely to the position advanced here, see Murad Saqafi, "Nou-andishan-i dini va mozal-i jamaah-yi madani" (Religious innovators and the question of civil society), *Goftogu*, 15 (1997): 114–20.

119. See especially ibid.

Chapter 8. Anwar Ibrahim

1. K. Das, "Chipping away at extremism," *Far Eastern Economic Review*, 8 February 1980, p. 10. (Subsequent references to this journal will abbreviate the title: *FEER*.)

2. See, for example, Judith Nagata, "Religious Ideology and Social Change: The Islamic Revival in Malaysia," *Pacific Affairs* 53, 3 (Fall 1980): 425, and Fred R. von der Mehden, "Malaysia in 1980: Signals to Watch," *Asian Survey* 21, 2 (February 1981): 246.

3. Ian Johnson, "How Malaysia's Rulers Devoured Each Other and Much They Built," *Wall Street Journal*, 30 October 1998, p. 1.

4. See, for example, "Malaysia on Trial," *New York Times*, 4 November 1998.

5. Keith B. Richburg, "New Voice in Malaysia," *Washington Post*, 19 June 1999.

6. For a discussion of these broader developments in the Malaysian political context, see John L. Esposito and John O. Voll, *Islam and Democracy* (New York: Oxford University Press, 1996), chap. 6, "Malaysia: The Politics of Multiculturalism."

7. Anwar Ibrahim, *The Asian Renaissance* (Singapore: Times Books International, 1996), p. 15.

8. Judith Nagata, *The Reflowering of Malaysian Islam* (Vancouver: University of British Columbia Press, 1984), p. 89.

9. Zainah Anwar, *Islamic Revivalism in Malaysia: Dakwah among the Students* (Petaling Jaya, Malaysia: Pelanduk Publications, 1987), p. 16.

10. Kamaruddin Muhammad Nor, as quoted in Anwar, *Islamic Revivalism*, p. 12.

11. Anwar Ibrahim, as quoted in Anwar, *Islamic Revivalism*, pp. 12–13.

12. See, for example, M. G. G. Pillai, "The Importance of Students' Status," *FEER*, 29 April 1974, pp. 14–15, and M. G. G. Pillai, "Graduating in Campus Confrontation," *FEER*, 4 October 1974, pp. 11–12.

13. Denzil Peiris, "The Emerging Rural Revolution," *FEER*, 10 January 1975, p. 30.

14. M. G. G. Pillai, "Taking up the Student Gauntlet, *FEER*, 13 December 1974, p. 14.

15. Peiris, "The Emerging Rural Revolution," p. 30.

16. Anwar Ibrahim, interviews with the authors, June 1990.

17. See Nagata, *Reflowering*, p. 93, and Henry Kamm, "Teacher Leads Malays Seeking Islamic Revival," *New York Times*, 23 March 1980.

18. Anwar, *Islamic Revivalism*, p. 13.

19. Ibrahim, interviews, June 1990.

20. Kamaruddin Muhammad Nur, quoted in Anwar, *Islamic Revivalism*, p. 20.

21. Anwar, *Islamic Revivalism*, p. 39.

22. Ibrahim, interviews, June 1990.

23. Esposito and Voll, *Islam and Democracy*, pp. 147–48.

24. Keith B. Richburg, "Malaysia's Pop-Off Leader," *Washington Post*, 13 October 1997.

25. "The True Struggle of the National Justice Party" (editorial, *New Straits Times*, 6–8 April 1999), Foreign Broadcast Information Service ; FBIS-EAS-1999-0408, 6 April 1999 (from http://wnc.fedworld.gov).

26. Richburg, "New Voice," 19 June 1999.

27. Shafruddin Hashim, "Muslim Society, Higher Education and Development: The Case of Malaysia," in *Muslim Society, Higher Education and Development in Southeast Asia*, ed. Sharom Ahmat and Sharon Siddique (Singapore: Institute of Southeast Asian Studies, 1987), pp. 45–46.

28. "Malaysians Seek Language Accord," *New York Times*, 16 April 1967.

29. Anwar, *Islamic Revivalism*, p. 16.

30. Ibrahim, *Asian Renaissance*, p. 22.

31. Peiris, "The Emerging Rural Revolution," p. 31.

32. Nagata, *Reflowering*, p. 95.

33. Henry Kamm, "Malaysia's Ethnic Fabric Is Beginning to Fray Again," *New York Times*, 20 March 1980.

34. Nagata, *Reflowering*, p. 92.

35. Ismail R. al Faruqi, preface to *Islamization of Knowledge: General Principles and Work Plan* (Herndon, VA: International Institute of Islamic Thought, 1982–1987), p. viii.

36. Anwar, *Islamic Revivalism*, p. 24.

37. Anwar, *Islamic Revivalism*, p. 38.

38. Kamm, "Teacher Leads Malays . . ."

39. Diane K. Mauzy, "Partai Islam Se-Malaysia," in *The Oxford Encyclopedia of the Modern Islamic World*, ed. John L. Esposito (New York: Oxford University Press, 1995), 3:305.

40. Ibrahim, interviews, June 1990.

41. Brief descriptions of this congress and speech can be found in Nagata, *Reflowering*, p. 95, and Jomo Kwame Sundaram and Ahmed Shabery Cheek, "The Politics of Malaysia's Islamic Resurgence," *Third World Quarterly* 10, 2 (April 1988): 853–54.

42. Nagata, *Reflowering*, p. 98.

43. Anwar Ibrahim, "The Need for Civilizational Dialogue," Occasional Papers Series, Center for Muslim-Christian Understanding, Georgetown University, Washington, DC, 1995, p. 8.

44. Anwar, *Islamic Revivalism*, pp. 63–64.

45. Khalijah Mohd Salleh, *Women in Development* (Kuala Lumpur: Institute for Policy Research, 1994), pp. 105, 124.

46. Anwar Ibrahim, "Development, Values and Changing Political Ideas," *Sojourn: Social Issues in Southeast Asia* 1, 1 (February 1986): 2.

47. Ibrahim, *Asian Renaissance* (Singapore: Times Books International, 1996), p. 74.

48. Ibrahim, "Development, Values," p. 1.

49. Ibrahim, *Asian Renaissance*, p. 81.

50. Ibrahim, "Development, Values," p. 5.

51. Anwar Ibrahim, address at the Ismail Faruqi Award presentation ceremony, International Islamic University, Kuala Lumpur, Malaysia, 28 February 1996.

52. Ibid.

53. Ibrahim, *Asian Renaissance*, p. 80.

54. Azizan Bahari, Chandra Muzaffar, et al., "Do Not Distort the Truth," *Commentary, International Movement for a Just World* (special issue) (October 1998): 15.

55. Anwar Ibrahim, "The Ardent Moderates," *Time*, 23 September 1996, p. 24.

56. Anwar Ibrahim, "We Believe in Engagement between the East and the West," interview in *Diplomat*, 15 February 1996, p. 18.

57. Ibrahim, *Asian Renaissance*, p. 100.

58. Ibid.

59. Anwar Ibrahim, address, "Islam and Confucianism: A Civilizational Dialogue," Kuala Lumpur, 13 March 1995.

60. Ibrahim, "Islam and Confucianism."

61. Anwar Ibrahim, "The Philosophy of Symbiosis," Remarks at the Intercultural Conference on the Ecomedia City 2020, Subang Jaya, Malaysia, 16 January 1995.

62. Ibrahim, *Asian Renaissance*, p. 24.

63. Ibrahim, "Ardent Moderates," p. 25

64. Ibrahim, *Asian Renaissance*, p. 58.

65. Surah 49:13. The translation is as it was presented in the text of Ibrahim, "Islam and Confusianism."

66. Ibrahim, "Islam and Confucianism."

67. Thomas F. Glick, "Convivencia: An Introductory Note," in *Convivencia: Jews, Muslims and Christians in Medieval Spain*, ed. Vivian B. Mann, Thomas F. Glick, and Jerrilyn D. Dodds (New York: George Braziller, 1992), pp. 1–2.

68. Ibrahim, *Asian Renaissance*, p. 30.

69. Samuel P. Huntington, "The Clash of Civilizations," *Foreign Affairs* 72, 3 (Summer 1993).

70. Samuel P. Huntington, *The Clash of Civilizations and the Remaking of World Order* (New York: Simon and Schuster, 1996), pp. 217–18.

71. Joyce M. Davis, *Between Jihad and Salaam: Profiles in Islam* (New York: St. Martin's Press, 1997), p. 309.

72. Ibrahim, "Need for Civilizational Dialogue," p. 4.

73. Ibid., p. 6.

74. Anwar Ibrahim, "Jose Rizal: Humanist and Renaissance Man," address in Kuala Lumpur, 3 October 1995.

75. Ibrahim, "Need for Civilizational Dialogue," p. 5.

76. Ibrahim, *Asian Renaissance*, p. 45.

77. Ibrahim, "Need for Civilizational Dialogue," p. 5.

78. Ibrahim, *Asian Renaissance*, p. 45.

Chapter 9. Abdurrahman Wahid

1. Abdurrahman Wahid, interview with the authors, Jakarta, July 1991.

2. Ibid.

3. Greg Barton, "The Liberal, Progressive Roots of Abdurrahman Wahid's Thought," in *Nahdatul Ulama, Traditional Islam and Modernity in Indonesia*, ed.

Greg Barton and Greg Fealy (Monash, Australia: Monash Asia Institute, 1996), p. 213.

4. Ibid., p. 202.

5. Ibid., p. 210.

6. Fred R. von der Mehden, "Malaysian and Indonesian Islamic Movements: The Iranian Connection," in *The Global Impact of the Iranian Revolution*, ed. John Esposito (Miami: Florida International University Press, 1990), p. 234.

7. Michael Vatikiotis, "Faith without Fanatics," *Far Eastern Economic Review* (14 June 1990): 25.

8. Abdurrahman Wahid, as quoted in Mujiburrahman, "Islam and Politics in Indonesia: The Political Thought of Abdurrahman Wahid," *Journal of Islam and Christian-Muslim Relations* 10, 3, (1999): 342.

9. Vatikiotis, "Faith," p. 30.

10. James Peacock, "Modern Movements in Insular Cultures," in *The Encyclopedia of Religion*, ed. Mircea Eliade (New York: Macmillan, 1987), 13:528.

11. For a discussion of these issues, see Albert Hourani, *Arabic Thought in the Liberal Age* (London: Oxford University Press), pp. 190–   , and Leonard Binder, *Islamic Liberalism: A Critique of Development Ideologies* (Chicago: University of Chicago Press, 1988), chap. 4.

12. Binder, *Islamic Liberalism*, pp. 158–59.

13. Abdurrahman Wahid, as quoted in Mujiburrahman, "Islam and Politics," p. 342.

14. Abdurrahman Wahid, "Reflections on the Need for a Concept of Man in Islam," memorandum to the rector of the U. N. University, 1 May 1983, p. 1.

15. Ibid., p. 2.

16. Abdurrahman Wahid, "Islam, the State, and Development in Indonesia," p. 41.

17. "Islam in Indonesia, Where To: Interview with Abdurrahman Wahid," *Inside Indonesia*, 8 October 1986, p. 3.

18. Abdurrahman Wahid, "Islam, Nonviolence and National Transformation: A Preliminary Overview from Historical Perspectives," February 1986, p. 3.

19. Abdurrahman Wahid, "Reflections," p. 3.

20. Ibid.

21. "Islam in Indonesia," p. 3.

22. "An Islamic Awakening," *Economist*, 17 April 1993.

23. "Yes, I Have Enemies. But It Is Important That I Do the Right Things," *Business Times (Singapore)*, 24 March 1999.

24. Wahid, "Reflections," p. 4.

25. "Government Stance on Confucianism Criticized," *Jakarta Post*, 13 August 1996.

26. "Gus Dur's Party Sitting Pretty after Indon Polls," *New Straits Times*, 10 June 1999.

27. Wahid, "Islam, Nonviolence and National Transformation," p. 4.

28. Douglas E. Rampage, "Democratization, Religious Tolerance and Pancasila: The Political Thought of Abdurrahman Wahid," in Barton and Fealy, *Nahdatul Ulama*, p. 227.

29. "Islam, Nonviolence and National Transformation," p. 3.

30. Abdurrahman Wahid, "Cultural Diversity and Religious Unity in Islam: The Indonesian Experience," *Bulletin* (1982–XVII 2): 256.

31. Ibid., p. 257.

32. Abdurrahman Wahid, "Islamic Fundamentalism: A Southeast Asian Perspective," (np/nd), p. 6.

33. Ibid., p. 7.

34. Ibid., p. 8.

35. "Religion, Ideology and Development," p. 4.

36. Douglas E. Rampage, "Democratization," p. 241.

37. Ibid., p. 254.

SUGGESTIONS FOR FURTHER READING

There are many places that the interested reader can look for further information on the subject of activist Islamic intellectuals. The following is obviously not a comprehensive bibliography but rather, a set of suggestions by the authors for further reading. Other sources are mentioned in the notes for the various chapters.

The general subject of the role of the intellectual has been viewed from many different perspectives. The classic study is Julien Benda, *The Treason of the Intellectuals* (trans., Richard Aldington; New York: W.W. Norton, 1969). A more recent analysis is provided in Edward W. Said, *Representations of the Intellectual* (New York: Vintage Books, 1994) and a study that places the topic within the framework of social science analysis is Ahmad Sadri, *Max Weber's Sociology of Intellectuals* (New York: Oxford University Press, 1992).

There are a number of important reference works and surveys that provide information about aspects of the Muslim world and the lives and contexts of the subjects of this book. An important basic reference work is the *Oxford Encyclopedia of the Modern Islamic World*, edited by John L. Esposito (New York: Oxford University Press, 1995). The authors of the book have also written more general surveys that place the intellectuals in their contexts. These books include John L. Esposito, *Islam and Politics* (4th ed.; Syracuse: Syracuse University Press, 1998), John L. Esposito, *The Islamic Threat: Myth or Reality?* (3rd ed.; New York: Oxford University Press, 1999), John Obert Voll, *Islam, Continuity and Change in the Modern World* (2nd ed.; Syracuse: Syracuse University Press, 1994), and John L. Esposito and John O. Voll, *Islam and Democracy* (New York: Oxford University Press, 1996). Other interpretive coverages can be found in Ibrahim M. Abu-Rabi', *Intellectual Origins of Islamic Resurgence in the Modern Arab World* (Albany: State University of New York Press, 1996) and Armando Salvatore, *Islam and the Political Discourse of Modernity* (Reading: Ithaca Press, 1997). Interesting interviews with some of the people discussed in this volume can be found in Joyce M. Davis, *Between Jihad and Salaam: Profiles in Islam* (New York: St. Martin's Press, 1997).

Further readings that would provide information about the countries and contexts of the activist intellectuals and some of their writings in translations can be found in the following books.

Ismail al-Faruqi

Ismail Ragi al-Faruqi, *On Arabism: Urubah and Religion* (Amsterdam: Djambatan, 1962).
———, *Islamization of Knowledge* (Herndon, VA: International Institute of Islamic Thought, 1982).
———, *Tawhid: Its Implications for Thought and Life* (Herndon, VA: International Institute of Islamic Thought, 1982).
M. Tariq Quraishi, *Ismail al-Faruqi: An Enduring Legacy* (Plainfield, IN: The Muslim Student Association, 1987).

Khurshid Ahmad

Khurshid Ahmad, *The Religion of Islam* (Lahore: Islamic Publications, 1967).
———, *Socialism or Islam* (Delhi: Hindustan Publications, 1969).
Seyyed Vali Reza Nasr, *The Vanguard of Islamic Revolution: The Jama'at-I Islami of Pakistan* (Berkeley: University of California Press, 1994).

Maryam Jameelah

Maryam Jameelah, *Islam and Western Society.*
———, *Islam in Theory and Practice.*
———, *Islam vs. the West.*
Seyyed Vali Reza Nasr, *Mawdudi and the Making of Islamic Revivalism* (New York: Oxford University Press, 1996).

Hasan Turabi

Abdelwahab El-Affendi, *Turabi's Revolution: Islam and Power in Sudan* (London: Grey Seal, 1991).
Mohamed Elhachmi Hamdi, *The Making of an Islamic Political Leader: Conversations with Hasan Al-Turabi* (Boulder: Westview, 1999).
Arthur L. Lowrie, ed., *Islam, Democracy, the State and the West: A Roundtable with Dr. Hasan Turabi* (Tampa: World & Islam Studies Enterprise, 1993).
Abdel Salam Sidahmed, *Politics and Islam in Contemporary Sudan* (New York: St. Martin's Press, 1996).

Rashid al-Ghanushi

Rached Ghannoushi, "The Battle Against Islam," *Middle East Affairs Journal 1,* 2 (Winter 1992/1413).
———, "Secularism in the Arab Maghrib," in *Islam and Secularism in the Middle East* (New York: New York University Press, 2000).
Emad Eldin Shahin, *Political Ascent: Contemporary Islamic Movements in North Africa* (Boulder: Westview Press, 1997).
Azzam Tamimi, *Rachid Ghannouchi: A Democrat Within Islamism* (New York: Oxford University Press, forthcoming).

Hasan Hanafi

Genieve Abdo, *No God But God: Egypt and the Triumph of Islam* (New York: Oxford University Press, 2000).

Hassan Hanafi, *Islam in the Modern World* (two volumes: Cairo: The Anglo-Egyptian Bookshop, 1995).

Shahrough Akhavi, "The Dialectic in Contemporary Egyptian Social Thought: The Scripturalist and Modernist Discourses of Sayyid Qutb and Hasan Hanafi," *International Journal of Middle East Studies 29*, 3 (August 1997): 377–401.

Anwar Ibrahim

Zainah Anwar, *Islamic Revivalism in Malaysia* (Petaling Jaya, Malaysia: Pelanduk Publications, 1987).

Robert W. Hefner, ed., *Islam in an Era of Nation-States: Politics and Religious Renewal in Muslim Southeast Asia* (Honolulu: University of Hawaii Press, 1997).

Anwar Ibrahim, *The Asian Renaissance* (Singapore: Times Books International, 1996).

Abd al-Rahman Wahid

Greg Barton and Greg Fealy, eds., *Nahdatul Ulama, Traditional Islam and Modernity in Indonesia* (Monash: Monash Asia Institute, 1996).

Robert W. Hefner, *Civil Islam* (Princeton: Princeton University Press, 2000).

"Islam in Indonesia: Where to: Interview with Abdurrahman Wahid," *Inside Indonesia* (October 8, 1986).

Majiburrahman, "Islam and Politics in Indonesia: The Political Thought of Abdurrahman Wahid," *Journal of Islam and Christian-Muslim Relations 10*, 3 (1999).

Abdolkarim Soroush

Mehrzad Boroujerdi, *Iranian Intellectuals and the West: The Tormented Triumph of Nativism* (Syracuse: Syracuse University Press, 1996).

Hamid Dabshi, *Theology of Discontent: The Ideological Foundations of the Islamic Revolution in Iran* (New York: New York University Press, 1993).

Reason, Freedom, and Democracy in Islam: Essential Writings of Abdolkarim Soroush, translated and edited by Mahmoud Sadri and Ahmad Sadri (New York: Oxford University Press, 2000).

INDEX

in Malaysia, 179, 184–85, 183
Christian Ethics (al-Faruqi), 33, 37
Christianity
 Abdurrahman Wahid's view of, 208, 211, 215
 Arabist view of, 25, 26
 Faruqi's analysis of, 33–34, 35, 36–37
 Hanafi's scholarship on, 76, 87
 Jameelah's view of, 60, 63
 Sudanese constitutional recognition of, 140, 143
 See also interreligious dialogue; Roman Catholic Church
Chuol, Gordon Kong, 147
citizenship, 115
civilizational dialogue, 191, 195, 196–98
civil society, 116, 151, 174, 175
"clash of civilizations" paradigm, 196–97
clerical establishment, 151, 155, 165–71, 234nn.84, 85, 92
 income of, 168–69
 See also ulama
colonialism, 17–18, 209–10
 Ahmad's (Khurshid) view of, 45
 Faruqi's view of, 25, 28
 Ghannoushi's view of, 106, 111, 112–13, 115
 Hanafi's view of, 88
 Jameelah's view of, 61–63
 See also France; Great Britain
Committee for the Development of Pesantrens, 201
Communism
 Egypt and, 70, 71, 73, 80
 Sudan and, 122, 124, 129, 136, 138, 227n.8
 Tunisia and, 102
Community of the Companions of the Prophet, 127–28
Confucianism, 193–94, 208
Confucius, 3, 7
conscientization, 211
"Consciousness Raising Campaign" (Malaysia; 1968), 178–79, 184
consensus. *See ijma*
Constitutional Democratic Rally (Tunisia), 105
consultation. *See shura*

convivencia (coexistence), 196, 198
Coon, Carleton, 65
Copts, 78
Corbin, Henri, 75
corruption, clerical, 168
cosmopolitan Islam, 207–8, 211
critics, intellectuals as, 10, 11
Cromer, Lord, 63
Crusades, 28, 111
Cultural Atlas of Islam, The (al-Faruqi and al-Faruqi), 27
Cultural Revolution (Iran), 150, 152, 171, 229–30n.4

Dabbagh, Hossein. *See* Soroush, Abdolkarim
dakwah (call to understanding), 187, 188
DAP. *See* Democratic Action Party
Dar al-Arqam movement, 184, 189
Darwin, Charles, 65
dawa (propagation of Islam), 43, 46
Deen, Imad ad, 214
democracy
 Abdurrahman Wahid's view of, 206, 209, 214
 Anwar Ibrahim's view of, 195
 Ghannoushi's view of, 112, 113–17
 Iran and, 151, 174
 Soroush's view of, 155, 158, 160–65, 170, 175
 Sudan and, 138–39, 140
Democratic Action Party (Malaysia), 183
Democratic Unionist Party (Sudan), 125, 126, 141
Deng, Francis, 124
Destourian Socialist Party (Tunisia), 96, 99
developing nations, 173, 191
development (social, political, economic), 191–94, 204, 210, 211–12
dhimmi ("protected" people), 64, 188
dictatorship, 113
din wa dawla (religion and state), 205
dissent, intellectuals and, 5
divorce, 35, 65, 66
DUP. *See* Democratic Unionist Party

Vatican II Ecumenical Council
(1964), 76, 87
vilayat-i faqih doctrine, 160, 167

Wad al-Turab, 119–20
Wahid, Abdurrahman. *See*
Abdurrahman Wahid
Wahid Hashim, 200
wahy (revelation), 32
Wan Azizah Ismail, 177, 182, 183,
190
Weber, Max, 4, 7, 8
Weiss, Leopold. *See* Asad,
Muhammad
Westernization, 12–14, 17, 18
Ahmad's (Khurshid) view of, 45
developing nations and, 173, 191
Faruqi's view of, 28
Ghannoushi's view of, 106, 113
Hanafi's view of, 88–89
Jameelah's view of, 60–67
Southeast Asian Muslims and,
209–10, 212
in Tunisia, 91–92
Western society
Anwar Ibrahim's view of, 193, 197
Faruqi's view of, 28
Ghannoushi's view of, 107, 108,
111–17

Hanafi's studies of, 79, 87–90
Jameelah's view of, 58–60
Mawdudi's view of, 45
Soroush's view of, 152, 171–73
will of the people. *See* popular
will
women's status and role in Islam
Anwar Ibrahim's view of, 186,
189–90
Ghannoushi's view of, 110–11
Jameelah's view of, 62, 66–67
in Tunisia, 92
Turabi's view of, 134–37
Women's Union (Sudan), 124
working class, 110
World Assembly of Muslim Youth
(1976–1982), 180
World Council of Churches, 33
World War II, 69

Yayasan Anda (Malaysian school),
180

zakat (alms tax), 51, 144
Zaytouna (Tunis), 92, 93–94, 97,
104
Zia ul-Haq, 46
Zionism, 28, 55, 72, 78, 83
Zurayk, Constantin, 26

KING ALFRED'S COLLEGE
LIBRARY